THE ILLUSTRATED
WORLD'S
RELIGIONS

Head and torso of the "Buddha of the Future" (Maitreya Bodhisattva), Chuguji temple, Nara. The timeless grace and serenity of this statue suggest the state of transcendence towards which all religions strive, regardless of specific doctrines or rituals.

THE ILLUSTRATED
WORLD'S
RELIGIONS

A GUIDE TO
OUR WISDOM TRADITIONS

Huston Smith

HarperSanFrancisco

A Division of HarperCollins*Publishers*

A Labyrinth Book

THE ILLUSTRATED WORLD'S RELIGIONS:
A GUIDE TO OUR WISDOM TRADITIONS.

HarperSanFrancisco
An imprint of HarperCollins*Publishers*

For information address HarperCollins Publishers,
10 East 53rd Street, New York, NY 10022.
HarperCollins Web Site: http://www.harpercollins.com

The Illustrated World's Religions: A Guide to Our Wisdom Traditions was produced by Labyrinth Publishing (UK) Ltd.
Consultant for visual imagery: Richard M. Carp, Ph.D. Picture editor: Patricia McCarver.
Printed & bound by L.E.G.O., Italy.
Art direction and design by Magda Valine.

FIRST HARPERCOLLINS PAPERBACK EDITION PUBLISHED IN 1995

A Previous Edition of This Book Was Cataloged as Follows:
Smith, Huston
    The illustrated world's religions: a guide to our
wisdom traditions / Huston Smith. – Ill. ed., 1st ed.
        p.cm.
    Includes index.
    ISBN 0-06-067453-9 (cloth)
    ISBN 0-06-067440-7 (pbk.)
    1. Religons. I.   Title
BL80.2.S6455   1994
291– dc20   93-24107

99 LAB 10 9 8 7

CONTENTS

PREFACE TO THE ILLUSTRATED EDITION

To **The Religions of Man** (1958), transformed by inclusive gender language into **The World's Religions** (1989), the present edition adds the world's religious art. This makes the book more faithful to its subject, for during most of human history people have found their sacred texts in song and dance and paintings and stone more than in writing.

The text of the book's 1989 edition is here reduced by half. This is partly to make room for art, but there is a supporting reason. In this book the text serves as something of a commentary on the art, outlining the visions that inspired it, the discernments which artists captured in color and form. It is fitting, therefore, for it to step somewhat aside.

Mention of vision is important here, for what distinguishes sacred art from other varieties is the window it opens onto another world – a world that is vaster, stranger, more real, and more beautiful than the world we normally encounter. Plato considered beauty *"the splendor of the true,"* and it is indeed the truth-value of sacred art that makes it great. Its subject matter need not be explicitly religious; in this book it tends to be, but that is because the book is about religion. What makes art sacred is not what it depicts, but the way it opens onto transcendence and carries the viewer into it, enabling him or her to see what it might be like to live in self-forgetfulness and timeless harmony. Few of Marc Chagall's subjects were explicitly religious, yet he is a religious artist because, inspired as he was by his Jewish heritage, everything his brush alighted on – flowers, fruit, birds – glowed and was miraculous. We see the whole world as color; rainbow-fresh as after a storm.

One editorial point. To help things flow, I have relieved this text of the footnotes that stud the 1989 edition. Readers who wish to know where quotations come from will find their sources noted in that unabridged version of the text.

Huston Smith
Berkeley, California

CHAPTER I

POINT OF DEPARTURE

Where are we?

Why are we here?

What does it all mean?

What, if anything, are we supposed to do?

Above: **Hypnos**, *the Greek god of sleep, was the twin brother of Death and the son of Night.* Right: *Two young monks from the Sonada Monastery in Darjeeling, India.*

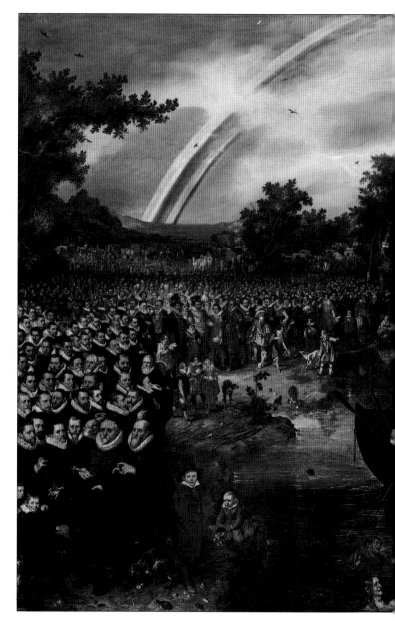

*T*RADITIONALLY, WHEN PEOPLE WANTED ANSWERS to life's ultimate questions – Where are we? Why are we here? What does it all mean? What, if anything, are we supposed to do? – they looked to their revealed texts; or to their ancestral myths if they were oral peoples (it comes to the same thing). Since the rise of modern science, however, they have turned increasingly to it for answers. This is understandable, for controlled experiments enable science to prove its theses; and with those theses it has remade the world. It is a signal feature of our century's close that we recognize that this turn to science was mistaken. Not entirely mistaken, for science (and its spin-off, technology) have their place. What was mistaken was to expect science to answer ultimate questions, for its method doesn't connect with them. Recognizing this clears the way for looking seriously again at the enterprise that does connect with them: religion.

Such serious looking and listening defines the object of this book. It may be wondered if this aim is not too broad. The religions we propose to consider belt the world. They stretch back thousands of years and are motivating more people today than ever before. Is it possible to listen seriously to them within the compass of a single book?

The answer is that it is possible, because we shall be listening for well-defined themes. These must be listed at the outset or the reader will be misled.

1. This is not a book about religious history. This explains the dearth of names, dates, and social influences in its pages. Historical facts are kept to the minimum that are needed to situate in time and space the *ideas* the book deals with.

2. Even respecting ideas, the book does not attempt to provide an inclusive overview of the religions included, for each hosts too many variations to make sense of in short compass. Instead of trying to catalogue them all, I try to do reasonable justice to the leading perspectives in each tradition.

3. The book is not a balanced account of its subject. The full story of religion is not rose-colored – often it is crude and barbaric. Wisdom and charity are intermittent, and the net result is profoundly ambiguous.

A balanced view of religion would include witch-

hunts and inquisitions, pogroms and persecution, the Christian Crusades and holy wars of Islam. The catalogue would have no end.

Why then do I only mention these things? My answer is so simple that it may sound ingenuous. This is a book about values. Probably as much bad art as good has been chiseled and painted, but no one would expect it to appear in these pages. Others will be interested in weigh-ing the virtues of religion against its atrocities. That has not been my concern.

"The Fishers for Souls" by Adriaen Pietersz van de Venne, 1614. This allegory represents the struggle for converts between the Catholics and Protestants. However, the eternal truths that have inspired religions have survived its frequent institutional follies.

*"**The Prophet Isaiah**" by Marc Chagall. The surest way to the heart of a people is through their faith.*

Having targeted my subject as the enduring religions at their best, let me say what I take that best to be. Their theological and metaphysical truths are, I am prepared to argue, inspired. Institutions – religious institutions included – are another story. Constituted as they are of uneven people (partly good, partly bad), institutions are built of vices as well as virtues, which has led one wag to suggest that the biggest mistake religion made was to get mixed up with people. This book skims the cream from religion's churning history by confining itself to its theological claims. When we limit ourselves to these, a cleaner side of the religions emerges. They begin to look like the world's wisdom traditions. (*"Where is the knowledge that is lost in information? Where is the wisdom that is lost in knowledge?"* – T.S. Eliot.) They look like data banks that house the winnowed wisdom of the human race.

4. Finally, this is not a book on comparative religions in the sense of comparing their worth. I have tried to let the best in each faith shine through. Readers are free to make their own comparisons if they are inclined to do so.

In saying what this book is not, I have already suggested what it is, but let me be explicit.

1. It is a book that seeks to embrace the world. That hope can only be approximated, of course. Arms are short and feet must be planted somewhere, so this book has a home. But it is a home whose doors swing in and out – in study and imaginings when not in overt travel. If it is possible to be homesick for the world, even places one has never been and knows one will never see, this book is the child of such homesickness.

In our century this global outreach is important, for lands around the planet have become our neighbors – China across the street, the Middle East at our back door. The change this new situation requires of us all – we who have been suddenly catapulted from town and country onto a world stage – is staggering. Twenty-five hundred years ago it took an exceptional individual like Diogenes to exclaim, *"I am not an Athenian or a Greek but a citizen of the world."* Today we must all be struggling to make those words our own. Anyone who is only Japanese or American, only Oriental or Occidental, is but half human. The other half that beats with the pulse of all humanity has yet to be awakened.

World understanding brings many rewards: it enables corporations to do business abroad, and diplomats to stumble less frequently. But its greatest gains need no tally. To glimpse what belonging means to the people of India; to sense with a Burmese grandmother what passes in life and what endures; to understand how Hindus can regard their personalities as masks that overlay the God within – to swing such things into view is to add dimensions to the glance of spirit. It is to have a larger world to live in.

These thoughts about world understanding lead directly to the world's religions, for the surest way to the heart of a people is through their faith if it has not fossilized. Which distinction – between religion alive and dead – brings us to the second constructive intent of this book.

2. It is (as has already been indicated) a book that takes religion seriously. There is no pandering here to curiosity seekers, or fixing on the sensational; no erotic sculpture, yogis on beds of nails, or penitente flagellants. Likewise avoided is a subtler form of disrespect which grants that religion is important, but for others – peoples of the past, or of other cultures, or whose egos need bolstering. The book's focus will be on others – Hindus, Buddhists, whoever – it will be "they" and "them" throughout. But behind those fronts, our deepest concern will be ourselves.

The chief reason I keep returning to the wisdom traditions (a phrase that will be explicated in the final chapter) is for the help they offer on problems I have not been able myself to parry. Given our common humanity, I assume that the reader has not been able to escape them either. Even the subtlest way of patronizing religion will be avoided: that which honors it, not for itself, but for its spin-offs – its contributions to art, or to peace of mind, or to group cohesion. This is a book about religion that exists, in William James' contrast, not as a dull habit but as an acute fever. It is about religion alive. And where religion lives, it takes over. All else, while not silenced, is thrown into a supporting role.

Religion alive confronts the individual with the most momentous option life can present. It calls the soul to the highest adventure it can undertake, a projected journey across the jungles, peaks, and deserts of the human spirit. The call is to confront reality, to master the self. Those who dare to hear and follow that secret call soon learn the dangers and difficulties of its lonely journey – *"the sharp edge of a razor, hard to traverse / A difficult path is this, the poets declare...." (Katha Upanishad)*. But they know its deliverances, too. When a lone spirit triumphs in this domain, it becomes more than a ruler. It becomes a world redeemer. Its impact stretches for millennia, blessing the tangled course of history for centuries. "Who are the greatest benefactors of the living generation of mankind?" Toynbee asked; and answered: "Confucius and Laotze, the Buddha, the Prophets of Israel and Judah, Zoroaster, Jesus, Mohammed and Socrates." The answer should not surprise, for authentic religion is the clearest opening through which the inexhaustible energies of the cosmos pour into human life.

3. Finally, this book makes a real effort to communicate. I think of it as a work of translation; one that tries not only to penetrate the worlds of Hindus, Bud-dhists, and Muslims, but to throw bridges from those worlds to the reader's world. "If you cannot – in the long run – tell everyone what you have been doing," Erwin Schrodinger wrote, "your doing has been worthless."

We are about to begin a voyage in space and time and eternity. The places will often be distant, the times remote, the themes beyond space and time altogether.

We shall have to use words that are foreign to us – Sanskrit, Chinese, and Arabic. We shall describe states of consciousness that words can only hint at. We shall use logic to try to corner insights that laugh at our attempt, and ultimately we shall fail. Being ourselves of a different cast of mind, we shall never quite understand the religions that are not our own. But if we take those religions seriously, we need not fail miserably. And to take them seriously, only two things are required. We need to see their adherents as men and women who face problems much like our own. And second, we must rid our minds of preconceptions that could dull our sensitivity to fresh insights.

A great anatomist used to close his opening lecture to beginning medical students with words that apply to our own undertaking as well. "In this course," he would say, "we shall be dealing with flesh and bones and cells and sinews, and there are going to be times when it's all going to seem terribly cold-blooded. But never forget: It's alive!"

Above: The winged eye, Egyptian symbol for divine omniscience, here adapted for use in a medal. Right: Dorset seascape. "Religion alive... calls the soul to the highest adventure it can undertake."

CHAPTER II

HINDUISM

"If I were asked under what sky the human mind has most deeply pondered over the greatest problems of life, and has found solutions to some of them which well deserve the attention even of those who have studied Plato and Kant — I should point to India.

And if I were to ask myself from what literature we who have been nurtured almost exclusively on the thoughts of Greeks and Romans, and of one Semitic race, the Jewish, may draw the corrective which is most wanted in order to make our inner life more perfect, more comprehensive, more universal, in fact more truly human a life,

again I should point to India."

Max Muller (19th century orientalist)

A stylized rendering of hrim, *the* bija *or seed syllable for the Divine Mother.*

WHAT PEOPLE WANT

THE QUESTION FOR THIS CHAPTER is how India (through its presiding religion, Hinduism) proposes to make life more perfect, comprehensive, universal, and truly human. It begins by asking what people want, and it is through this question that we will enter this first religion.

Hindus hold that people want four things. They begin by wanting pleasure. This is natural; we are born with built-in pleasure-pain reactors. If we ignore these, leaving our hands on hot stoves or stepping out of second-storey windows, we soon die. What could be more appropriate than to follow the promptings of pleasure and entrust our lives to it?

Having heard that India is ascetic, other-worldly, and life-negating, we might expect her attitude toward hedonists to be scolding, but it is not. To be sure, she has not made pleasure her highest good, but this is different from condemning enjoyment. To the person who wants pleasure, India says in effect: go after it. There is nothing wrong with it; it is one of the four legitimate ends of life. The world is awash with beauty and heavy with sensual delights. Moreover, there are worlds above this one where pleasures increase by a factor of a million at each rung, and these worlds, too, we shall experience in due course. Like everything else, hedonism requires good sense. Small immediate goals must be sacrificed for long range gains, and impulses that would injure others must be curbed to avoid antagonisms and remorse. Only the stupid will lie, steal, cheat, or succumb to addictions. But as long as the basic rules of morality are observed, you are free to seek all the pleasure you want. To simple persons who seek little else, Hinduism presents itself primarily as a regimen for insuring health and prosperity;

while at the other end of the spectrum, for sophisticates, it elaborates a sensual aesthetic that shocks in its explicitness. If pleasure is what you want, do not suppress the desire. Seek it intelligently.

This India says, and waits. It waits for the time — it will come to everyone, though not to everyone in this lifetime — when one realizes that one wants more than pleasure. The reason everyone eventually comes to this discovery is because pleasure is too trivial to satisfy us. Pleasure is essentially private, and the self is too small an object for perpetual enthusiasm. Sooner or later everyone wants more from life than pleasant sensations. When this discovery arrives, interest usually shifts to the second major goal of life, namely worldly success in the form of wealth, fame, and power. This goal too should not be repressed or condemned. Its satisfactions are more substantial than pleasure, for they are social. Their scope is larger for involving other people.

This does not have to be argued for a contemporary Western audience. Anglo-Americans are not sybarites. They do not give themselves over to pleasure — they are too busy, too driven. What takes arguing in the West is not that pleasure has limitations, but that social achievements are likewise limited — that *"what am I worth?"* isn't synonymous with *"how much have I got?"*

India grants, not only that success is a requisite for supporting a household and discharging one's civic responsibilities, but that its achievements confer dignity and self-respect. In the end, however, these rewards too harbor limitations we can enumerate.

1. Wealth, fame, and power are exclusive, hence competitive, hence precarious. Unlike mental and spiritual treasures, they cannot be dispensed without diminishing one's own portion. If I own a dollar, that dollar

is not yours; to be in the limelight presupposes an audience in the darkened hall. Similarly with fame and power. From the competitiveness of these goods to their precariousness is a short step, for as other people want them too, who knows when fortune will change hands?

2. The drive for success is insatiable. A qualification is needed, for many people *are* content with their income, visibility, and authority. It is people who place these things first in their lives who cannot be satisfied, and for a discernible reason. These are not the things people really want, and you can never get enough of what you do not really want. To try to extinguish greed with money is like trying to quench fire by pouring butter over it. The parable of the driver who kept his donkey plodding by attaching a carrot to its harness comes from India.

3. The third problem with worldly success is one it shares with hedonism. Success, too, centers meaning in one's finite self which proves to be too small for enduring interest. Neither the size of one's fortune nor the height of one's station can conceal the smallness of their possessor.

Above: *Shiva with his consort Uma. To the person who wants pleasure, Hinduism instructs not to suppress the desire but to seek it intelligently.*

4. The final reason why worldly success cannot satisfy us is that its rewards are ephemeral. "You can't take it with you," we say; and because we can't, its glitter fades. For we are creatures who can envision eternity, and must rue by contrast brief dividends.

Before proceeding to the other two things that Hinduism sees people wanting, it will be well to summarize the ones that have been mentioned. Hindus locate pleasure and success on the Path of Desire. They use this phrase because natural desires have thus far dictated life's course. To understand that satisfying these desires still leaves us unfulfilled is not to condemn them; this has already been said. Desires should not be turned from until they turn from us, for Hinduism regards the objects on the Path of Desire as if they were toys. There is nothing wrong with toys. Quite the contrary; the thought of children without toys is sad. Even sadder, though, is the prospect of adults who remain fixated at their level.

But what more satisfying interests are there? Two, say the Hindus. Before naming them we can note that together they constitute the Path of Renunciation.

The word renunciation has a negative ring, and India's frequent use of it has earned her the reputation of being a life-denying

An 11th-century stone icon from western India showing an infant Jain saint in his mother's arms.

spoilsport. But everything turns on what is renounced. In waiving away the desert tray, an athlete in training renounces a momentary pleasure for a more significant goal. When a man of the world praised an Indian ascetic for his powers of renunciation, the yogi responded: *"Your renunciation is far greater than mine, for I have renounced the finite for the Infinite whereas you are renouncing the Infinite for the finite." If people could be satisfied by following their impulses, the thought of renunciation would never arise.*

Let us be clear. Hinduism does not say that everyone in his present life will find the Path of Desire wanting; for against a vast time scale, Hinduism draws a distinction between chronological and psychological age. Two persons, both forty-six, are the same age chronologically, but psychologically one may be immature and the other not. Hindus extend this distinction to cover multiple life spans, as we shall see when we come to their doctrine of reincarnation. As a consequence, we shall find men and women who play the game of desire with all the zest of nine-year-old cops and robbers; though they know little else, they will die with the sense of having had a good life. Others, though, will be just as good at this game but find its laurels paltry. Why the difference? The enthusiasts are caught up in the flush of novelty, whereas the others, having played the game many times, seek other worlds to conquer.

These other worlds lie beyond self-centeredness, for the emptiness that remains after one rakes in what one wants for oneself derives from the smallness and insignificance of the integumented self.

This suggests that identification with something larger might relieve the sense of triviality. That thought announces the birth of religion, for all true religion begins with the quest for meaning and value beyond oneself. It renounces the ego's claims to finality.

In stepping out of self-centeredness, what do we step into? Hinduism has planted two markers which together constitute the Path of Renunciation.

The first reads, "Community." In supporting at once our own life and the lives of others, the community has an importance no individual life can command. Let us, then, transfer our allegiance to it, giving its claims priority over our own.

This transfer marks the first significant step in religion. It produces the religion of duty — after pleasure and success the third great aim of life in the Hindu outlook. Its attraction for the mature is major. Myriads have transformed the will to get into the will to give, the will to win into the will to serve. Not to triumph but to acquit themselves responsibly in the task at hand, has become their watchword.

Hinduism abounds in directives to persons who would put their shoulders to the collective wheel. It details duties appropriate to age, temperament, and social status; they will be examined in subsequent sections. Here we need only repeat what was said in connection with pleasure and success: duty, too, yields notable rewards, only to leave the human spirit unfilled. Its rewards require maturity to be appreciated, but given maturity, they are substantial. Faithful performance of duty brings respect and gratitude from one's peers. More important, however, is the self-respect that comes from doing one's share. In the end, though, even these rewards prove insufficient.

For even when time converts communities into history, history, standing alone, is finite and hence ultimately tragic. It is tragic not only because it must end — *"this too must pass away"* — but in its refusal to be perfected. Hope and history are always light years apart. The final good must lie elsewhere.

WHAT PEOPLE REALLY WANT

"There comes a time when one asks, even of Shakespeare,
even of Beethoven, is this all?"
Aldous Huxley

IT IS DIFFICULT TO THINK of a sentence that identifies Hinduism's attitude toward the world more precisely. The world's offerings are substantial enough to satisfy us for many lifetimes, but eventually everyone realizes with Simone Weil that *"there is no true good here below, that everything that appears to be good in this world is finite, limited, wears out, and once worn out, leaves necessity exposed in all its nakedness."*

If what "wears out" – finite things – can't satisfy us completely, what can? Only its alternative, the infinite. Infinitude, though, is a highly abstract notion. To link it to human satisfactions we need to connect it to the wants we have been discussing.

Pleasure, success, and duty are not what we really want, the Hindus say; what we really want is to be, to know, and to be happy. No one wants to die, to be in the dark about things, or to be miserable. Pleasure, success, and duty are only approximations of what we really want; they are apertures through which our true wants come through to us. Come through provisionally, though, we must add; for as windows they can admit only so much being, knowledge, and happiness, and what we really want is those things in infinite degree. The Hindus call this fourth, final and true want for which we are programmed liberation *(moksha)* – liberation from everything that distances us from infinite being, infinite awareness, and infinite bliss.

This brings us to the most startling claim of Hindu anthropology. That which we most truly want, we can have. As if that were not enough, though, the anthropology adds: you already have it.

For what is a human being? A body? Certainly, but anything else? A personality that includes mind, memories, and propensities? This, too, but anything more? Some say no, but Hinduism disagrees. Underlying the human self, and animating it, is a reservoir of being that never dies, is never exhausted, and is unrestricted in consciousness and bliss. This infinite center of every life, this hidden self or *Atman,* is no less than *Brahman,* the Godhead. Body, personality, and *Atman-Brahman* – a human self, is not completely accounted for until all three are entered.

But if this is true and we really are infinite in our being, why is this not apparent?

The answer, say the Hindus, lies in the depth at which the Eternal is buried within us, under an almost impenetrable mass of distractions, delusions, and self-serving instincts that comprise our surface selves. A chimney can be covered with dust, dirt, and mud to the point where no light pierces it at all. The human project is to clean one's "chimney" to allow the light within to radiate in full display.

Above: **Ganesh**, *one of the most beloved Hindu deities.* Right: **"Cosmogenesis"** *Kangra, Himachal Pradesh, 18th century. The evolution of the universe from dense matter, symbolized here by elephants, into the ethereal spheres of the cosmos.*

Cosmogenesis Kangra Himachal Pradesh 18th cent

THE BEYOND WITHIN

"*THE AIM OF LIFE,*" Justice Holmes said, "*is to get as far as possible from imperfection.*" Hinduism holds that it is possible to transcend imperfections completely, and it reduces them to three: ones that limit the joy, knowledge, and being that we basically want. To begin with the strictures on joy, these fall into three subgroups: physical pain, thwarted desire, and ennui — an emptiness that breeds apathy, and depression. The sense of life's vanity. About physical pain we can be brief, for it derives from our bodies which we shall eventually outgrow — the spiritual character of the Hindu self is growing pronounced.

Psychological disappointments, for their part, occur when our egos don't get what they want, so they will decline as egos stop insisting. As for emptiness, it will

abate as interests turn outward, for the cosmic drama is too stupendous to pall when our egos don't eclipse it.

Life's second limitation is ignorance. The Hindus claim that this, too, is removable. The *Upanishads* speak of a *"knowing of That the knowledge of which brings knowledge of everything."* It is not likely that "everything" here refers here to factual knowledge. More probably, it refers to an insight that lays bare the meaning of things at large.

As for restricted being, life's third limitation, this needs to be approached by asking how the self is to be defined. Not, certainly, by the physical space we occupy – the amount of water we displace in the bathtub. It makes more sense to gauge our being by the size of our spirits, the range of reality that engages us. By this criterion, people who could identify with being as a whole would be unlimited, yet this seems hardly right, for they would still die. The object of their concerns would continue, but they themselves would have vanished. We need, therefore, to approach this question of being not only

spatially, so to speak, but also in terms of time. Strictly speaking, every moment of our lives is a dying; the I of that moment dies, never to be reborn. Yet despite the fact that in this sense my life consists of nothing but funerals, I do not think of *myself* as dying with each moment, for I do not equate myself with those moments. I thread them as if they were beads on my string, experiencing them without considering myself identical with them. Hinduism carries this notion to its

logical limit. It posits a self that threads successive lives in the way a single life threads successive moments.

This is the basic point in the Hindu estimate of human nature. Depth psychology has accustomed us to the notion that there is more to our minds than we consciously realize. Hinduism extends this notion and considers the mind to be infinite. Infinite in being, our minds are infinite in awareness as well, for there is nothing beyond them that remains to be known.

And they are infinite in joy, for there is nothing alien to them to thwart their beatitude.

Hindu literature is studded with metaphors that are designed to awaken us to the realms of gold that are hidden in the depths of our being. We are like kings who, falling victim to amnesia, wander our kingdoms in tatters not knowing who we really are. Or like a lion cub which, having been separated from its mother, is raised by sheep and takes to grazing and bleating like them. We are like a lover who, in his dream, searches the wide world in despair for his beloved, oblivious of the fact that she is lying at his side throughout.

In Kathmandu, Hindu temples and Buddhist stupas appear side by side. Opposite: *Vasundhara Temple next to Swayambhunath.* Above: *Hindu shrine in front of Bauddhanath.*

FOUR PATHS TO THE GOAL

ALL OF US DWELL on the brink of the infinite ocean of life's creative power. We carry it within us: supreme strength, the fullness of wisdom, and unquenchable joy; but it is deeply hidden. What if we could bring it to light and draw from it unceasingly?

Hinduism's discoveries for actualizing the human potential come under the heading of *yoga,* a word that derives from the same root as the English word 'yoke' and carries connotations of uniting (yoking together), and placing under discipline (as in "take my yoke upon you"). Yoga is a method of training designed to lead to integration or union. It includes physical exercises, but its ultimate goal is union with God. The spiritual trails that Hindus have blazed toward this goal are four. At first this may seem surprising; if there is one goal, should there not be one path to it? This might be the case if we all started from the same point; but in actuality people approach the goal from different angles, so multiple paths are needed. Different starting points here really refers to different types of people. All the religions in this book recognize different spiritual personality types, but Hinduism is exceptional in the attention it has given the matter; it identifies the principal types, and delineates the programs that are suited to each.

The result is a recognition, pervading the entire religion, that there are multiple paths to God, each calling for its distinctive mode of approach.

Since the paths that Hinduism charts are four, the types they are intended for are likewise four. Some people are primarily reflective. Others are emotional. Still others are active and energetic. Finally, some like to experiment.

For each of these personality types, Hinduism prescribes a distinct yoga that is designed to capitalize on the type's strong suit. The types are not separated into watertight compartments. Every human being possesses some talent in all four directions in the way most hands of cards include all four suits. But one normally leads with one's strongest suit.

All four paths begin with moral preliminaries. As the aim of the yogas is to discern the self's deep-lying divinity, the scum on its surface must be removed. Selfishness muddies the water, ill-will skews objectivity.

The first step of every yoga, therefore, involves the dismantling of bad habits and the acquisition of good ones, such as non-injury, truthfulness, non-stealing, self-control, cleanliness, contentment, self-discipline, and a compelling desire to reach the goal. Keeping these common preliminaries in mind, we proceed to the yogas' distinctive directives.

Above: *God is depicted in this image with "a thousand heads and a thousand hands."* Opposite: *Jain* **Tirthankara,** *or great teacher, in the Vimala Sha Temple, Mount Abu, India.*

THE WAY TO GOD THROUGH KNOWLEDGE

*J*NANA YOGA INTENDED for spiritual aspirants who have a strong reflective bent, is the path to oneness with God through knowledge. Such knowledge has nothing to do with factual information. It is an intuitive discernment that transforms the knower into the likeness of what it knows. Reflection is important for such people; their thoughts grasp their lives and transform them. For these knowing types, Hinduism proposes a series of demonstrations designed to convince one that there is more to oneself than had been supposed. The key to the project is discrimination, the power to distinguish between the surface self that crowds the foreground of attention and the larger self that is latent and out of sight.

Cultivating this power proceeds through three stages, the first of which is hearing. Through listening to sages and scriptures, the aspirant is introduced to the prospect that one's essential being is Being itself. The second step is thinking. By prolonged, intensive reflection, that which the first step introduced as a hypothesis assumes life. Several lines of thought are proposed for this project. The disciple may be advised to examine his everyday language and ponder its implications.

The word *"my"* always implies a distinction between the possessor and what is possessed; when I speak of my book or my jacket, I do not suppose that I am those things. But I also speak of my body, my mind, and my personality, which suggests that in some sense I think of myself as distinct from them as well.

From a different angle, science tells me that there is almost nothing in my body that was there seven years ago, and my mind and my personality have changed even more. Yet throughout these changes I have remained in some sense the same person. What is the something in my makeup that has endured? Our word "personality" comes from the Latin *persona* which originally referred to the mask an actor donned as he or she stepped onto the stage. The mask depicted the actor's role, while behind it the actor remained hidden and anonymous. Hindus see this as an apt analogy for the roles our enduring souls are cast to play in their various lifetimes.

If the yogi is able and diligent such reflections will eventually induce a lively sense of the enduring Self that underlies the transient self. The two will become increasingly distinct, separating like water and oil where formerly they mixed like water and milk. One is then ready for the third step on the path of knowledge which consists in shifting self-identification to one's abiding part. One effective way to do this is to think of one's nominal self in the third person. Instead of "I am walking down the street," one thinks, "There goes Sybil walking down Fifth Avenue," and backs up the assertion by trying to visualize Sybil from a distance.

This exercise does two things. It drives a wedge between one's self-identification and one's surface self, and at the same time forces this self-identification to a deeper level until at last — through a knowledge that is identical with being — one becomes in full what one always was at heart.

"That thou art, other than Whom there is no other seer, hearer, thinker, or agent" (Upanishads).

THE WAY TO GOD THROUGH LOVE

*T*HE YOGA OF KNOWLEDGE is said to be the shortest path to divine realization but also the steepest, for on the whole life is powered less by reason than by emotion, the strongest of which is love. The aim of bhakti yoga – the yoga of love and devotion – is to direct toward God the love that lies at the base of every heart.

"*As the waters of the Ganges flow incessantly toward the ocean,*" says God in the *Bhagavata Purana*, "*so do the minds of the bhakta move constantly toward Me, the Supreme Person residing in every heart, when they hear about My qualities.*"

Bhakti yoga is the most popular of the four yogas. One of its best known advocates was a sixteenth century mystical poet named Tulsidas.

During his early married life he was so inordinately fond of his wife that he could not abide her absence for even a day, which led her to remark: "How passionately attached to me you are! If only you could shift your attachment to God, you would reach him in no time."

Tulsidas took her suggestion to heart, and it worked.

The *bhakta* envisions God differently from the *jnana*. In *jnana* yoga the guiding image was of an infinite sea of being underlying the wavelets of our finite selves. Thus envisioned, God is impersonal, or rather transpersonal, for personality (being definite) seems to be finite whereas the *jnanic* God is infinite. To the *bhakta*, for whom feelings are more important than thoughts, God appears different on each of these counts.

First, as healthy love is out-going, the *bhakta* will reject all suggestions that the God one loves is oneself, even one's deepest Self, and insist on God's otherness. As a Hindu devotional classic puts the point, "I want to taste sugar; I don't want to be sugar."

> *"Can water quaff itself?*
> *Can trees taste of the fruit they bear?*
> *He who worships God must stand distinct from Him,*
> *Only so shall he know the joyful love of God."*

Second, being persuaded of God's otherness, the *bhakta's* goal, too, will differ from the *jnana's*. The bhakta will strive, not to identify with God but to adore God with every element of his or her being. All we have to do in this yoga is to love God dearly — not just claim such love, but love God in fact; love God only (other things being loved in relation to God), and love God for no ulterior reason (not even to be loved in return) but for love's sake alone. Insofar as we succeed in this project we know joy, for no experience can compare with that of being fully and authentically in love.

How is such love to be engendered? The task is not easy, for the world clamors so loudly that an invisible God is not easily perceived.

Enter Hinduism's myths, her magnificent symbols, her several hundred images of God, her rituals that keep turning night and day, like never-ending prayer wheels. Valued as ends in themselves these could, of course, usurp God's place, but this is not their intent. They are matchmakers, whose vocation is to introduce the human heart to what they represent but themselves are not. It is obtuse to confuse Hinduism's images with idolatry, and their multiplicity with polytheism. They are runways from which the sense-encumbered human spirit can rise for its *"flight of the alone to the Alone."* A symbol such as a multi-armed image can represent God's power; myths can plumb depths that are closed to the intellect; parables and legends present ideals in ways that make hearers long to embody them. The value of these things lies in their power to recall our minds from the world's distractions to the thought of God and God's love. In singing God's praises, praying to God with wholehearted devotion, meditating on God's majesty and glory, reading about God in the scriptures and regarding the entire universe as God's handiwork, we move our affections steadily in God's direction.

Three features of the *bhakta's* approach deserve mention: *japam,* ringing the changes on love, and the worship of one's chosen ideal.

Japam is the practice of repeating God's name. It finds a Christian parallel in the Jesus Prayer which a classic of Russian spirituality, *The Way of a Pilgrim*, describes. *"Keep the name of the Lord spinning in the midst of all your activities"* is a favorite bhakti maxim. Washing or weaving, planting or shopping, sacred vocables penetrate the subconscious mind to infuse it with holiness.

Left: *Hindu woman in East Africa worshipping Hanuman.*

Ringing the changes on love puts to religious use the fact that love assumes different nuances according to the relationships involved. The love of the parent for the child carries overtones of protectiveness, whereas a child's love includes dependence. The love of friends is different from the conjugal love of woman and man. Different still is the love of a devoted servant for its master. Hinduism holds that all of these modes have their place in strengthening the love of God and encourages *bhaktas* to make use of them all in different contexts.

We come finally to the worship of God in the form of one's chosen ideal, or *ishta*. The Hindus have represented God in innumerable forms. They all point equally to God, but it is advisable for each devotee to develop an abiding attachment to one of them. Only so can its presence deepen and its power be fully assimilated. For most persons the most effective *ishta* will be one of God's incarnations, for the human heart is naturally tuned to loving people.

Left: *A ritual of purification in the waters of the Ganges.* Above: *Shopping for garlands to celebrate one of the many Hindu holy days.*

THE WAY TO GOD THROUGH WORK

THE THIRD PATH TOWARD GOD, intended for persons of energetic bent, is *karma yoga* , the way through work.

Work is life's staple. The point is not simply that people must work to survive; most people like to be constructively engaged – they find it satisfying. To such persons Hinduism says, You don't have to retire to a cloister to realize God; he can be found in the world of everyday affairs as readily as anywhere. All you need do is learn how to work in ways that carry you toward God, not away from God.

How this is to be done depends on the other components in the worker's nature. By choosing the path of work the karma yogi has already declared his taste for activity, but there remains the question of whether this supporting disposition is predominantly affective or reflective. The answer to that question determines whether the yogi will approach work reflectively or in the spirit of love. In the first case, *karma yoga* is practiced thoughtfully, in *jnanic* mode; while in the second, it is performed as loving service *(bhakti)*. We need to see how the spiritual dynamics operate in the two cases.

According to Hindu doctrine, every action directed toward the external world reacts on the doer. Everything I do for my private benefit adds another layer to my ego, and in thus thickening it separates me further from God. Conversely, every act that is done without thought for myself diminishes my self-centeredness until nothing separates me from the divine. In keeping with this principle, persons who are emotionally inclined should work for God's sake instead of their own. *"He who performs actions without attachment, resigning them to God, is untainted by their effects as the lotus leaf by water"* (Bhagavad-Gita). Such a one is as active as before but works in a different spirit, from dedication. Acts are no longer undertaken for their personal rewards. Not only are they now performed as service to God; they are regarded as prompted by God's will and powered by God's energy which courses through the devotee. *"Thou art the Doer, I am the instrument."* Performed in this spirit, actions lighten the ego instead of encumbering it. Each task becomes a sacred ritual, performed as a loving sacrifice for God's glory.

For persons of reflective rather than emotional bent, God-oriented work proceeds differently. They too work unselfishly, but in a different way. We have seen that philosophers tend to find the idea of Infinite Being in one's deepest center more meaningful than the thought of a Heavenly Father who watches over the world with love. It follows that they will approach work less relationally, seeking through it enlightenment rather than a deepening love relationship.

The way they do this is through working in the spirit of detachment. They draw a line between their finite selves and the Infinite Self that underlies them, and then systematically disidentify with the former. In terms of work, this means cultivating an active disinterest in "what's in it for me," whether the reward be cash or recognition. Those emoluments are pleasant, but the *karma yogi* knows their price: if he is invested in them, they inflate his ego. In doing so they thicken the insulation between his current and his true Self, and increase his isolation.

The alternative is work performed detachedly, in virtual dissociation from the empirical self. Identifying with the Eternal, the worker continues to work, but as the deeds are performed by the empirical self, the True Self has nothing to do with them. *"He who performs his task dictated by duty, caring nothing for the fruit of the action, he is a yogi"* (Bhagavad-Gita). Having given his best to what's to be done, he lets the chips fall where they may. *"One to me is loss or gain, / One to me is fame or shame, / One to me*

is pleasure, pain" (Bhagavad-Gita). Those who are proficient in this way of working are calm, even while busy, like the center of a spinning wheel. It is the stillness of absolute motion. Though philosophically and affectionately inclined persons practice *karma yoga* differently, it is easy to see their practices as pointed in the same direction.

Both yogis are engaged in radical reducing diets, designed to starve the finite ego by withdrawing interest from the bearing of their work on their finite selves.

THE WAY TO GOD THROUGH PSYCHOPHYSICAL EXERCISES

BECAUSE OF THE DAZZLING HEIGHTS to which it leads, *raja yoga* is known in India as *"the royal (raj) road to reintegration."* Designed for persons of experimental bent, it is the way to God through psychophysical experiments. Unlike experiments in the natural sciences, those of *raja yoga* are on one's self. No dogmas need be accepted, but experiments do require hypotheses they are designed to confirm or disprove. The hypothesis that underlies *raja yoga* is the Hindu doctrine of the human self which can be restated as·follows: The self has four layers. First and most obviously, we have bodies. Next comes the conscious layer of our minds. Underlying these two is a third region, the individual subconscious, which consists of deposits from our individual histories. We don't remember most of those deposits, but they continue to shape us. The West is familiar with these first three segments of the self. The distinctive feature of the Hindu view comes in its inclusion of a fourth component. Underlying the other three, less perceived by the conscious mind than even its private subconscious (though related to it fully as much) stands Being Itself – infinite, unthwarted, eternal.

"I am smaller than the minutest atom, likewise greater than the greatest. I am the whole, the diversified-multicolored-lovely-strange universe. I am the Ancient One, the Lord. I am the Being-of-Gold. I am the very state of divine beatitude."

The purpose of *raja yoga* is to demonstrate the validity of this fourfold estimate of the human self by leading the inquirer to direct personal experience of "the Beyond within." Its method is willed introversion; its intent, to drive the psychic energy of the self to its deepest part. With raja yoga's hypothesis before us, we are prepared to outline the eight steps of its experimental attempt to verify that hypothesis; most pointedly its final, most exuberant claim.

1. and 2. The first two steps concern the moral preliminaries common to all four yogas, for unless one's personal life is in reasonable order and one's relationships harmonious, there can be no hope of deeper self-knowledge; the surface waters will be too choppy. Step one involves the practice of five abstentions (from injury, lying, stealing, sensuality, and greed); step two, the five observances (cleanliness, contentment, self-control, studiousness, and contemplation of the divine).

3. Although *raja yoga* is mainly interested in the mind, it works with the body as well. More precisely, it works through the body to the mind. Beyond general health, its chief concern for the body is to keep it from

Above: *Steatite seal illustrating a yogi in meditation with a trident symbol at his back depicting his transcendence of the seven planes of existence* Opposite: *Yogi meditating at the Kumbha Mela festival near the Ganges.*

distracting the mind when it concentrates. India's most famous discovery here is the *"lotus position"* in which the *yogi* sits — ideally on a tiger skin symbolizing energy, overlaid with a deerskin symbolizing calm — with legs crossed in such a way that each foot rests sole up on its opposing thigh. With allowance for its natural curvature, the spine is erect. Hands are placed, palms up, in the lap, one atop the other with thumbs touching lightly. The eyes may be closed or allowed to fall unfocused on the ground or floor.

4. Having positioned the body in an alert but relaxed position, the yogi turns to his breath, for random breathing can shatter the mind's repose. Evenness and breath reduction are the general aims here; a typical exercise calls for breathing so gently across goose down touching the nostrils that an observer cannot tell if air is moving in or out. Prolonged abstention from breathing is important too, for at such times the body approaches a state of suspended animation and the mind seems disembodied. These are cherished moments for the task at hand. *"The light of a lamp does not flicker in a windless place"* (*Bhagavad-Gita*).

5. Composed, body at ease, its breathing regular, the *yogi* sits in contemplation. Suddenly a door creaks, a sliver of moonlight shimmers on the ground ahead, or a mosquito whines, and he is back in the world. *"Restless the mind is, so strongly shaken by the grip of the senses. Truly I think that the wind is no wilder"* (*Bhagavad-Gita*).

The object of the fifth step of *raja yoga* is to unplug one's sense receptors, so to speak; or put them on hold so the clatter of the world's boiler factory won't disturb the *yogi's* concentration. That this can be done without bodily mutilation is a common experience. A man calls his wife to remind her that they should leave for a social engagement. Five minutes later she insists that she did not hear him; he, that she must have heard, for he was in the adjoining room and spoke distinctly. Who is right? It is a matter of definition.

If hearing means that sound waves of sufficient amplitude beat on healthy eardrums, she heard; if it means that they were noticed, she did not. There is nothing esoteric about such occurrences; their explanation is simply concentration — the woman was at her computer and deeply engrossed. There is nothing mysterious about this fifth step. It seeks to carry the yogi beyond the point the wife had reached: first, by turning concentration from a chance occurrence into a controlled skill; and second, by raising the skill to a point where drumbeats in the same room can escape notice.

6. At last the *yogi* is alone with his mind, but the battle is not yet won, for the mind's fiercest antagonist is itself. Closeted, it still shows not the slightest inclination to settle down or obey. The *yogi* wants it to be still, to mirror reality in the way a quiet lake reflects the moon. Instead, its surface is choppy at best. Hinduism likens its restlessness to a crazed monkey cavorting about its cage. Or rather, a drunken, crazed monkey. But more! — a drunken, crazed monkey that has St. Vitus' Dance. Even this is insufficient. The mind is like a drunken crazed monkey with St. Vitus' Dance who has just been stung by a wasp.

Those who have seriously tried to meditate will not find this metaphor extreme. I tell my hand to rise and it obeys. I tell my mind to be still and it mocks my command. Psychotic minds are even less controlled than normal ones; fantasies overtake them at the slightest provocation. The *raja yogi* works for powers of concentration that excel those of the normal mind in the way that mind excels psychotic minds.

Opposite: *Illustration of a yogi showing the seven chakras.*

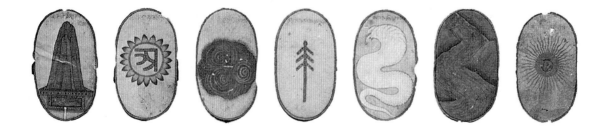

"When all the senses are stilled, when the mind is at rest, when the intellect wavers not – that, say the wise, is the highest state" (Katha Upanishad).

The method for reaching this state is not exotic, only arduous. One begins by relaxing the mind to allow repressed thoughts and emotions to exorcise themselves through free association. Then one selects something to concentrate on – the glowing tip of a joss stick, an imaged sea of infinite light, the object does not much matter – and practices keeping the mind on the object until success increases.

7. The last two steps are stages in which this process of concentration progressively deepens. In the previous step the mind was brought to the point where it could stay with its object, but it continued to be aware that it was attending to it. In the seventh step, the knower drops from view. The object occupies his entire attention, leaving no remainder for self awareness.

8. In the eighth, climactic stage (known as *samadhi*) the object likewise vanishes. It was useful as a device for focusing the attention, but now that that purpose has been achieved, it has no further function. Objects by their very nature are limited. They are composed of properties that make them what they are by excluding from them the properties of the things they are not; a cup would not be round if it were also square. But the "object" the raja yogi is seeking excludes nothing, for it is infinite, and hence formless – *"separated from all qualities, neither this nor that, without form, without a name" (Upanishads)*. The knower is confronted with total being, and for a spell is immersed in it.

We have presented the four yogas as alternatives, but to conclude with a point that was made at the start, Hinduism does not consider them as exclusive of one another. No individual is solely reflective, emotional, active, or experimental, and different life situations call for different resources to be brought into play. Most persons will find that they make better time on one road than the others, so will keep close to it; but Hinduism encourages people to test all four and combine them in the ways they find most productive.

Right: Rajasthani painting illustrating the ascending and descending planes of experience. The center circle is the plane of normal reality. Above: A set of seven gouache paintings illustrating various phases of cosmic evolution and involution. (Rajasthan, 18th century).

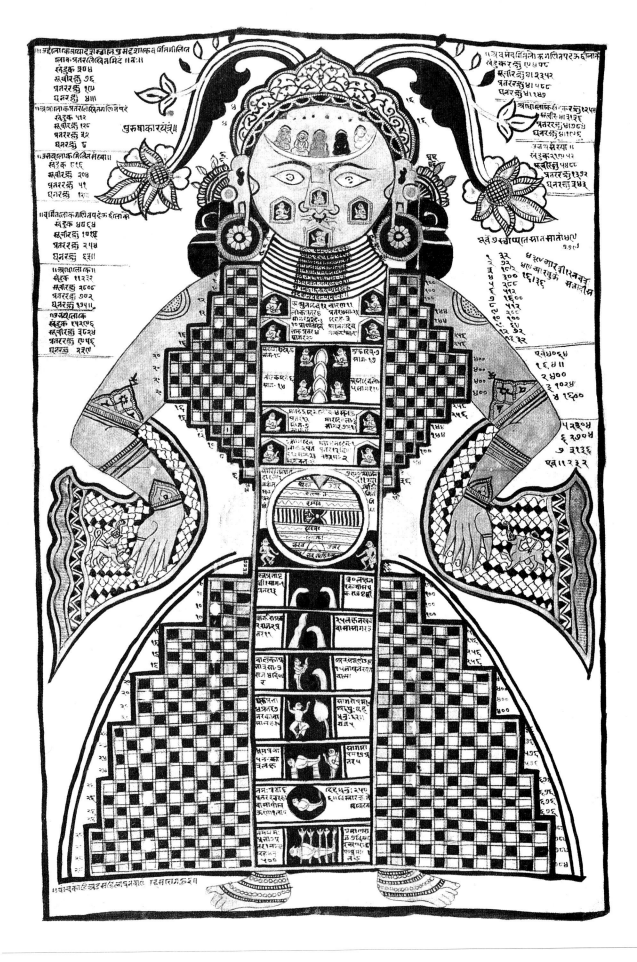

THE STAGES OF LIFE

EOPLE ARE DIFFERENT. Few observations could be more banal, yet serious attention to it is one of Hinduism's distinctive gifts. The preceding sections traced its insistence that differences in human nature call for a variety of paths toward life's fulfillment. We have now to note the same insistence pressed from another quarter. Not only do individuals differ from one another; each individual moves through different stages of life that call for their own agendas.

The first stage India identifies as that of the student. Traditionally this stage began after the rite of initiation, between the ages of eight and twelve, and lasted for twelve years during which the student typically lived in the home of a teacher, rendering service for instruction received. It was an apprenticeship in which habits of character were acquired along with skills and information.

The second stage, which typically begins with marriage, is that of the householder. Here, during life's noonday, interests naturally turn outward. There are three channels into which they appropriately flow — family, vocation, and the community — and attention will normally be divided between the three. This is the time for satisfying the first three human wants: pleasure through marriage and one's family, success through vocation, and duty through civic responsibilities.

Hinduism smiles on the happy fulfillment of these wants but does not try to prolong their satisfactions when they ebb. Those who do try to hang onto them are not a pretty spectacle, for pursuits appropriate in their day become grotesque when obsessively clung to. Still, we cannot censure those who continue to cling, for they see no promising alternative. The question they forthrightly raise is, is old age worthwhile?

The answer to that question depends on who we think we are. If we are basically bodies, nothing can compare with sensory pleasures. If we are personalities, personal achievements will fulfill us most. But if we are spirits, nothing can rival the excitement of discovering the awe-inspiring unknown world within. Because India took our spirituality seriously, she looked forward to life's second half, staking it out as the time for one's true adult education. *"Leave all and follow the Self! Enjoy its inexpressible riches" (Upanishads).*

Life's second half also divides into halves, the first of which is retirement. Anytime after the arrival of a first grandchild the individual may claim the license of age and withdraw from social obligations that were thus far willingly shouldered. For many years society has exacted its dues; now relief is in order lest life end before we understand it. Traditionally those who took full advantage of this call to spiritual adventure were known as forest dwellers, for — husband and wife together if she wished to go, husband alone if she did not — they would take leave of their family and home and seek out forest solitudes in which to pursue their tasks of self-discovery. Retirement looks beyond the stars, not to the village streets. It is the time for working out a philosophy, and then working that philosophy into a way of life.

The quest that was commenced in that third stage, continues through the fourth, the stage of renunciation, but here it acquires a new wrinkle. Geography ceases to be important. In the state of retirement, geography *was* important, for if one didn't pull up stakes and move, associates would treat you as they always had, which

would keep as you always were. A clean break was needed. In time, though – the time of retirement – one becomes inner directed to the point where it doesn't matter where you are. The market place, or one's former village, is now as hospitable to the spirit as the forest. But if one reenters the world, one does so as a different person. Having discovered the release from limitations that is synonymous with anonymity, the *sannyasin* (as those in this final stage are called) can distinguish his true from his finite self wherever he happens to be.

A Shiva sadhu at the Kumbha Mela festival in Nashik, India.

*Streetsweepers such as this one in Kathmandu are members of the
sudra caste under the Hindu system.*

THE STATIONS OF LIFE

EOPLE ARE DIFFERENT — we are back a third time to this cardinal Hindu tenet. We have traced its import for the different paths people should follow toward God and the different agendas that are appropriate at different stages of life. We come now to its implications for the social order. This means that we must talk about caste, the topic on which Hinduism is probably best known by the outside world and most roundly denounced.

We shall skirt the cloudy issue of how caste arose, and record at once perversions that have entered with time if they were not there from the beginning: the wretched state of outcastes (untouchables) who are excluded from the caste system altogether; the proliferation of subcastes which now number over three thousand; massive proscriptions against intermarriage and interdining; gross inequities which favor the higher castes; and a heredity system which all but forces people to remain in the castes into which they were born.

With these heavy counts against it, it may come as a surprise to find that there are contemporary Indians, thoroughly familiar with Western alternatives, who defend caste — not, to be sure, in its entirety, especially what it has become, but in its basic format. What lasting values could such a system possibly contain?

We can begin with the suggestion that with respect to the ways they can best contribute to society, as well as best develop their own potentials, people fall into four groups.

1. The first group India called *Brahmins* or *seers*. Reflective, and with keen intuitive grasp of what matters most in human life, these are civilization's intellec-

tual and spiritual leaders. Into their province fall the functions our more specialized society has distributed among philosophers, artists, religious leaders, and teachers. Things of the mind and spirit are their raw materials.

2. Others are born administrators or organizers, with a genius for orchestrating people and projects in ways that maximize available talents.

3. Others find their vocation as producers; they are artisans and farmers, and in our time engineers who are skillful in creating the material things on which life depends.

4. Finally there are some who are best described as followers; hired hands, unskilled laborers, and currently factory workers would be other names for them. These are persons who, if they had to carve out careers for themselves, commit themselves to long periods of training, or go into business for themselves, would flounder. Having short attention spans, they are not good at foregoing present gratification for the sake of future rewards. Supervised, though, they are capable of hard work and devoted service. Such persons are better off (and actually happier) working for others than being on their own. It goes against modernity's democratic, egalitarian instincts to grant that this fourth type of person exists, to which traditional Hindus reply: What we might like people to be is not the point. The question is what they are.

Within each caste there was considerable equality, opportunity, and social insurance, but the castes themselves were ranked hierarchically. Even here, though, there was an underlying egalitarianism, for it was assumed that in the course of their manifold incarnations all *jivas* (individual souls) would move through all four castes, beginning with the lowest. More interesting, however, is the way in which the system sought in one specific respect to equalize the castes. All four should be equally rewarded for their services, but this does not mean that they should receive the same pay, for that would assume that pay is the reward everyone values most. This is not the case, so people should be paid in different coin, so to speak. Producers, being occupied with things, should receive what they most prize: wealth and the things money can buy. Administrators are more invested in human relationships: the structures and dynamics of social institutions. Power, therefore, — social, political, administrative power — should be their distinctive reward. Neither wealth nor power interest Brahmins most — if they do they are wrongly cast — so the reward they should receive is respect from the castes that are still glued to those things. There remain the followers. In theory, they should have the fewest responsibilities and greatest freedom. Wage earners need not indenture themselves to a lifetime at a single job, and when checkout time comes they are through for the day — their jobs "colonize" their lives less. India never confused democracy with egalitarianism; justice was defined as a state in which privileges were proportionate to responsibilities. The upper three castes — "twice-born" because religiously initiated — were more honored, affluent, and powerful, but their obligations were also greater. In reverse of the European doctrine that the king could do no wrong, the Hindu view came very near to holding that followers (the lowest, *shudra* caste) could do

Brahmin priests in Benares. Brahmins are the philosophers, scholars and religious leaders of Hinduism.

no wrong, its members being regarded more or less as children from whom less should be expected. Classical legal doctrine stipulated that for the same offense the punishment of the *vaishya* (producer) should be twice as heavy as that of the shudra, that of the *kshatriya* (administrator) twice as heavy again, and that of the *Brahmin* twice or even four times as heavy. In India the lowest caste was exempt from many of the forms of probity and self-denial that the upper castes were held to. Its widows might remarry, and proscription against meat and alcohol were less exacting.

Something like this was, and is, caste *de jure,* in principle. *De facto,* in actuality, ideals never work out as intended. Insofar as caste today means rigidity, exclusiveness, and undeserved privilege, Hindus are working to clear the corruption from their polity. There continue to be some, however, who believe that in looking to the problem no country has yet solved—the problem of how society might be ordered to insure the maximum of both fair play and creativity—the basic assumptions of caste continue to warrant attention.

Up to this point we have approached Hinduism in terms of its practical import. Beginning with its analysis of what people want, we have traced its suggestions concerning the ways these wants might be met and the responses appropriate to various stages and stations of human life. The remaining sections of this chapter shift the focus from practice to theory, indicating the principal philosophical concepts that rib the Hindu religion.

Right: *Shiva's warlike consort Durga subduing the buffalo demon.* Opposite: *This mandala on the ceiling of Adi Nath Temple in Ranakpur shows the primordial sound at the center of the universe expanding outward into the material realm. Overleaf, page 48: A statue of the deity Mahesamurti, in Elephanta.*

"Thou Before Whom All Words Recoil"

THE FIRST PRINCIPLE OF JAPANESE *ikebana* flower arrangement is to learn what to leave out. This is also the first principle in speaking of God, the Hindus insist. Because thoughts and things are finite and God is infinite, the only literally accurate description of the Unsearchable is *neti...neti,* "not this...not this." If you traverse the length and breadth of the universe saying of everything you see and conceive, "not this...not this," what remains will be God. A famous Hindu prayer begins, *"Oh Thou, before whom all words recoil."* And yet, words and concepts are of course inevitable, for without them we get nowhere. They are indicators that point us in the right direction without delivering us to our destination. The Sanskrit name for God is Brahman which has a dual etymology deriving from *br,* to breathe, and *brih,* to be great. The chief attributes to be linked with the name are *sat*, *chit*, and *ananda;* God is being, awareness, and bliss. Utter reality, utter consciousness, and utterly beyond all possibility of frustration and futility — this is the basic Hindu view of God as long as we keep in mind that our understanding of these attributes only approximates the way they inhere in God.

This is as far as some minds need go. Most persons, however, find such abstractions empty. C. S. Lewis was among them; as a child, he tells us, he was warned by his parents against attaching concrete attributes to God, for these would hem him in and restrict his infinity. He tried his best, but the closest he could come to a notion of a formless God was an infinite sea of grey tapioca.

This anecdote suggests that most minds need pictures, almost, to provide traction. Hinduism encourages persons of this nature to think of God as the noblest instance of what they find in the sensible world. This means thinking of God as the supreme person, for persons are nature's noblest crown.

Thus conceived, *Brahman* is *Saguna Brahman,* or God with attributes, as distinct from the sages' more abstract *Nirguna Brahman* or God-without-attributes.

Nirguna Brahman is the ocean without a ripple; *Saguna Brahman* that same ocean alive with waves and swells. In the language of theology, the distinction is between personal and transpersonal conceptions of God. Hinduism includes superb champions of each view, but on the whole accepts them both, in something of the way scientists accept both wave and particle depictions of matter. God's relation to the world varies according to the symbolism that is espoused. Conceived in personal terms, God will stand in relation to the world as an artist to his or her handiwork. He will be Creator (*Brahma*), Preserver (*Vishnu*), and Destroyer (*Shiva*) who in the end resolves all finite forms back into the primordial being from which they sprang.

Alternatively, conceived transpersonally, God works less deliberately. The world will still be God-dependent. It will have emerged in some unfathomable way from the divine plenitude and be sustained by its power: *"He shining, the sun, the moon and the stars shine after Him; by His light all is lighted."*

But God will not have intentionally willed the world, nor be scarred by its inherent ambiguity, imperfections, and finitude.

COMING OF AGE IN THE UNIVERSE

WITH GOD IN PLACE, WE CAN return to human beings to see how Hindus trace their odysseys.

Individual souls, or *jivas*, enter the world mysteriously; by God's power we may be sure, but how or for what reason we are unable fully to fathom. Like bubbles that form on the bottom of boiling teakettles, they make their way through the water (universe) until they burst into freedom in the limitless air. They begin as the souls of the simplest forms of life, but they do not vanish with the death of their original bodies. In the Hindu view, spirit no more depends on the body it inhabits than bodies depend on the clothes they wear or the houses they live in. *"Worn-out garments are shed by the body / Worn-out bodies are shed by the dweller" (Bhagavad-Gita).*

The process by which an individual *jiva* passes through a sequence of bodies is known as reincarnation, or transmigration. On the subhuman level the passage proceeds automatically; the soul is on an escalator, so to speak, and ascends through increasingly complex animal forms until a human body is attained. With this attainment things change dramatically. For the first time the *jiva* knows itself, and with its reflexive awareness come freedom and responsibility.

The mechanism that ties these new acquisitions together is the law of *karma*. The literal meaning of karma (as we saw in *karma yoga*) is work, but as a doctrine it means, roughly, the moral law of cause and effect. The law is not foreign to the West; *"As a man sows, so shall he reap."* What India does is tighten the law to the point where it brooks no exceptions. The present condition of each interior life – how happy it is, how confused or serene, how much it sees – is an exact product of what it has wanted and done in the past. Equally, one's present thoughts and decisions determine one's future experiences. Each act that is directed upon the world reacts on oneself, delivering a chisel blow that sculpts one's destiny.

This notion of a completely moral universe commits the Hindu to complete personal responsibility. It allows no toehold for psychological projection (blaming others for one's troubles) or appeals to bad luck. It is not, however, fatalistic. Karma decrees that every decision must have its inexorable consequences, but the decisions themselves are freely arrived at. The hand that a card player picks up he dealt in a former life; now he is free to play it as he chooses. The course that a soul follows is charted by its wants and deeds at each stage of its journey.

What those wants are can be quickly rehearsed. A *jiva* that has reached the human level wants nothing more at first than to taste widely of the sense delights its new physical equipment affords it. With repetition, however, these fall prey to habituation and gradually pall, whereupon the *jiva* turns to social conquests. As long as wealth, fame, and power remain exciting, they satisfy; but when novelty wears off – when the winner has acknowledged with the same bow and pretty little speech the honors he has received so many times before – he begins to look for something new and more deeply satisfying. Duty, the total dedication of one's life to one's community, can fill the need for a while, but the ironies and anomalies of history make this object, too, a revolving door. Lean on it and it gives, but in time one discovers that it is going in circles. After social dedication, the only good that can satisfy is the Infinite and Eternal:

Moksha. Total release. Progress through these ascending wants zigzags, but the general direction is upward. Eventually, everyone gets the point.

Never during its pilgrimage is the human spirit alone. From start to finish its nucleus is the *Atman,* the God within that seeks release like a jack-in-the-box. Or in bhaktic understanding, God is one's constant companion, the Friend who understands.

What happens when the goal is reached? Some say the individual soul passes into complete identification with God and loses every trace of its former separateness. Others, wishing to taste sugar, hope that some slight differentiation between the soul and God will remain – a thin line that retains the two-ness that is required for love and the beatific vision.

There is an Indian fable that capsules this process of coming of age in the universe. An old man seated on a lawn with a group of children tells them of the magic Kalpataru tree that fulfills all wishes. "If you speak to it and tell it a wish, the wish will be granted," the old man says, adding that he once obtained such a tree and planted it in his garden. "In fact, that is the Kalpataru over there."

At once the children rush to the tree and start showering it with requests. Most of these turn out to be unwise, ending in indigestion or tears. But the Kalpataru grants them indiscriminately. It has no interest in giving advice.

Years pass and the Kalpataru is forgotten. The children have now grown into men and women and are trying to fulfill the new wishes they have found. At first they want their wishes to be fulfilled instantly, but later they search for wishes that can be satisfied only with ever-increasing difficulty.

The point of the story is that the universe is one gigantic Wishing Tree, with branches that reach into every heart. The cosmic process decrees that sometime or other, in this life or another, each of these wishes will be granted – together, of course, with consequences.

There was one child from the original group, however, the story concludes, who did not spend his years skipping from desire to desire, from one gratification to another. For from the first he had understood the real nature of the Wishing Tree. For him, the Kalpataru was not the pretty magic tree of his uncle's story. It did not exist to grant the foolish wishes of children – it was unspeakably terrible and grand. It was his father and his mother. Its roots held the world together, and its branches reached beyond the stars. Before the beginning it had been, and always would be.

Above: *Red sandstone torso of a Bodhisattva from Sanci, created during the Gupta period, 5th-9th century.* Opposite: *This Hindu cosmogenesis celebrates the boundless variety of the universe.*

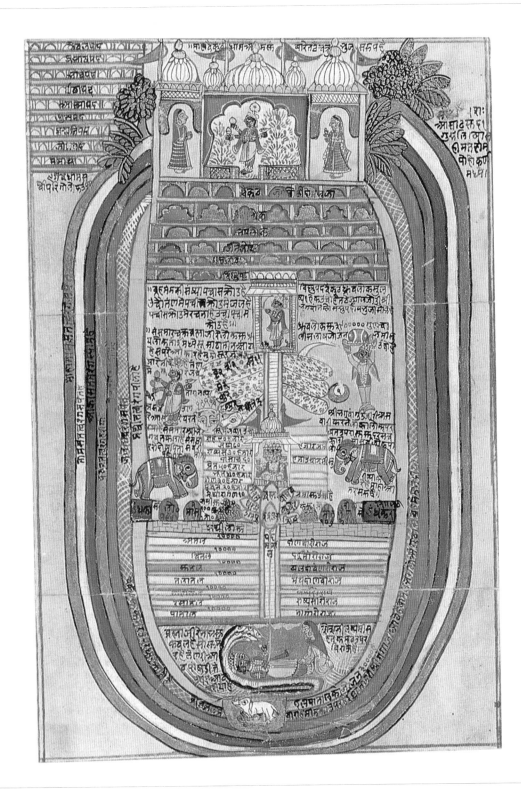

THE WORLD ~ WELCOME AND FAREWELL

*T*HE GROUND PLAN of the Hindu world looks something like this: There are innumerable galaxies comparable to our own, each centering in an earth from which people wend their ways to God. Ringing each earth are a number of finer worlds above, and coarser ones below, to which souls repair between incarnations according to their just deserts.

All these worlds issue from God, for *"just as the spider pours forth its thread from itself and takes it back again, even so the universe grows from the Imperishable" (Upanishads).*

Periodically, however, the thread is withdrawn; the cosmos collapses into a Night of Brahma and all phenomenal being is returned to a state of pure potentiality. Switching metaphors: exhaled and then inhaled, the world is God's respiration. The oscillation is built into the scheme of things; the universe had no beginning and will have no end. The time scale in all this is staggering. The Himalayas are made of solid granite. Once every thousand years a bird flies over them, brushing the range with its wings. When by this process the Himalayas have been worn away, one day of a cosmic cycle will have elapsed.

When we turn from cosmology to moral concerns, we have seen that the law of karma renders the cosmos just. Even so, ours is a middling world, and in two senses. It is positioned between better worlds (heavens) above and worse worlds (hells) below, and it is woven of good and evil, pleasure and pain, knowledge and ignorance in about equal proportions. And so things will remain; the fourth grade remains the fourth grade while different pupils move through it. Dreams of utopia are, therefore, not just doomed to disappointment; they misjudge the world's purpose, which is not to double for paradise but to provide a training ground for the human spirit. The world can develop character and prepare people to look beyond it – for these it is admirably fashioned. But it cannot be perfected. *"Said Jesus, blessed be his name, this world is a bridge: pass over, but build no house upon it."* It is not surprising that this apocryphal saying comes from India.

If we ask about the world's metaphysical status, we shall have to continue the distinction we have watched divide Hinduism on every major issue; namely, the one between dual and non-dual points of view. On the conduct of life, this distinction divides *jnana yoga* from *bhakti;* on God's nature it divides the personal from the transpersonal view; on the issue of salvation it divides those who anticipate merging with God from those who aspire to God's company. In cosmology the same line divides those who see the world as completely real from those who think it only semi-real. If we ask if dreams are real, our answer must be qualified. They are real in that we have them, but most of their images do not exist in the real – i.e., waking – world. Strictly speaking, a dream is a psychological construct, a mental fabrication. The Hindus have something like this in mind when they characterize the world as *maya*. The world *appears* the way we see it, but that is not the way it really is.

Maya comes from the same root as magic. In saying the world is *maya*, non-dual Hinduism is saying that there is something tricky about it. The trick lies in the way the world's materiality and multiplicity pass themselves off as being independently real – real apart from the stance from which we see them – whereas in fact reality is undifferentiated *Brahman* throughout, in the way a rope lying in the dust remains a rope while being mistaken for a snake. *Maya* is also seductive in the attractiveness with which it decorates the world, trapping us for a long time within it and postponing our wish to journey on.

If we ask why Reality which is in fact one and perfect is seen by us as many and marred, why the soul (which is actually united with God throughout) experi-

ences itself as sundered, why the rope so often looks like a snake, we confront questions that have no answer. The most that we can say is that the world is *lila,* God's play. Children playing hide and seek place themselves in situations from which they must escape. Why do they do so when they could free themselves by simply withdrawing from the game? The only answer that can be given is that the game is its own reward. So too, in some mysterious way, must it be with the world. Like a child playing alone, God is the cosmic dancer whose routine is all creatures and all worlds. From the tireless stream of divine energy the cosmos flows in endless, graceful reenactment.

Those who have seen images of the goddess Kali dancing on a prostrate body while holding in her hands a sword and severed head; those who have heard that more Hindu temples are dedicated to Shiva (God in his aspect of destroyer whose haunt is the crematorium) than to God as creator and preserver combined – those who know these things will not jump quickly to the conclusion that the Hindu world view is gentle.

Opposite: *Lingam representing the divine creative power, carved with Shiva's face.* Above: *Shiva in his guise of Nataraj, the cosmic dancer.*

But while they force us to look terror straight in the eye, Shiva and Kali ask us to see that what they destroy is the finite, to make way for the infinite.

Seen in perspective, the world is benign. It has no permanent hell or eternal damnation. It may be loved without fear, as long as we do not try to appropriate it. For all is *maya* and *lila,* the spellbinding dance of the cosmic magician, beyond which lies the boundless good which all will experience in the end. It is no accident that the only art form India did not produce was tragedy.

In sum: to the question "What kind of world do we have?" Hinduism answers:

1. A multiple world that includes innumerable galaxies horizontally, innumerable tiers vertically, and innumerable cycles temporally.

2. A moral world in which the law of *karma* is inexorable.

3. A middling world that will never replace paradise as the spirit's destination.

4. A world that is *maya,* deceptively tricky in passing off its multiplicity, materiality and dualities as ultimate when they are actually provisional.

5. A gymnasium for developing spiritual capacities — what Keats called *"a vale for soul-making."*

6. A world that is *lila,* the play of the divine in its cosmic dance — untiring, unending, resistless, yet ultimately beneficent with a grace born of infinite vitality.

Opposite: *Candles and incense burning in a humble village temple.* Below: *Preparing a funeral pyre.* Above: *A vulture feeds on a corpse thrown into the sacred Ganges.*

Because Thou lovest the Burning-ground,
I have made a Burning-ground of my heart —
That Thou, Dark One, hunter of the Burning-ground,
Mayest dance Thy eternal dance.

(Bengali hymn).

MANY PATHS TO THE SAME SUMMIT

THAT HINDUISM HAS SHARED HER LAND for centuries with Jains, Buddhists, Parsees, Muslims, Sikhs, and Christians may help explain a final idea that comes out more clearly through her than through the other great religions; namely, her conviction that the various major religions are alternate paths to the same God. *"Truth is one; sages call it by different names"* (Vedas). As tone is as important as idea here, we shall let a major nineteenth century saint, Ramakrishna, express the point in his own words:

"God has made different religions to suit different aspirations, times, and countries. All doctrines are only so many paths; but a path is by no means God Himself. Indeed, one can reach God if one follows any of the paths with whole-hearted devotion. One may eat a cake with icing either straight or sidewise. It will taste sweet either way. As one can ascend to the top of a house by means of a ladder or a bamboo or a staircase or a rope, so diverse are the ways and means to approach God, and every religion in the world shows one of these ways.

Bow down and worship where others kneel, for where so many have adored, the kind Lord must manifest himself, for he is all mercy.

People partition off their lands by means of boundaries, but

no one can partition off the all-embracing sky overhead. The indivisible sky surrounds all and includes all. So it is in ignorance that people say, "My religion is the only one, my religion is the best." When a heart is illumined by true knowledge, it knows that above all these wars of sects and sectarians presides the one indivisible, eternal, all-knowing bliss.

There was a man who worshipped Shiva, but hated all other deities. One day Shiva appeared to him and said, "I shall never be pleased with you as long as you hate other gods." The man, though, was stubborn. After a few days Shiva again appeared to him and repeated, "I shall never be pleased with you while you hate." The man kept silent.

Several more days elapsed, after which Shiva made a third appearance. This time one side of his body was Shiva and the other Vishnu. Half pleased and half displeased, the man shifted his offering to the side representing Shiva. Shiva gave up, saying, "This man's bigotry is incorrigible."

Above: *A portrait of Shiva adorns a water tank in the city of Benares.* Right: *Celebrants carrying an effigy of Vishnu.*

CHAPTER II

BUDDHISM

Buddhism begins with a man. In his later years, when India was afire with his message, people came to him asking what he was. Not "Who are you?" but "What are you?"

"Are you a god?" they asked.

"No."

"An angel?"

"No."

"A saint?"

"No."

"Then what are you?"

Buddha answered, "I am awake."

Shrine at Bodh Gaya, the place of Buddha's enlightenment.

THE MAN WHO WOKE UP

BUDDHISM BEGINS WITH A MAN. In his later years, when India was afire with his message, people came to him asking what he was. Not "Who are you?" but "*What* are you?"

"Are you a god?" they asked. "No." "An angel?" "No." "A saint?" "No." "Then what are you?" Buddha answered, "I am awake." His answer became his title, for this is what Buddha means. The Sanskrit root *budh* means to awake and to know. While the rest of humanity was dreaming the dream we call the waking human state, one of their number roused himself. Buddhism begins with a man who woke up.

His life has become encased in loving legend, but the basic facts are straightforward. He was born around 563 B.C. in what is now Nepal. Siddhartha was his given name and Gautama his family name. His father ruled one of the petty kingdoms that comprised India then, so Siddhartha's upbringing was luxurious. He appears to have been exceptionally handsome, and at sixteen married a neighboring princess, Yasodhara, who bore a son, Rahula.

Here, in short, was a man who seemed to have everything: social standing, appearance, wealth, a model wife, a child, and a throne he would soon inherit. Despite all this, however, there settled over him in his twenties a despond that was to lead him to abandon his lucky lot.

The cause of his discontent is impounded in the legend of The Four Passing Sights. When Siddhartha was born his father summoned fortunetellers to discern his future. All agreed that this was no usual child, but his career was crossed with an ambiguity. If he succeeded his father he would unify India and become a world conqueror, but if he forsook the world he would become a world redeemer. His father wanted the former destiny, so he spared no effort to keep his son on course. Palaces and dancing girls were placed at his disposal, and orders were given that no unpleasantness be allowed into his courtly life. When he left the palace, runners were stationed to clear the roads of the old, the diseased, and the dead. One day, however, this order was neglected and Siddhartha saw an old man — gaunt, broken-toothed, trembling as he leaned on his staff. On another day he saw a body racked with disease, lying by the roadside. On a third outing he encountered a corpse. Having thus discovered the facts of aging, disease, and death, he saw on a fourth ride a monk with shaven head, ocher robe, and bowl; and learned from him of a path that renounces the world. It is a legend, this story, but it impounds the truth that it was the body's inescapable involvement with disease, decrepitude, and death that made him despair of finding fulfillment on the physical plane.

Once he had perceived the inevitability of pain and passage, fleshly pleasures lost their charm and he determined to follow the calling of a truth-seeker. One night in his twenty-ninth year he effected his Great Going Forth. Taking silent farewell of his sleeping wife and child, he mounted his great white steed and set off for a forest. Reaching its edge, he discarded his royal attire, shaved his head, and entered the forest to seek enlightenment.

Six years followed, during which his energies were directed to this end. The search was difficult, and moved through three phases. It began with his seeking out two of the foremost Hindu masters of the day and learning what he could from their tradition.

His next step was to join a band of ascetics and give their way a try. Was his body holding him back? He

Opposite: *Chinese painting of one of the* **"The Four Passing Sights"** *which prompted Buddha to take up the spiritual path and seek enlightenment.*

爾時太子出城南門見一病人問因緣時

would crush its interference. In every austerity he outdid his teachers, and eventually grew so weak that had his companions not rescued him with some warm rice gruel he would have died. This experience taught Gautama the futility of asceticism and inspired what was to become the first constructive plank of his program: the principle of The Middle Way between the extremes of asceticism and indulgence.

Having renounced mortification, Gautama devoted the final phase of his quest to a combination of rigorous thought and mystic concentration along the lines of Hinduism's raja yoga. Sensing at length that a breakthrough was near, he sat down one evening under what has come to be known as the Bo Tree (short for *Bodhi* or enlightenment), vowing not to arise until he had gained his goal.

"The Death of Buddha and his Entry into Nirvana."
Painting on a 14th century Japanese scroll.

The records offer as the first event of the night a temptation scene reminiscent of Jesus in the desert. Seeking to disrupt Gautama's concentration, Mara, the Evil One, first paraded voluptuous women, and when they failed in their purpose assailed the future Buddha with torrents of flaming rocks. These, though, turned into blossom petals when they entered the field of his yogic concentration. In final desperation, Mara challenged Gautama's right to do what he was doing, but he touched the earth with his right fingertip and the earth thundered, *"I bear you witness."* Mara fled in rout and raptures descended from heaven to clothe the victor.

Thereafter, while the Bo Tree rained red blossoms that full-mooned night of May, Gautama's meditation deepened until, as the morning star glittered in the transparent eastern sky, his mind pierced the world's bubble, collapsing it to nothing; only, wonder of wonders, to find it restored with the effulgence of true being. The Great Awakening had arrived. Gautama was gone. He had been replaced by the Buddha.

Mara was waiting for him with one last temptation. How could the Buddha expect people to understand truth as profound as that which he had discovered? Why not wash his hands of the whole hot world, be done with the body, and slip at once into perpetual nirvana? The argument almost prevailed, but at length the Buddha answered, *"There will be some who will understand,"* and Mara was vanquished forever.

Nearly half a century followed in which the Buddha accomplished his mission. He founded an order of monks, challenged the deadness of *Brahmin* society, and accepted in return the resentment, queries, and bewilderment his stance provoked. His daily routine was staggering. In addition to training monks and overseeing the affairs of his Order, he maintained an interminable schedule of public preaching and private counseling. What saved him from burning out under these pressures was his pattern of withdrawal and return. In overview, he withdrew for the six years of his quest and returned to the world for the next forty-five. But each year was likewise divided between nine months of teaching and three months in retreat with his monks during the rainy season. His daily cycle, too, followed this mold. Three times each day he withdrew from his duties to meditate.

After an arduous ministry of forty-five years, at the age of eighty and around the year 483 B.C., Buddha died after eating some poisoned mushrooms that had gotten into a dish by accident. His valedictory has echoes through history: *"All compounds grow old. Work out your own salvation with diligence."*

Above: *Chinese depiction of Buddha's farewell to his horse and groom, as he sets out on his search for enlightenment.*

THE SILENT SAGE

IT IS IMPOSSIBLE TO READ the accounts of Buddha's life without gaining the impression that one has been in touch with one of the greatest personalities of all time.

Perhaps the most striking thing about him was his combination of a cool head and a warm heart. Clearly, he was a great rationalist. Every problem that came his way was subjected to cool, dispassionate analysis. But this objective, critical talent was balanced by a Franciscan tenderness so strong that it has caused his message to be subtitled "a religion of infinite compassion." Whether he actually risked his life to free a goat that was snagged on a precipice may be historically uncertain, but the act would certainly have been in character, for his life was one continuous gift to the famished crowds.

Socially, his royal lineage was of great advantage. "Fine in presence," he moved easily among kings and potentates, for he had been one of them. Yet his poise and sophistication seem not to have distanced him from simple villagers. Surface distinctions meant so little to him that he often failed to notice them. There was an amazing simplicity about this man before whom kings bowed. Even when his reputation was at its highest he would be seen, begging-bowl in hand, walking through streets and alleys with the patience of one who knows the illusion of time.

It is perhaps inaccurate to speak of the Buddha as modest, for he knew he had risen to a plane of understanding above others. But this is different from vanity or humorless conceit. At the final assembly of one of his *sangha's* (order's) annual retreats, the Exalted One surveyed the silent company and asked, openly and sincerely, for criticism. *"I summon you, disciples, to tell me: have you any fault to find with me in word or in deed?"*

Notwithstanding his own objectivity toward himself, there was constant pressure during his lifetime to turn him into a god. This he rebuffed categorically, insisting that he was human in every respect. He made no attempt to conceal his temptations and weaknesses — how difficult it had been to attain enlightenment, how narrow the margin by which he had won through, how fallible he still remained. He admitted that the months when he was first alone in the forest had brought him to the brink of mortal terror. As one biographer remarks, *"One who thus speaks need not allure with hopes of heavenly joy. One who speaks like this of himself attracts by that power with which the Truth attracts all who enter her domain."*

The Buddha's talents for leadership and organization were evidenced not only by the size to which his order grew, but equally by the perfection of its discipline. A king visiting one of their assemblies which was prolonged into the full-moon night burst out at last, "You are playing me no tricks? How can it be that there should be no sound at all, not a sneeze, nor a cough, in so large an Assembly, among 1250 of the Brethren?" Watching the Assembly, seated as silent as a clear lake, he added, "Would that my son might have such calm."

Like other spiritual geniuses, the Buddha was gifted with preternatural insight into character. Able to size up, almost at sight, the people who approached him, he seemed never to be taken in by appearances but would move at once to what was essential. We find a beautiful instance of this in his encounter with Sunita the flower-scavenger. Though Sunita was an outcaste, the Buddha saw the marks of sainthood *"shining within him like a lamp in a jar,"* and invited him to join his community.

The Buddha's entire life was powered by a strong sense of mission. Immediately after his enlightenment, he saw in his mind's eye the whole of humanity — people milling and lost, desperately in need of help and guidance. His acceptance of his mission without regard for personal cost won India's heart as well as her mind. *"Giving up family and treasure, in the beauty of his early manhood the monk Gautama went forth into the homeless state."* But after his disciples had done their best with their

praise, they found in their master depths their words could not reach. They revered what they understood, but there was more than they could exhaust. To the end he remained for them half light, half shadow, defying complete intelligibility. So they called him Sakyamuni, "silent sage (*muni*) of the Sakya clan," symbol of something that could not be described.

And they called him Tathagata, the "Thus-come," the "Truth-winner," the "Perfectly Enlightened One," "he who alone thoroughly knows and sees, face to face, this universe." *"Deep is the Tathagata, unmeasurable, difficult to understand, even like the ocean."*

Above: *Chinese painting of Buddha's first sermon at Sarnath.*

THE REBEL SAINT

I N MOVING FROM BUDDHA THE MAN to Buddhism the religion, we must see it against the background of the Hinduism from which it sprang and from which it split. Unlike Hinduism, which emerged by slow, spiritual accretion, the religion of the Buddha appeared overnight. In large measure it was a reaction to Hindu perversions. To understand the Buddha's teachings, therefore, we shall need to understand the Hinduism that provoked it, and for that some observations about religion are in order. Six features of religion appear so regularly as to suggest that their seeds are in the human makeup. One of these is *authority*. Religion is as complex as government or medicine, so it stands to reason that talent and attention to its workings will lift some persons above the masses in matters of spirit. Their advice will be sought, and their counsels treasured.

A second normal feature of religion is *ritual*. Religion arose out of celebration and its opposite, bereavement, both of which cry out for collective expression. When tragedy strikes or we all but explode with joy, we want not only to be with people; we want to be with them in ways that strengthen our bonds and relieve our isolation, making us more than the sum of our parts.

Religion may begin in ritual, but *explanations* are soon called for. From whence do we come, whither do we go, why are we here? The questions call for answers, and theories soon enter the religious domain.

A fourth religious constant is *tradition*. In human beings it replaces instinct in conserving what past generations have learned and bequeath to the present.

A fifth feature of religion is *grace* — the belief and assurance that reality is on our side and can be counted on.

Finally, religion traffics in *mystery*. Being finite, the human mind cannot fathom the Infinite that envelops it.

Each of these six things contributes to religion while being able to clog its works. In the Hinduism of the Buddha's day they had done that. Authority had become hereditary and exploitative as *Brahmins* took to hoarding their religious secrets and charging exorbitantly for ministrations. Rituals had become mechanical means for working miracles. Explanations had lost their experiential base and devolved into arguments. Tradition had become a dead weight. God's grace was being misread in ways that undercut human responsibility, and mystery was confused with mystification — perverse obsession with miracles, the occult, and the fantastic.

Opposite and above: *Statues in a Chinese temple representing various of the Buddhist patriarchs.*

Onto this sullied landscape stepped the Buddha, determined to clear the ground that truth might spring anew. The outcome was startling, for what emerged was (in its beginning) a religion almost entirely devoid of each of the above mentioned ingredients without which, we might have supposed, religion could not take root.

1. Buddha preached a religion devoid of authority. He worked to break the *Brahmins'* monopoly on religion, and at the same time challenged individuals to take responsibility for their lives. *"Do not accept what you hear by report. Be lamps unto yourselves."*

2. Buddha preached a religion devoid of ritual. Repeatedly he ridiculed the rigmarole of *Brahmanic* rites as superstitious petitions to ineffectual gods. They were trappings – irrelevant to the hard, demanding job of ego-reduction.

3. Buddha preached a religion that skirted speculation. He could have been one of the world's great metaphysicians, but "the thicket of theorizing" was not for him. Whether the world is eternal or not eternal, whether it is finite or infinite, whether a Buddha exists after death or not – *"on such questions the Buddha maintains a noble silence,"* for opinions here *"tend not to edification."* To drive the point home he told a parable that has become famous:

"It is as if a man, wounded by an arrow thickly smeared with poison, were to say to his surgeon: I will not have this arrow removed until I know who shot it, his caste, his height, his color, where he comes from; the kind of bow the arrow was shot from, the wood of which the shaft was made and the species of bird whose feathers adorn it. Verily, before these questions were settled, that man would have died."

4. Buddha preached a religion devoid of tradition. He stood atop the past and its peaks extended his vision enormously, but he saw his contemporaries as buried beneath those peaks. So he counseled his followers: *"Do not go by what is handed down, nor by the authority of your traditional teachings. When you know of yourselves, 'These teachings are good or not good,' only then accept or reject them."*

5. Buddha preached a religion of intense self-effort. We have noted that a mood of discouragement and defeat had settled over the India of his century. Many

had come to accept the round of birth and rebirth as unending, which was like resigning oneself to a sentence to hard labor that would never end. Nothing struck the Buddha as more pernicious than this fatalism. There was only one assertion, he said, that he denied categorically: that of the "fools" who say that we can do nothing about our lot. *"There is a path to the end of suffering. Tread it!"* Each individual must tread this path himself or herself, through determination and strenuous exertion. *"Those who, relying upon themselves only, not looking for assistance to anyone besides themselves, it is they who will reach the topmost height."*

6. Buddha preached a religion devoid of the supernatural. He condemned all forms of divination, soothsaying, and forecasting as low arts; and, though he concluded from his own experience that the human mind was capable of powers now referred to as paranormal, he refused to allow his monks to play around with those powers. *"By this ye shall know that a man is not my disciple – that he tries to work a miracle."*

After the Buddha's death, all the accouterments that he had labored to protect his religion from came tumbling into it, but as long as he lived he kept them at bay. As a consequence, original Buddhism presents us with a version of religion that is unique and therefore instructive.

1. It was empirical. Never has a religion presented its case with such unswerving appeal to direct validation. *"Do not go by reasoning, nor by inferring, nor by argument. A true disciple must know for himself."*

2. It was scientific. It took as its final test the quality of lived experience, and sought indefatigably for the causes of experience. *"That being present, this becomes; that not being present this does not become."*

3. It was pragmatic. The Buddha likened his teachings to tools whose value is in their usefulness; and to rafts that help people cross rivers but are burdens thereafter.

4. It was therapeutic. *"One thing I teach,"* said the Buddha: *"suffering and the end of suffering. It is only ill and the ceasing of ill that I proclaim."*

5. It was psychological. The word is used here in

contrast to metaphysical. Instead of beginning with the universe and moving to the place of human beings within it, the Buddha began with the human predicament and the solution it called for.

6. It was egalitarian. With a breadth of view unparalleled in his age and infrequent in any, he insisted that women were as capable of enlightenment as men. And he rejected the caste system's assumption that aptitudes were hereditary.

7. It was directed to individuals. The Buddha was not blind to the social side of human nature — not only did he found a religious order; he insisted on its importance in reinforcing individual resolves. But in the end he appealed to the secret workings of the inward heart. *"Betake yourselves to no external refuge. Work out your own salvation with diligence."*

Above: *A Western woman meditating near the bodhi tree under which Buddha achieved enlightenment. Buddha rejected both the inequalities of the Hindu caste system and the traditional prejudice against women.*

THE FOUR NOBLE TRUTHS

AFTER HIS ENLIGHTENMENT the Buddha proceeded directly to India's holy city of Benares. Six miles short of it, in a deer park at Sarnath, he preached his first sermon. It proclaimed his key discoveries, which came to be known as the Four Noble Truths.

The First Noble Truth is that life is *dukkha*. The word is usually translated "suffering," and because the Buddha took it as his starting point, his religion has been charged with being pessimistic. That charge would hold, though, only if the Buddha thought the suffering he acknowledged was unrelievable; whereas in fact he was certain that it could be relieved. This shows that the "life" he diagnosed as suffering is unregenerate life, or life as it is normally lived. The Buddha did not doubt that it is possible to have a good time, but two questions obtruded. First, *how much* of life is enjoyable. And second, *at what level* of our being does enjoyment proceed. Buddha thought the level is superficial. Beneath the neon dazzle is darkness; at the core – not of all life but of unregenerate life – is the "quiet desperation" that Thoreau thought characterizes most lives. *"Lo! as the wind is, so is mortal life:/A moan, a sigh, a sob, a storm, a strife"* (Dhammapada).

Dukkha names this pain that to some degree skews all finite existence. The word was used in Buddha's day to refer to wheels whose axles were off-center, and bones that had slipped from their sockets. (A modern metaphor might be a shopping cart we try to steer from the wrong end.) The exact meaning of the First Noble Truth, therefore, comes down to this: Life as typically lived is out of joint. Something is awry. Its pivot is not true. This restricts movement (blocks creativity), and causes undue friction (interpersonal conflict).

Having an analytical mind, the Buddha was not content to state this First Truth in general terms. He pinpointed four moments when life's dislocation becomes especially evident: in the birth trauma, in illness, in old age with its decrepitude, and in the fear of approaching death. To these he added: to be separated from what one loves, and to be saddled with what one hates.

No one denies that life's shoe pinches in these six places, which shows that it doesn't fit. Why doesn't it? Dropping metaphor in favor of the Buddha's straightforward question: What causes *dukkha*, life's suffering? The Second Noble Truth answers that question. The cause of *dukkha* is *tanha.*

Tanha is usually translated as desire, but here too it is wise to stay close to the original word, for *tanha* is a specific kind of desire, the desire for private fulfillment. When we are selfless we are free, but that is precisely the difficulty, to maintain that state. *Tanha* is the ego oozing like a secret sore. It consists, not of all inclinations, but of those that pull against life as a whole; selfish inclinations that make demands for oneself at the expense, if necessary, of others. These demands bring suffering, because the law of life calls for seeing others as extensions of ourselves, not our rivals.

This is not the way people normally see others. Given a group photograph, whose face does one scan for first? It is a small but telling symptom of the devouring cancer that causes sorrow. Where is the man who is as concerned that no children go hungry as that his own children have food? Where is the woman who rejoices as much in her colleague's promotion as in her own? Coddling our individual identities, we lock ourselves inside our skin-encapsulated egos and seek fulfillment through their enlargement. Fools to suppose that imprisonment can bring release! Can we not see that *"tis the self by which we suffer"*? Far from being the door to abundant life, the ego is a strangulated hernia; the more it swells, the tighter it shuts off the free-flowing circulation on which health depends, and pain increases.

The Third Noble Truth follows logically from the Second. If the cause of life's dislocation is selfish craving, its cure lies in the overcoming of *tanha*, such craving. If we could be released from the narrow limits of self-interest into the vast expanse of universal life, we would be relieved of our torment. The Fourth Noble Truth prescribes how the cure can be accomplished. The overcoming of tanha, the way out of our captivity, is through The Eightfold Path.

Opposite: Swayambhunath, a Buddhist temple near Kathmandu.

THE EIGHTFOLD PATH

THE BUDDHA'S APPROACH to the problem of life in the Four Noble Truths is essentially that of a physician. He begins by noting the symptoms that provoke concern: we experience more pain, less creativity, and more conflict than we feel there should be. From there he proceeds to diagnosis: what is causing these symptoms? His answer is *tanha*, the drive for private fulfillment. The prognosis is hopeful, for the cause of the symptoms can be removed. The Eightfold Path is his prescription for accomplishing its removal. It is a course of treatment, but not from without through pills or radiation. It is, rather, a course of training, like those that athletes undertake but with a moral aim. Its intent is to pick one up where one is and set one down a different human being, one that is cured of life's crippling disability.

The course consists of eight steps, but they are prefaced by a preliminary step that isn't explicitly stated but which the Buddha mentions so often elsewhere that we may assume that here he was simply presupposing it. This preliminary step is right association. No one has recognized more clearly than the Buddha the extent to which we are social animals, influenced at every turn by the "companioned example" of our associates. When a wild elephant is to be tamed, the way to begin is by yoking it to one that has already been through the ropes. By contact, the wild one comes to see that what is expected of it is not wholly incompatible with being an elephant. Training for the life of the spirit is not different. Without palpable evidence that progress is possible, discouragement is inevitable. Bees cannot make honey alone, and comparably, human beings will not persist on the Way outside the field of confidence and support that fellow travelers generate.

Worshippers outside Swayambhunath.

With this assumed step in place we may proceed to the steps of the path that are formally numbered.

1. Right knowledge.

To journey purposefully one needs a map, a sense of the lay of the land. We need to have some idea as to where we are and in which direction to proceed. It is this knowledge that the first step of the Path calls for and provides. Its substance has already been covered, for it consists of the Four Noble Truths. Those truths and the Path they lead to lock together. The fourth noble truth is the Eightfold Path, and the first step on that path is knowledge of the Four Noble Truths.

2. Right aspiration.

Whereas the first step summoned us to understand what life's problem is, the second counsels us to decide what we really want. Is it truly enlightenment, or do our affections swoop this way and that, dipping like kites with every current of distraction? Not until liberation is sought single-mindedly will our steps change from sliding sandbank scrambles into ground-gripping strides.

3. Right speech.

In the next three steps we take hold of the switches that control our destinies, beginning with attention to language. Here our first task is to *notice* our speech and what it reveals about our character. Instead of resolving right off to speak truthfully, we will do better to start with the easier exercise of noticing how often each day we find it necessary to deviate from the truth, for invariably we will find that we do so to protect something in us that is soft, flabby, and unattractive. Besides truth, our speech should proceed toward charity. False witness, idle chatter, gossip, slander, and abuse are to be avoided, not only in their obvious forms but also in their covert ones, for the latter – subtle, belittling, "accidental" tactlessness and barbed wit – are often more vicious because their animus is veiled.

4. Right behavior.

The Buddha detailed this directive in the Five Precepts that constitute the Buddhist version of the ethical half of the Ten Commandments:

Do not kill. Strict Buddhists extend this proscription to animals and are vegetarians.

Do not steal.

Do not lie.

Do not be unchaste.

For monks and the unmarried, this means continence. For the married it means restraint in proportion to one's interests in, and distance along, the Path.

Do not take drugs or drink intoxicants.

5. Right livelihood.

The word "occupation" is well advised, for our work does indeed occupy most of our waking attention. Buddha considered spiritual progress to be impossible if the bulk of one's doings pull against it. *"The hand of the dyer is subdued by the dye in which it works."*

For those who are intent enough on liberation to give their entire lives to the project, right livelihood prescribes joining the monastic order and following its discipline. For the layperson it calls for engaging in occupations that promote life instead of destroying it. Some of the professions the Buddha considered incompatible with serious seeking were poison peddler, slave trader, prostitute, butcher, brewer, arms maker, and tax collector, wherein (in his day) profiteering was routine.

6. Right effort. The Buddha laid tremendous stress on moral exertion. The only way fetters can be shaken off is by what William James called *"the slow dull heave of the will."*

"Those who follow the Way," the Buddha said, *"might well follow the example of an ox that marches through the deep mire carrying a heavy load. He is tired, but his steady, forward-looking gaze will not relax until he comes out of the mire. Only then does he relax. O monks, remember that passion and sin are more than the filthy mire, and that you can escape misery only*

by earnestly and steadfastly persevering in the Way."

7. Right mindfulness.

No teacher has credited the mind with more influence over life than did the Buddha. The best loved of all Buddhist texts, *The Dhammapada*, opens with the words, *"All we are is the result of what we have thought."* Among Western philosophers, it is Spinoza who stands closest to the Buddha on the mind's potential. His dictum – *"to understand something is to be delivered of it"* – comes close to summarizing the entire Buddhist ethic. Both these thinkers saw ignorance, not sin, as life's prime adversary.

To gradually overcome this ignorance, the Buddha counsels such continuous self-examination as to make us wilt (almost) at the prospect, but he thought it necessary because he believed that freedom – liberation from unconscious, mechanical existence – is a product of self-awareness. To this end, he asks us to see everything *"as it really is."* If we maintain a steady attention to our thoughts and feelings, we see that they are not permanent parts of us. Everything, especially our moods and emotions, are to be witnessed non-reactively, neither condemning some nor holding on to others. A miscellany of other practices is recommended, some of which are these: The aspirant is to keep the mind in control of the senses and impulses, rather than being driven by them. Fearful and disgusting sights are to be meditated on until one no longer experiences aversion toward them. The entire world should be pervaded with thoughts of loving kindness.

Here is a Western observer's description of monks in Thailand practicing this seventh step:

"One of them spends hours each day slowly walking about the grounds of the wat in absolute concentration upon the minutest fraction of every action connected with each step. The procedure is carried into every single physical act of daily life until, theoretically, the conscious mind can follow every step that goes into the generation of a feeling, perception or thought. A fifty-year-old monk meditates in a small graveyard adjoining his wat, because he's undisturbed there. He seats himself, cross-legged and immobile but with his eyes open, for hours on end – through the driving rain at midnight or the blistering heat of noonday. His usual length of stay is two or three hours."

8. Right absorption.

This involves substantially the techniques we have already encountered in Hinduism's *raja yoga* and leads to substantially the same goal.

In his later years the Buddha told his disciples that his first intimations of deliverance came to him before he left home when, still a boy and sitting one day in the cool shade of an apple tree in deep thought, he found himself caught up into what he later identified as the first level of the absorptions. It was his first faint foretaste of deliverance, and he said to himself, *"This is the way to enlightenment."* It was nostalgia for the return and deepening of this experience, as much as his disillusionment with the usual rewards of worldly life, that led him to his decision to devote his life completely to spiritual pursuits. The result, as we have seen, was not simply a new philosophy of life. It was regeneration: change into a different kind of creature who experiences the world in a new way. Unless we see this, we shall be unequipped to fathom the power of Buddhism in human history. Something happened to the Buddha under that Bo tree, and something has happened to every Buddhist since who has persevered to the final step of the Eightfold Path. Like a camera, the mind had been poorly focused, but the adjustment has now been made. With the *"extirpation of delusion, craving, and hostility,"* the three poisons, we see that things were not as we had supposed. Indeed, suppositions of whatsoever sort have vanished, to be replaced by direct perception. The mind reposes in its true condition.

Above: *Tibetan Tanka (painted wall hanging) representing the Wheel of Life.* Overleaf, page 79: *A Tibetan man reciting his prayers outside Swayambunath in Nepal.*

BASIC BUDDHIST CONCEPTS

THE BUDDHA'S TOTAL OUTLOOK ON LIFE is not easy to come by for three reasons: he did not commit his teaching to writing; a century and a half elapsed before the first written records appear; and when they do appear they pour forth in bewildering variety and number. Even so, memories were good in those days, and within the welter of materials we can detect an assemblage of ideas that are consistent enough to permit us to think that they came from the Buddha himself. This section targets those that are most important.

We can begin with *nirvana,* the word the Buddha used to name life's goal. Etymologically it means "to blow out," or "to extinguish," not transitively, but as a fire ceases to draw. Deprived of fuel the fire goes out, and this is *nirvana.* From such imagery it has been widely supposed that the extinction to which Buddhism points is annihilation pure and simple, but this is not so. We must be precise as to what is to be extinguished, and it turns out to be the boundaries of the finite self. Negatively, *nirvana* is the state in which the faggots of private desire have been consumed and everything that restricts the boundless life is exhausted. Affirmatively, it is that boundless life itself.

Buddha parried every request for a positive description of the unconditioned, insisting that it was *"incomprehensible, indescribable, inconceivable and unutterable;"* for after we eliminate every aspect of the only consciousness we have known, how can we speak of what is left? One of Buddha's heirs, Nagasena, used the analogy of wind. Asked what *nirvana* is like, Nagasena asked his questioner to show him the wind — its color and configuration; whether it is thick or thin, long or short. When the questioner protested that this was impossible, Nagasena asked, rhetorically, whether this was grounds for con-

cluding that wind doesn't exist. Assured that it was not, he concluded, *"Even so, there is nirvana, but it is not possible to show nirvana."* The Buddha did assert, though, that nirvana is bliss. *"Bliss, yes bliss, my friends, is nirvana."*

Is *nirvana* God? That depends on how the word is defined. If it designates a personal being who created the universe by deliberate design, *nirvana* is not God and Buddhism is atheistic.

The word has a second meaning, however, which theologians sometimes call the Godhead. The idea of personality, which is definite and therefore in ways limiting, is not part of this second concept. When the Buddha declared, *"There is, O monks, an Unborn, neither become nor created nor formed. Were there not, there would be no deliverance from the formed, the made, the compounded,"* he seemed to be speaking in this tradition. Buddologists have compiled a list of characteristics of *nirvana* that seem to place it in the Godhead camp. *Nirvana* is permanent, stable, imperishable, immovable, ageless, deathless, unborn, and unbecome; it is power, bliss and happiness, the secure refuge, the shelter, and the place of unassailable safety; it is the real Truth and the supreme Reality; it is the Good, the supreme goal and the one and only consummation of our lives; the eternal, hidden and incomprehensible peace.

Turning from *nirvana* to the human self, the most startling thing the Buddha said about it is that it has no soul. Coming from a religion, this *anatta* (no soul) doctrine sounds as odd as his denial of a personal God, but again the word the Buddha used must be carefully examined. What was the *atta* (Pali for the Sanskrit *atman* or soul) which the Buddha denied? At the time it had come to signify (a) a spiritual substance which, in keeping with the dualistic position in Hinduism, (b) retains its separate identity forever. Buddha rejected both these beliefs.

The body houses no homunculus or ghostly wraith that animates and outlasts it.

His alternative view of selfhood comes to light through his thoughts on transmigration. Authentic child of India, he did not doubt that reincarnation was a fact, but he disagreed with the way his *Brahmanic* contemporaries conceived of it – as some sort of psychic pellet that migrated from body to body. His alternative view is captured by the image of a wave.

Suppose we are in a boat and notice that a wave is approaching us. Here it comes all right; when it reaches us we rise for a moment, then descend when it passes. Eventually it breaks on the shore and is gone. What are we to make of this? We speak of it as *a* wave, for in a sense it *is* single; from the gentle swell that sets it in motion to its crashing death on the beach, it is a single, identifiable wave that runs its course. Yet at no two moments are its molecules identical. *Pari passu*. Nothing that is *in* my next incarnation will be identical with what is in me now, but I will still be "me" in the way the wave retained its identity while moving through its successive stages. What continues from life to life and unites them is a trajectory, a four-dimensional form, a causal chain of karmic propensities. Causal connection is solidly affirmed; but no entity – no physical or psychic substantial substrate – passes from life to life. Hume and James were right: if there is an enduring self, subject always, never object, it does not show itself.

This denial of a substantial soul was only an aspect of Buddha's wider denial of substances of every sort. Verbs rather than nouns fit his world view, for everything is in process, everything is in change. This gives a certain poignancy to Buddhist descriptions of the natural world, for everything is impermanent, transitory, and yes, dying. *"Waves follow one another in eternal pursuit." "Life is a journey; death is a return to earth./The universe is an inn; the passing years are like dust."*

Thus, to the first two of the Three Marks of Existence, or characteristics shared by everything in the natural world, that have already been covered – *dukkha* or suffering, and lack of permanent identity *(anatta)* – we must now add impermanence, or *anicca*. To underscore life's fleetingness, Buddha called the components of the human self *skandas* – skeins that hang together as loosely as yarn – and the body a "heap," its elements no more solidly assembled than grains in a sandpile. Why did the Buddha belabor this point that may seem obvious? Because he believed that we will stop clutching for permanence only if its non-existence is driven into the marrow of our being. Look upon this phantom world, he said:

> *"As a star at dawn, a bubble in a stream.*
> *A flash of lightning in a summer cloud.*
> *A flickering lamp, a phantom and a dream."*

Given this sense of the radical impermanence of things, we might expect the Buddha's answer to the question of whether human beings survive bodily death to be a flat no, but actually his answer was equivocal. Ordinary persons when they die leave strands of finite desire that can only be realized in other incarnations; in this sense at least these persons live on. But what about the *arhat*, one who has extinguished all such desires. Does such a one continue to exist? When the Buddha was asked this question he said, *"Profound, measureless, unfathomable is the arhat, even as the mighty ocean. Reborn does not apply to him nor not-reborn, nor any combination of such terms."*

We may assume that this cryptic response was designed to call attention to the fact that language poses some questions so clumsily as to preclude solution by their very formulation. The question of a realized soul's existence after death is a case in point. If the Buddha had said, *"Yes, it does live on,"* his listeners would have assumed the persistence of our present mode of consciousness which the Buddha did not intend. On the other hand, if he had said, *"The enlightened soul ceases to exist,"* his hearers would have assumed that he was consigning it to total oblivion, which he also did not intend. On the basis of

this rejection of extremes we cannot say much with certainty, but something can be ventured. The ultimate destiny of the human spirit is a condition in which all identification with the historical experience of the finite self will disappear, while experience as such will not only remain but be heightened beyond recognition. As an inconsequential dream vanishes completely on awakening, as the stars go out in deference to the morning sun, so individual awareness will be eclipsed in the blazing light of total realization. Some say *"the dewdrop slips into the shining sea."* Others prefer to think of the dewdrop as opening to welcome the sea itself.

If we try to form a more detailed picture of the state of *nirvana,* we shall have to proceed without the Buddha's help, not only because he realized almost to despair how far the condition transcends the power of words, but also because he refused to wheedle his hearers with previews of coming attractions. A thousand questions remain, but the Buddha is silent.

> *Others abide our questions.*
> *Thou art free.*
> *We ask and ask.*
> *Thou smilest and art still.*

BIG RAFT AND LITTLE

*T*HUS FAR WE HAVE BEEN LOOKING at Buddhism as it appears from its earliest records. We turn now to Buddhist history, which shows how variations enter when a tradition ministers to masses of people who are differently endowed.

When we approach Buddhist history with this interest, what strikes us immediately is that it splits. The Buddha dies, and before the century is out the seeds of schism have been sown. They related to questions that have always divided people, three of which are apposite here.

First, there is the question of whether people are independent or interdependent. Some persons are most aware of their individuality, with the consequence that they see themselves as making their own ways through life. "I was born in the slums, my father was an alcoholic, all of my siblings went to the dogs – don't talk to me about heredity or environment. I got to where I am by myself!" This is one attitude. On the other side of the fence are persons for whom mutuality prevails. To such persons, the separateness of people seems tenuous. "Send not to ask for whom the bell tolls, it tolls for thee."

A second question concerns the relation in which human beings stand, this time not to their fellows, but to the universe. Is the universe friendly? Or is it indifferent, if not hostile?

A third demarcating question is: What is the best part of the human self, its head or its heart? Classicists rank thoughts above feelings; romantics do the opposite. The first seek wisdom; the second (if they had to choose) prefer compassion.

Here are three questions that have probably divided people as long as they have been human, and divided the Buddhists. One group took as its motto the Buddha's valedictory, *"Work out your own salvation with diligence."* It sought progress through wisdom, not cosmic grace. The other group placed compassion above wisdom, sought help from compassionate Buddhas, and sought to enlighten others.

Other differences gathered around these fundamental ones. The first group insisted that Buddhism was a full-time job, so those who were serious about it should become monks. To the second group Buddhism was as relevant for laypersons as for professionals. This difference left its imprint on the names of the two outlooks. Both came to be called *yanas*, rafts or ferries for carrying people across life's river. The second group, however, stressing cosmic grace and the larger place it made for laypersons, claimed to be "Buddhism for the people" and the larger of the two transports. Accordingly, it preempted the name *Mahayana*, the Big Raft, *maha* meaning "great." As the name caught on, the first group came to be known (by default), as *Hinayana*, or the Little Raft.

Not exactly pleased with this invidious name, the Hinayanists have preferred to call their Buddhism *Theravada*, the Way of the Elders. In doing so they regained the initiative by claiming to represent original Buddhism, the Buddhism taught by Gautama himself. The claim is justified if we confine ourselves to the explicit teachings of the Buddha as they are recorded in the earliest texts, the Pali Canon, for on the whole those texts do support the Theravada position. But this fact has not discouraged the Mahayanists from their counterclaim that it is they who represent the true line of succession. For, they argue, the Buddha taught more eloquently and profoundly by his life and example than by the words the Pali Canon records, and the decisive fact about his life is that he did not remain in *nirvana* after his enlighten-

Page 80: *Buddhist monks outside the religious school at Swayambunath.* Above and right: *Prayerflags and chortens in Muktinath.*

ment but returned to devote his life to others.

We can leave to the two schools their dispute over apostolic succession; our concern is to understand their positions, not weigh their claims. The differences that have come out thus far may be summarized by the following pairs of contrasts if we keep in mind that they are not absolute but denote differences in emphasis.

1. For Theravada Buddhism, progress rests with the individual – the extent of his informed exertion. For Mahayanists, it is a field phenomenon.

"He findeth not who seeks his own,
The soul is lost that's saved alone."
(John Whittier)

2. Not only are individuals on their own respecting other people; Theravadins see them as on their own in the universe. No gods exist to help us over the humps. *"No one saves us but ourselves; no one can and no one may. We ourselves must tread the Path; Buddhas only show the way."* For Mahayanists, in contrast, grace is a fact. Buddhas and bodhisattvas work on our behalf.

3. In Theravada Buddhism the prime attribute of enlightenment is wisdom *(bodhi)*, meaning profound insight into the nature of reality, the causes of anxiety and suffering, and the absence of a separate, self-existent core of selfhood. From these realizations flow automatically the Four Noble Virtues: loving kindness, compassion, equanimity, and joy in the happiness and well-being of others. From the Mahayana perspective *karuna* (compassion) is not an automatic byproduct; even more than wisdom, it must be actively cultivated. *"A guard I would be to them who have no protection,"* runs a typical Mahayana invocation; *"a guide to the voyager, a ship, a well, a spring, a bridge for the seeker of the other shore."*

4. The *sangha* (Buddhist monastic order) is at the heart of Theravada Buddhism. Monasteries (and to a lesser extent nunneries) are spiritual dynamos in lands where it predominates. They remind people of higher truths that underlie visible reality, and their monks and nuns are accorded great respect. Mahayana Buddhism, on the other hand, is primarily a religion for laypersons. Its priests usually marry, and they are expected to make service to the laity their primary concern.

5. It follows from these differences that the ideal type the two groups project will also differ. For the Theravadins the ideal is the *arhat*, the perfected disciple who strikes out alone for *nirvana* and with prodigious concentration proceeds toward that goal. The Mahayana ideal, on the contrary, is the *bodhisattva*, "*one whose essence (sattva) is perfected wisdom (bodhi)*" — a being who, having reached the brink of *nirvana*, voluntarily renounces that prize and returns to the world to make it available to others. The difference between the two types is illustrated in the story of four men who, crossing a desert, come upon a compound surrounded by high walls. One of the four scales the wall and on reaching the top gives a whoop of delight

Buddha statue in Sarnath. Mahayanists say Buddha is a world savior who draws all creatures toward him "by the rays of his jeweled hands."

and jumps over. The second and third do likewise. When the fourth man gets to the top and sees a garden with streams and fruit trees, he remembers other wayfarers and climbs down to report the oasis to them. A *bodhisattva* is a person who vows not to enter *nirvana* "until the grass itself is enlightened."

6. This difference in ideal floods back to color the two schools' estimates of the Buddha himself. For one he was essentially a saint, for the other a savior. Theravadins revere him as a supreme sage who through his own efforts awakened to the truth and became an incomparable teacher, but his personal influence ceased with his entrance into *nirvana*. The reverence the Mahayanists felt for him could not be satisfied with this humanness. For them, the Buddha was a world savior who continues to draw all creatures toward him *"by the rays of his jeweled hands."*

These differences are the central ones, but several others may be mentioned to piece out the picture. Whereas the Theravadins followed their founder in considering speculation a useless diversion, Mahayana spawned elaborate cosmologies replete with multi-leveled heavens and hells. The only kind of prayer the Theravadins countenanced was meditation and invocations to deepen faith and lovingkindness, whereas the Mahayanists added supplication, petition, and calling on the name of the Buddha for spiritual strength. Finally, whereas Theravada remained conservative to the point of an almost fundamentalistic adherence to the early Pali texts, Mahayana was liberal in almost every respect. It accepted later texts as equally authoritative, was less strict in interpreting disciplinary rules, and had a higher opinion of the spiritual possibilities of women and the laity in general.

Thus in the end the wheel comes full circle. The religion that began as a revolt against rites, speculation, grace, and the supernatural, ends with all of them back in force and its founder (who was an atheist as far as a personal God was concerned) transformed into such a God himself.

Which one wins? Inwardly there is no such thing as winning, but outwardly (in terms of numbers) the answer is Mahayana.

We have dwelt on doctrinal differences, but there is a significant socio-political difference between Theravada and Mahayana that should be added. Theravada sought to incarnate a feature of the Buddha's teachings that has not thus far been mentioned: his vision of an entire society – a civilization if you will – that was founded like a tripod on monarchy, the monastic community *(sangha)*, and the laity, each with responsibilities to the other two and meriting services from them in return. South Asian countries that remain to this day Theravadin – Sri Lanka, Burma, Thailand, and Cambodia – took this political side of the Buddha's message seriously, and remnants of his model are discernible in those lands right down to today. China's interest in Buddhism (which she transmitted to the other lands that were to become Mahayanist: Korea, Japan, and Tibet) bypassed its social dimensions which included education as well as politics. In East Asian lands, Buddhism appears as something of a graft. Buddhist missionaries persuaded the Chinese that they possessed psychological and metaphysical profundities the Chinese were ignorant of, but Confucius had thought a lot about the social order, and the Chinese were not about to be lectured to on that topic. So China discounted the political proposals of the Buddha and took from his corpus its psycho-spiritual components with their cosmic overtones.

THE SECRET OF THE FLOWER

FTER BUDDHISM SPLIT INTO Theravada and Mahayana, Theravada continued as a fairly unified tradition whereas Mahayana divided into a number of schools. The most popular of these, the Pure Land School, relies on faith in a compassionate Buddha to carry devotees to the Pure Land of the Western Paradise, a kind of heaven. Another important Mahayana school (*Ti'en Tai* in China; *Tendai* in Japan) introduced into Buddhism the Confucian predilections for learning and social harmony. We shall not go into these and smaller sects of Mahayana Buddhism. Instead, we shall reserve our space for, first, the Buddhism that Taoism profoundly influenced, namely *Ch'an* (*Zen* in Japanese), and second, the Buddhism that evolved in Tibet. This is partly because these are the branches of Buddhism that have attracted the most attention in the West, but there is the added advantage that they will take us to two quite different lands in which Buddhism has flourished.

Because the Communist takeover of China disrupted its religious life, we shall pursue the Ch'an/Zen sect in its Japanese guise. Like other Mahayanist sects, this one claims to trace its perspective back to Gautama himself. His teachings that found their way into the Pali Canon, it holds, were those the masses seized upon, but his more perceptive followers discerned in his message a higher, subtler teaching. The classic instance of this is the Buddha's Flower Sermon. Standing on a mountain with his disciples around him, the Buddha did not on this occasion resort to words. He simply held aloft a golden lotus. No one understood the meaning of this eloquent gesture save Mahakasyapa whose quiet smile, indicating that he had gotten the point, caused the Buddha to appoint him his successor. The insight that prompted the smile was transmitted in India through twenty-eight patriarchs and carried to China in 520 A.D. by Bodhidharma. Spreading from there to Japan in the twelfth century, it contains the secret of Zen.

Entering Zen is like stepping through Alice's looking glass. One finds oneself in a topsy-turvy wonderland where everything seems quite mad — charmingly mad for the most part, but mad all the same. It is a world of bewildering dialogues, obscure conundrums, stunning paradoxes, flagrant contradictions, and abrupt non sequiturs, all carried off in the most urbane, cheerful, and innocent style imaginable. Here are some examples:

Opposite: A fresco in one of the cave temples of Ajanta shows Buddha during his famous Flower Sermon, which is said to mark the beginning of Zen. Above: A Burmese conception of Buddha.

Whenever a certain master was asked the meaning of Zen, he lifted his index finger. That was all. Another kicked a ball. Still another slapped the inquirer.

A novice who makes a respectful allusion to the Buddha is ordered to rinse his mouth and never utter that dirty word again.

A group of Zen masters, gathered for conversation, have a great time declaring that there is no such thing as Buddhism, or Enlightenment, or anything even remotely resembling *nirvana.* They set traps for one another, trying to trick someone into an assertion that might imply the opposite. Practiced as they are, they always elude these traps, whereupon the entire company bursts into glorious, room-shaking laughter.

What goes on here? Is it possible to make any sense out of what at first blush looks like Olympian horseplay if not a direct put-on? Are Zennists serious in this kind of double-talk, or are they simply pulling our legs? The answer is that they are completely serious, though they are seldom solemn. And though we cannot hope to capture their perspective completely, it being of Zen's essence that it cannot be impounded in words, we can give some hint as to what they are up to.

We can begin with the point just alluded to, the limitations of language. We all know that menus are not meals, or maps the terrains they depict. The distinctive thing about Zen is its preoccupation — obsession even — with this distinction, and its alertness to how often spiritual nourishment (if we may put the matter this way) stops with menu reading. When the Buddha made his point by holding up a flower and Mahakasyapa got that point, no words intervened. And when (a thousand years later) Bodhidharma brought that "point" to China, he defined the treasure he had brought as "a special transmission *outside* the scriptures." Zen continues this experiential emphasis. Heirs are validated by their masters, and granted permission to teach, only when their masters (*roshis*) see them as having attained the insight-experience that flashed wordlessly from Buddha to Mahakasyapa in the Flower Sermon.

How is this insight-experience to be acquired? Limiting ourselves to the *Rinzai* sect — the other main branch of Zen is *Soto* — its method can be unfolded through four of its key terms: *zazen, koan, sanzen,* and *satori. Zazen* literally means "seated meditation." The bulk of Zen training takes place in a meditation hall where monks sit for hours on end in the lotus posture they inherited from India. Their eyes are half closed as their gaze falls unfocused on the tawny straw mats beneath them. Thus they sit, hour after hour, day after day, year after year, seeking to waken the Buddha-mind that will then reshape their daily lives.

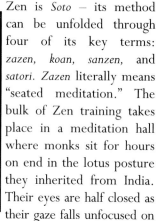

The most distinctive feature of their meditation is the *koans* they attend to. In a general way *koan* means problem, but the problems Zen devises are surreal.

What is the sound of one hand clapping?

What was the appearance of your face before your ancestors were born?

A monk asked Jo Shu (a famous Chinese master), *"Does a dog have a Buddha-nature?,"* to which Jo Shu replied, *"Mu."* (To recognize the seeming contradiction here, we need to know that the Buddha had said that

even grass has a Buddha-nature, and that the word *mu* means no.)

Our impulse is to dismiss such conundrums as absurd, but the Zen practitioner is not permitted to do this. He is ordered to train his full mind on them, but not (in the initial stages at least) in the way we call thinking or reasoning. The mind has other ways of working than its normal, rational way, Zen is convinced; and it is these latent ways that *zazen* is designed to call into action.

This requires explaining. From the Zen perspective, reason is too short a ladder to reach to truth's full height. In must be supplemented, and it is that supplementation that *koans* are designed to assist. If they look scandalous to reason, we must remember that Zennists aren't out to placate reason; they want to put it in its place. By forcing reason to wrestle with what (from the rational perspective) is absurd, the *koan* rouses the mind to a state of agitation wherein it hurls itself against its logical cage with the desperation of a cornered rat. By paradox and non sequitur it provokes, excites, exasperates and eventually exhausts the rational mind until it sees that thinking is never more than thinking *about*. Then, having gotten the rational mind where it wants it – reduced to an impasse – it counts on a flash of insight to bridge the gap between secondhand and firsthand life.

"Light breaks on secret lots....
Where logics die
The secret grows through the eye."
(Dylan Thomas)

Opposite: *Monks practicing zazen at an English zendo.*
Right: *Statue of the priest Kuyo, with a string of little Buddhas issuing from his mouth, from the early Kamakura period in Japan.*

Struggling with his *koan,* the Zen monk is not alone. Fellow monks are engaged in the same pursuit, and twice a day (on average) he confronts his master in *sanzen,* or private "consultation concerning meditation." These meetings are invariably brief. The trainee repeats the koan he is working on and follows it with his answer to date, which the master either validates or rejects.

To what does the method lead? The first important breakthrough is an intuitive experience called *satori.* Though its preparation may take years, the experience itself comes in a flash, exploding like a silent rocket in the unconscious mind to throw new light on everything. Here is an example:

"Ztt! I entered. I lost the boundary of my physical body. I had my skin, of course, but I felt I was standing in the center of the cosmos. I saw people coming toward me, but all were the same man. All were myself. I had never known this world before. I had believed that I was created, but now I must change my opinion: I was never created; I was the cosmos. No individual existed."

From this and similar descriptions we can infer that *satori* is Zen's version of the mystical experience which, wherever it appears, brings joy, at-one-ment, and a sense of reality that defies ordinary language. But whereas the tendency is to consider such experiences as the culmination of the religious quest, Zen places them close to its starting point.

Drawing half its inspiration from the practical, this-worldly orientation of the Chinese (to balance the mystical other-worldly half it derived from India), Zen refuses to permit the human spirit to withdraw into mysticism completely. Once we achieve *satori,* we must get out of its "sticky morass" and return to the world. The genius of Zen lies in its determination to fuse the temporal and the eternal; to widen the doors of perception

Above: *A garden made of sand and rocks graces the 15th century Ryonji Temple in Japan, illustrating the simplicity and purity that lie at the heart of Zen.*

so the wonder of the *satori* experience can flood every-day life.

With the possible exception of the Buddha himself, the process is never altogether accomplished. Yet by extrapolating from hints in the Zen corpus, we can form some idea of what *"the man who has nothing further to do"* would be like.

First, he would find life distinctly good. Asked what Zen training leads to, a Western student who had been practicing for seven years answered, *"No paranormal experiences that I can detect. But you wake up in the morning and the world seems so beautiful you can hardly stand it."*

Along with this sense of life's goodness there comes, secondly, an objective outlook on one's relation to others; their welfare seems as important as one's own. Dualisms dissolve, and one feels grateful to the past and responsible to the present and future.

The third point has already been mentioned. Zen doesn't lead away from the world, not for long. It returns the practitioner to a world newly perceived. *"What is the most miraculous of all miracles? That I sit quietly by myself."* The advanced stages of Zen wear an air of divine ordinariness. *"Have you eaten? Then wash your bowls."* If you cannot find the meaning of life in an act as simple as that of doing the dishes, you will find it nowhere.

> *My daily activities are not different,*
> *Only I am naturally in harmony with them.*
> *Taking nothing, renouncing nothing,*
> *In every circumstance no hindrance, no conflict.*
> *Drawing water, carrying firewood,*
> *This is supernatural power, this the marvelous activity.*

With this discovery of the infinite in the finite there comes, fourthly, an attitude of generalized agreeableness. *"Yesterday was fair, today it is raining."* The adept has passed beyond the opposites of preference and rejection. As a poem by Seng Ts'an puts the point:

> *The perfect way knows no difficulties*
> *Except that it refuses to make preferences;*
> *A tenth of an inch's difference,*
> *And heaven and earth are set apart.*

Finally, as the dichotomies between self and other, finite and infinite, acceptance and rejection are transcended, even that between life and death disappears. As one adept stated, "When Zen realization is achieved, never again can one feel that one's individual death brings an end to life. One has lived from an endless past and will live into an endless future."

As we leave Zen to its future we may note that its influence on the cultural life of Japan has been enormous. Though its greatest influence has been on pervasive life attitudes, four ingredients of Japanese culture carry its imprint indelibly. In *sumie* or black ink landscape painting, Zen monks, living their simple lives close to the earth, have rivaled the skill and depth of feeling of their Chinese masters. In landscape gardening, Zen temples surpassed their Chinese counterparts and raised the art to unrivaled perfection. Flower arrangement began in floral offerings to the Buddha, but developed into an art which until recently was a part of the training of every refined Japanese girl. Finally there is the celebrated tea ceremony in which an austere but beautiful setting, a few fine pieces of old pottery, a slow, graceful ritual, and a spirit of utter tranquility combine to epitomize the harmony, respect, clarity, and calm that characterize Zen at its best.

THE DIAMOND THUNDERBOLT

W E HAVE SPOKEN of two *yanas* or paths in Buddhism but we must now add a third. If Hinayana literally means the Little Way and Mahayana the Great Way, Vajrayana is the Diamond Way.

Vajra was originally the Indian Thunder-God, but when Mahayana turned the Buddha into a cosmic figure, it turned this god into his diamond scepter. This added beauty and supremacy to *Vajra's* original link with power, for the diamond cuts other substances but cannot itself be cut. The Vajrayana, then, is the way of adamantine strength – strength to realize the Buddha's wisdom and compassion. Its Indian roots spread primarily to Tibet, where it became the third major Buddhist path. Tibetan Buddhism is essentially the Vajrayana, to which we must immediately add that the essence of the Vajrayana is Tantra.

Tantra has two Sanskrit roots, one of which is *"extension."* In this meaning, it adds to or extends the Buddha's teachings. The other root associates the word with weaving and by implication interpenetration, for woven threads intersect. Tantric texts focus on the interrelatedness of things.

The Tibetans do not see their path as distinctive in its goal. Its originality lies in its practices, which enable adepts to reach *nirvana* in a single lifetime. The acceleration is accomplished by utilizing all of the energies latent in the human make-up, physical ones emphatically included.

The energy that interests the West most is sex, so it is not surprising that Tantra is best known abroad for its sacramental use of this force. Actually, though, its teachings on the subject are not particularly distinctive. All religions include sex in some way, for sexual love is the divine's clearest epiphany. At the moment of mutual climax, where what each most wants is what the other most wants to give, it is impossible to say whether the experience is more physical or spiritual, or whether the lovers sense themselves to be two or one. What distinguishes Tantra is the way it wholeheartedly espouses sex as a spiritual ally, working with it intentionally and explicitly. Beyond squeamishness and titillation, Tantrics keep the physical and spiritual components of the love-sex splice in strict conjunction – through their art (which shows couples in coital embrace), in their fantasies (the ability to visualize should be actively cultivated), and in overt sexual engagement (for only one of the four Tibetan priestly orders is celibate).

With Tantra's sexual side addressed, we can proceed to more general features of its practice. Having noted that its distinctive practices involve the body, we can now add that they focus on speech, vision, and gestures. Zen and *raja yoga* think these distract, and try to suppress (or rise above) them. Tantrics grant that sounds, sights, and movements can distract, but deny that they must do so. Skillfully utilized, they can empower the spiritual quest. *Mantras* fashion sounds into holy formulas. *Mudras* choreograph hand gestures, turning them into sacred dances. *Mandalas* treat the eyes to icons whose holy beauty empowers.

The liturgy that integrates these devices proceeds like this: Seated in parallel rows, wearing headgear that ranges from crowns to wild shamanic hats, garbed in maroon robes which they periodically smother in sumptuous vestments of silver, scarlet, and gold, the monks chant in modes that range from deep, guttural, metric monotones to a unique multiphonic chanting that sounds like chords. Concomitantly, their hands perform stylized gestures that augment the states of consciousness that are

being accessed. Throughout, the monks visualize the deities they are invoking with an intensity that makes them seem physically present. It is a spiritual technology, designed to lift the human spirit to the level of the gods in order to partake of their power.

To complete this profile of Tibetan Buddhism, we must mention a unique institution. When in 1989 the Nobel Peace Prize was awarded to His Holiness the Dalai Lama, that institution received worldwide attention.

The Dalai Lama is not accurately likened to the Pope, for he does not define doctrine. Even more misleading is the designation God-King, for though temporal and spiritual authority converge in him, this does not define his essential function. That function is to incarnate on earth the celestial principle of which compassion or mercy is the defining feature. The Dalai Lama is the *bodhisattva* who in India is known as *Avalokiteshvara,* in China as the Goddess of Mercy *Kwan-yin,* and in Japan as *Kannon. As Chenrezig* (his Tibetan name) he has for the last several centuries incarnated himself thirteen times for the empowerment and regeneration of the Tibetan tradition. Through him there flows a current of spiritual compassion. Whether the Dalai Lama will reincarnate himself again after his present body is spent is uncertain, for currently the Chinese invaders are determined that there will be no distinct people for him to serve. If there are not, something important will have withdrawn from history. For as rain forests are to the earth's atmosphere, someone has said, so are the Tibetan people to the soul of this planet in this time of their desperate ordeal.

Left: *18th century Nepalese bronze of a couple in the embrace known as the Padmalinga-asana.*

THE IMAGE OF THE CROSSING

W E HAVE LOOKED AT THREE MODES of transport in Buddhism: the Little Raft, the Big Raft, and the Diamond Raft. These vehicles are so different that it makes sense in closing to ask what they have in common. Without being exhaustive, two things stand out. All revere a single founder, and they share a common metaphor – the simple, everyday experience of crossing a river on a ferryboat.

Before technology spanned rivers with bridges, every major journey involved ferryboats. Buddhism played on this fact, for Buddhism is a voyage across life's river – a journey from the common-sense bank of ignorance, grasping, and death, to the further shore of wisdom and enlightenment. Differences within Buddhism are no more than variations in the kind of vehicle – *yana* – one chooses, and the stage one is at in the journey. What are these stages and vehicles?

While we are on the first bank, it is virtually our entire world. Its earth beneath our feet is solid and reassuring, whereas the opposite shore barely exists and has little impact on our dealings.

If, however, something prompts us to see what the other side is like, we may decide to find out. If we opt to make the journey alone, our temperament is Theravadic; we follow the Buddha's design for a sturdy craft and build it ourselves. Most of us, however, have neither the time nor the talent for a project of such proportions. Mahayanists, we move down the bank to where a ferryboat is expected. As the group of explorers clambers aboard there is an air of excitement. Attention focuses on the farther shore, but the voyagers are still very much citizens of this side of the river.

As the ferry pushes off and moves across the water, the bank we are leaving loses its substance. Its shops and streets and antlike figures are blending together and releasing their hold on us. As yet, though, the other side is not in focus either. At this interval the only tangible realities are the water with its treacherous currents and the boat that is stoutly but precariously contending with them. This is the moment for Buddhism's Three Vows:

I take refuge in the *Buddha* — there was an explorer who made this trip and proved that it can succeed. I take refuge in the *dharma*, this ship to which we have committed our lives in the conviction that it is seaworthy. I take refuge in the *sangha*, the order; our crew that is navigating the ship in whom we have confidence.

The further shore draws near, becomes real. The craft jolts onto the sand and we step onto solid ground.

The land which had been misty and insubstantial is now fact, and the shore that we left behind, formerly so palpable and real, is now only a slender horizontal line, a visual patch, a memory without hold on us.

Impatient to explore our new surroundings, we nevertheless remember our gratitude for the splendid ship and crew who have brought us safely to what promises to be a rewarding land. It will not be gratitude, however, to insist on packing the boat with us as we plunge into the woods. *"Would he be a clever man,"* the Buddha asked, "if, having reached the other shore, he were to cling to his raft, take it on his back, and walk about with the weight of it?"

This announces the *Prajnaparamita* or *Perfection of Wisdom* sutras which are widely considered to be Buddhism's culminating texts. The Five Precepts and the Eightfold Path; concepts like *dukkha, karma, nirvana;* the committed order and the person of the Buddha himself — all these are vitally important to the individual while he is making the crossing, but they lose their relevance for those who have arrived. Indeed, to the traveler who moves into the interior of his new domain there comes a time when not only the craft but the river and its former bank drop from view. When such a one turns around to look for the land that has been left behind, what appears? What of that land *can* appear to one who has crossed a horizon beyond which the river itself has vanished? One looks back and, there being no river, there is no opposite shore, no craft, no ferryman. These things are not a part of the new world.

Above: Narrative relief from Borobudur depicting the Buddha's teachings being carried across the seas to other lands.

Before the river was crossed the two shores, human and divine, seemed as different as night and day, but once the crossing has been effected, no dichotomy remains. The realm of the gods is no distinct place; it is where the traveler now stands. And if he returns to his original home, he sees it from the perspective his travels have imparted: it is transmuted. It is in this light that we are to read the avowals in *The Perfection of Wisdom* that "*this our worldly life is an activity of nirvana itself. Not the slightest distinction exists between them.*" Travel having introduced a land called (positively) Nirvana, and negatively Emptiness because it erases lines of division, the "stream-winner" now sees in his original world the Emptiness he had to travel to first discover. "*Form is emptiness, emptiness is form.*" The noisy disjunction between acceptance and rejection having been stilled, every moment is affirmed for what it actually is. It is Indra's cosmic net, laced with jewels at every intersection; each jewel reflects the others, together with the reflections *in* the others.

> "*This earth on which we stand, is the promised Lotus Land,
> And this very body is the body of the Buddha.*"

This new-found shore throws light on the *bodhisattva's* vow not to enter *nirvana* "*until the grass itself be enlight-*

ened." As grass keeps coming, does this mean that the *bodhisattva* will never be enlightened? Not exactly. It means, rather, that he has risen to the point where the distinction between time and eternity has lost its force. Insight has dissolved the opposites that reason pushed apart. "*The jewel of eternity is in the lotus of birth and death.*"

From the standpoint of normal, worldly consciousness there must always remain an inconsistency between this climactic insight and worldly prudence. This, though, should not surprise us, for it would be odd to say the least if the world looked exactly the same to those who have crossed the river of ignorance. Only they can dissolve the world's differences — or perhaps we should say take them in their stride, for the distinctions persist, but now without differences. Where to eagle vision the river can still be seen, it is seen as connecting the two banks, rather than separating them.

Above: *Small bronze figure of a bodhisattva from the Kamakura period.* Right: *Gilded stone carving of the Buddha in Dazu, east central China.*

The Confluence of Buddhism and Hinduism in India

*T*O THE BASIC paradox of Buddhism — a religion that began by repudiating ritual, speculation, grace, mystery, and a personal God, and ended by embracing them all — another should be added. Today Buddhists abound in every Asian land except India. Buddhism triumphs in the world at large, only to be vanquished in the land of its birth.

Thus it might seem, but the fact is that Buddhism was not so much defeated by Hinduism as accommodated within it. Up to around the year 1000 A.D., Buddhism persisted in India as a distinct movement, but by then its differences with Hinduism softened to the point where separate institutions seemed unnecessary.

Hindus admitted the legitimacy of many of the Buddha's reforms, and in imitation of the Buddhist *sangha,* orders of Hindu *sadhus* (wandering ascetics) were established.

From the other side, Buddhist teachings came to sound increasingly like Hindu ones as the baroque embellishments of the Mahayana moved into place.

Only if one assumes that Buddhist principles left no mark on Hinduism can the merger be considered a Buddhist defeat. In fact, almost all of Buddhism's affirmative doctrines found their place or parallel. Its contributions accepted by Hindus (in principle if not always practice) included its stress on kindness to all creatures, on non-killing of animals, on the elimination of caste barriers in matters religious and their reduction in matters social, and its strong ethical emphasis generally. The *bodhisattva* ideal left its mark in prayers like this one by Santi Deva: *"I desire of the Lord only the power to relieve the pain of others and make them happy."* The Buddha was recognized as an avatar, or a divine incarnation; *nirvana* was more or less assimilated to the non-dual view of *moksha;* and the *Prajnaparamita's* perforating of the line between *samsara* and *nirvana* found an echo in Hindu Tantric proclamations like this one:

"This very world is a mansion of mirth;
here I can eat, here drink and make merry."
(Ramakrishna).

CHAPTER *IV*

C O N F U C I A N I S M

"How dare I allow myself to be taken as sage and humane!"

he said. "It may rather be said of me that I strive

to become such without ceasing."

Confucius

Above: *Stone engraving of Confucius followed by one of his disciples.*
Left: *Etched glass portait of Confucius in Qu Fu, China.*

THE FIRST TEACHER

*I*F THERE IS ONE NAME with which Chinese culture has been associated it is Confucius' — Kung Fu-tzu or Kung the Master. Chinese reverently speak of him as The First Teacher, not chronologically but because he stands first in rank. No one claims that he crafted Chinese culture singlehandedly, but he was its supreme editor.

The reader who supposes that such an achievement could come only from a dramatic life will be disappointed. Confucius was born around 551 B.C. in what is now Shantung province. His early home life was modest. His father died before he was three, leaving his upbringing to a loving but impoverished mother. He was not a bookworm, but he did like school and did well in his studies.

In his early twenties, having held several insignificant government posts and contracted a not too successful marriage, he established himself as a tutor. This was obviously his vocation. His reputation spread rapidly, and he attracted a circle of ardent disciples who were devoted to him. Even so, his career was a disappointment. His goal was public office, for he believed that his theories would not take hold unless he demonstrated that they worked. Rulers, though, were too afraid of his candor and integrity to appoint him to positions that carried power.

At the age of fifty, he set out on a thirteen year trek in which he wandered from state to state, proffering unsolicited advice to rulers on how to improve their governing and seeking always a chance to put his ideas into practice. The opportunity never came. State after state disregarded his counsels, and only a small band of faithful disciples stood by him through rebuff, discouragement, and near starvation.

In time, with a change of administration in his own state, he was invited to return. There, recognizing that he was now too old for office anyway, he spent his last five years quietly teaching and editing the classics of China's past. In 479 B.C., at the age of seventy-three, he died. A failure as a politician, Confucius was undoubtedly one of the world's greatest teachers. Prepared to instruct in virtually all the disciplines of his day, he was a one-man university. His method of teaching was Socratic. Always informal, he seems not to have lectured but instead to have conversed on problems his students posed, citing readings and asking questions. The openness with which he interacted with his students was striking. Not for a moment assuming that he was himself a sage — sagehood being for him a matter of comportment, not a stock of knowledge — he presented himself to his students as their fellow learner. On the importance of the task on which they were together embarked, however, he was uncompromising. This led him to expect much from his students

Opposite: *Palace life as seen by a Sung dynasty artist. Above: Traditionally, the dead were buried with all they might need in the afterlife, including statues of attendants like this one. Page 102/3: Images of a Chinese scribe and a warlord reflecting the two social extremes of Confucius' time.*

for he saw their mission as nothing less than the revitalization of their entire society. The passion with which he plied that mission made him a zealot, but humor and a sense of proportion saved him from being a fanatic. There was nothing other-worldly about him. He loved to be with people, to dine out, to join in the chorus of a good song, and to drink, though not in excess. His disciples reported that *"he was affable, yet firm; dignified yet pleasant."* His democratic bearing has already been remarked upon. Not only was he always ready to champion the cause of common people against the oppressive nobility of his day; in his personal relations he cut scandalously across class lines — as one example, he never slighted his poorer students even when they couldn't pay.

To the end he remained more exacting of himself than he was of others. *"How dare I allow myself to be taken as sage and humane!"* he said. *"It may rather be said of me that I strive to become such without ceasing."* Power and wealth could have been his for the asking if he had been willing to compromise his principles, but he preferred his integrity. He never regretted the choice. *"With coarse food to eat, water to drink, and my bended arm for a pillow, I still have joy in the midst of these things. Riches and honors acquired by unrighteousness mean no more to me than the floating clouds."*

With his death began his glorification. Among his disciples the move was immediate, and from them it steadily spread. What would have pleased him more was the attention given to his ideas. Until this century, every Chinese school child for two thousand years raised his clasped hands each morning toward a table in the schoolroom that bore a plaque bearing Confucius' name. Virtually every Chinese student has pored over his sayings for hours, with the result that they have become a part of the Chinese mind and trickled down to the illiterate in spoken proverbs. Chinese government, too, has been influenced by him, more deeply than by any other figure. Since the start of the Christian era a large number of governmental offices, including some of the highest, have required of their occupants a knowledge of the Confucian classics. There have been a number of attempts, some of them quasi-official, to elevate him to the stature of divinity.

What produced this influence? — so great that until the Communist takeover sinologists were still regarding Confucianism as the greatest single intellectual force among one-quarter of the world's population. It could hardly have been his personality, for as exemplary as that was, it was too undramatic to explain his impact. If we turn instead to his teachings, our puzzle only deepens. As edifying anecdotes and moral maxims, they are unexceptionable; but how a collection of sayings so patently didactic, so pedestrian that they often appear commonplace, could have rallied a civilization, appears at first glance to be one of history's standing puzzles. Here are some samples:

"Is not he a true philosopher who,
though he be unrecognized, cherishes no resentment?
What you do not wish done to yourself,
do not do to others.
I will not grieve that others do not know me.
I will grieve that I do not know others.
Do not wish for quick results, nor look
for small advantages."

There is certainly nothing wrong with such moralisms. But where is their power?

THE PROBLEM CONFUCIUS FACED

FOR THE CLUE TO CONFUCIUS' influence we must understand the desperate problem he faced, which was social anarchy. Early China was neither more nor less turbulent than other maturing societies, but from the eighth to the third centuries B.C. the Chou Dynasty's ordering power progressively deteriorated. Rival barons ranged unchecked, and their interminable wars produced political chaos. In earlier days codes of chivalry were honored, but by Confucius' time warfare had descended to the unrestrained horror of the Period of the Warring States. Contests between charioteers gave way to cavalry with its surprise attacks and sudden raids. Instead of holding prisoners for ransom, conquerors had them put to death in mass executions. Whole populations were beheaded, including women, children, and the aged. We read of mass slaughters of 60,000, 80,000, and even 400,000. There are accounts of the conquered being thrown into boiling caldrons and their relatives forced to drink the human soup. In such a time, the burning question in everyone's mind was: How can we keep from destroying ourselves?

As Confucius' impact lies in his answer to this question, we need to place it in historical perspective. Confucius lived at a time when his society was going to pieces; its glue was no longer holding. What had held it together until then?

Up to the human level, the answer was instinct. The cooperation it produces among ants and bees is legendary, but throughout subhuman kingdoms it insures reasonable stability. The human species, however, lacks this mechanism, for man has been defined as "the animal without instincts." What takes its place to maintain the social order? In tribal societies the answer is tradition — what anthropologists call "the cake of custom." Through generations of trial and error, ways of interacting evolve that keep tribes stable, and these ways catch on. Once their patterns are in place, they are transmitted from generation to generation unthinkingly — *cum lacte*, with the mother's milk, as the Romans used to say.

The individualism of modern life makes it difficult for us to realize how completely such mores can dictate behavior, but fashions provide a clue. If a corporation executive were to forget his necktie he would have trouble getting through the day.

His problem would not be indecent exposure, but simply that he had violated his peer group's dress code. This would make him look like an outsider, and he would feel uncomfortable. That discomfort is the source of convention's power.

If we envision a society in which all behavior is regulated by the equivalent of corporate dress codes, we will be close to how traditional societies function. To summarize the important points:

(a) The degree to which tradition rules them is astonishing; there are Eskimo and aboriginal tribes that do not even have words for disobedience.

(b) Tradition exerts its influence tacitly – spontaneously and unthinkingly. No laws are formulated or penalties affixed; no plans for moral education are intentionally devised. Group expectations are so strong that the young internalize them automatically.

Pre-Confucian China had been traditional in this strong sense. To cite but a single piece of evidence, we have the report of a noble lady who was burned to death in a palace fire because she refused to violate convention and leave the house without a chaperon. The historian (a contemporary of Confucius) who recorded the incident glossed it in a way that shows that convention had lost some of its force in his thinking but was still very much intact. He suggested that if the lady had been unmarried, her conduct would have been beyond question. But as she was not only married but elderly as well, it "might not have been altogether unfitting under the circumstances" for her to have left the burning mansion unaccompanied.

Few people in Confucius' day would have paid even this much respect to tradition, for China had reached a point in its evolution where individuals were emerging in large numbers. Self-conscious rather than group-conscious, they were guided more by self-interest than social expectations. The mortar that had held society together was chipping and flaking. In working their way out of the "cake of custom," individuals had cracked it beyond repair.

Liu Pang, victor in the civil war following the collapse of the Ch'in Dynasty (221-207 BCE) enters the Imperial Capital.

RIVAL ANSWERS

WHEN TRADITION LOSES ITS STRENGTH to hold society together, human life faces the gravest crisis it has encountered. What can replace it? The Enlightenment proposed reason; educate citizens and inform them, and they can be counted on to behave sensibly. This is the Jeffersonian-Enlightenment faith. As it has still to prove itself, it is of more than antiquarian interest to consider the options that were proposed in ancient China.

One of these was put forward by a group of thinkers that came to be called Realists. What do you do when people don't behave? Hit them. It's a classic answer to a classic question. What people understand best is force, so devise laws that establish clearly what will and will not be tolerated, and attach to them penalties that are severe enough to deter infractions. In short, laws with teeth in them.

The estimate of human nature from which this political philosophy proceeded was low in two respects. First, it assumed that base impulses predominate over noble ones. People are naturally lustful, greedy, and jealous. To the extent that virtue is possible, it must be built into people as wood is straightened in a press. Second, people are short-sighted. Rulers must envision long-range goals, but subjects can't do this. They will not voluntarily trade present satisfactions for future gains. Suppose a baby has a scalp disease. *"If the baby's head is not shaved, the malady will return. But while the shaving is in process, the baby will howl in protest even if its mother holds it lovingly. The child cannot comprehend the gain that will derive from its momentary discomfort."* Similarly, the masses "want security, but hate the means that produce security."

An altogether different answer to the social problem was propounded by Mo Ti, who advocated the opposite of force, namely love. Peace can only come through the spread of kindness and good will toward all. One should *"feel toward all people exactly as one feels toward one's own people,"* he insisted. *"Mutual attacks among states, mutual usurpation of houses, mutual injuring of individuals, arise out of want of mutual love. How can this condition be altered? By regarding the state of others as one's own, the houses of others as one's own, the persons of others as one's self. When all the people in the world love one another, then the strong will not overpower the weak, the many will not oppress the few, and the wealthy will not mock the poor."*

Mo Ti's confidence in love was not empirically derived. It flowed from his theism, the clearest instance of it that China affords. The universe is good because it is presided over by Shang Ti, a personal god who *"loves people dearly. He rewards the virtuous and punishes the wicked, and has prepared everything for the good of humankind."* It is inconceivable that in a world thus ordered, love would not pay.

Opposite: *Confucius admired the harmony of the early Chou Dynasty which produced works of art like this jade symbol of the North.* Right: *Eunuchs, who were often castrated criminals pressed into service at the court.*

CONFUCIUS' ANSWER

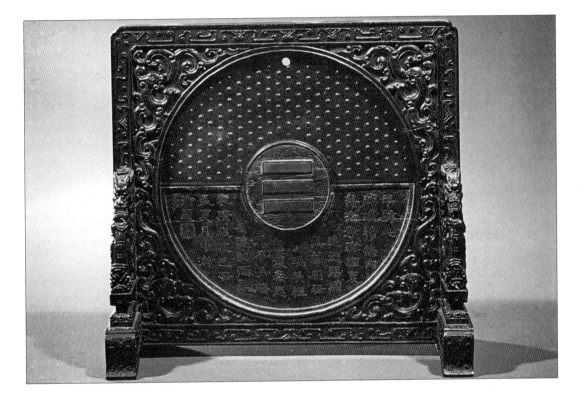

NEITHER OF THESE SOLUTIONS to the turmoil of Confucius' day impressed him. The Realists' force could restrain gross misconduct, but it would not change attitudes. Mo Ti was closer to the mark in recognizing that attitudes had to change, but his total reliance on love was unrealistic. To be effective on a large scale, love needs the help of social structures and a collective ethos; without these, it preaches ends without means. As for reason – the modern, Enlightenment prescription for social ills – it probably never crossed Confucius' mind; but if it did, he would have dismissed it as not thought through. The Chinese character for "mind" designates "heart" as well, which shows that the Chinese took it for granted that reason functions in a context of attitudes and emotions. Unless our hearts prompt us to cooperate, reason will devise clever stratagems to further self-interest.

Agonizing over the inhumanity of his day, Confucius looked in an altogether different direction for its cure. He became obsessed with tradition and its power to civilize. His studies convinced him that about five hundred years earlier, in the opening phase of the Chou Dynasty, China had achieved a truly golden age. Calling it the Age of the Grand Harmony, Confucius reflected on what had brought this happy state into being and concluded that it was the way of life (another way of saying tradition) that its ancestors had perfected and transmitted to their

*Confucian principles of tolerance and social responsibility enabled
China to accommodate a rich variety of religious beliefs including
Buddhism.*

offspring as naturally as they had given them life itself.

Confucius stood in awe of the Chou way of life, and longed for its peace and harmony that mocked his own age by contrast. To recover its secret became his obsession. How, though, could this be done when the force that created it – a model, spontaneous tradition – had crumbled? His answer can be put succinctly. When spontaneous tradition loses its power, shore it up with deliberate tradition – tradition now consciously attended to and given reasoned support. He wouldn't have couched his program in these words, but this in effect was what it came to.

Simple to the ear, the proposal had the marks of social genius. In times of transition, an effective program must meet two conditions. It must be continuous with the past, for only by tying in with what people are familiar with does it stand a chance of being accepted. At the same time the answer must take clear-eyed account of developments that render the old answer unworkable. Confucius' proposal met both requirements brilliantly. His repeated reference to his heroes, the founding father of Chou, kept tradition stage center; as did his transparently honest claim that he was "a lover of the ancients." With the predictability of a politician taking his stand on the Constitution, he appealed to the Classics as establishing the guidelines for his platform. Yet all the while he was interpreting, modifying, and reformulating. Unknown to his people, and largely to himself we may assume, he was effecting a momentous reorientation by shifting tradition from unconscious to conscious status.

The shift required that deliberate thought be given to two things: keeping the force of tradition intact, and determining which ends it should now serve. This meant that his countrymen needed first to decide what values they wanted to move into place, and then turn every device of education – formal and informal, womb to tomb – to seeing that these values were universally internalized. Moral ideals were to be imparted by every conceivable means – temples, theatres, homes, toys, proverbs, schools, history, stories – until they became habits of the heart. Even festivals and parades were to be religious in this comprehensive sense. By such means, even a society constituted of individuals could (if it put itself to the task, Confucius was confident) spin a power of suggestion, that would prompt its members to behave socially even when the law was not looking.

It was a powerful routine, perhaps the only one by which distinctively human values ever permeate large groups. For nearly two thousand years the first sentence every Chinese child was taught to read was, *"Human beings are by nature good."* We may smile at the undisguised moralizing, but every people needs it. The United States has its story of George Washington and the cherry tree and the moralisms of the McGuffey Reader. The Romans' renown for discipline and obedience fed on their legend of the father who condemned his son to death for winning a victory against orders. Did Lord Nelson actually say, *"England expects every man to do his duty,"* or Francis I exclaim, *"All is lost save honor"*? It doesn't much matter. The stories express national ideals, and shape peoples to their image. It is in this light that we should approach Confucius' interminable anecdotes and maxims, which his pupils compiled in the *Analects*. They forged the prototype of what he hoped the Chinese character would become.

Tsu King asked: *"What would you say of the person who is liked by all his fellow townsmen?"* *"That is not sufficient,"* Confucius replied. *"What is better is that the good among his fellow townsmen like him, and the bad hate him."*

The Master said: *"The well-bred are dignified but not pompous. The ill-bred are pompous, but not dignified."*

Once when Fan Ch'ih was rambling along with the Master under the trees at the Rain Altars, he asked, *"How may one improve one's character, correct one's personal faults, and discriminate in what is irrational?"* *"An excellent question,"* the Master replied. *"If one puts duty first and success after, will not that improve one's character? If one attacks one's own failings instead of those of others, will that not remedy personal faults?"*

Confucius was creating in his countrymen their second nature, which is what civilization comes to.

THE CONTENT OF DELIBERATE TRADITION

MAXIMS AND ANECDOTES such as the ones just cited abound in the Confucian corpus. Here we shall distill from them five ideals that structured Confucius' thought.

1. *Jen* defines the ideal relationship which should pertain between individuals – the character is comprised of the character for *"human being"* joined to the character for *"two."* Variously translated as goodness, man-to-man-ness, benevolence, and love, it is perhaps best rendered as human-heartedness. *Jen* was the virtue of virtues in Confucius' eyes. It was a capacity so sublime, even transcendental, that one "cannot but be chary in speaking of it." Confucius confessed that he had never seen it fully incarnated. In public life it prompts untiring diligence. In private life it induces courtesy, unselfishness, and empathy – the capacity to *"measure the feelings of others by one's own."* It knows no national boundaries for it understands that "within the four seas all men are brothers."

2. The second ideal is the *chun tzu*. If *jen* is the ideal relationship between human beings, *chun tzu* refers to the ideal term in such relations. It has been translated the Superior Person and Humanity-at-its-Best. Perhaps the Mature Person is as faithful a rendering as any.

The *chun tzu* is the opposite of a petty person. Adequate and poised, the *chun tzu* has toward life as a whole the approach of an ideal hostess who is so at home in her surroundings that she is relaxed and, being so, can turn full attention to putting others at their ease. Or to switch genders, having come to the point where he is at home in the universe at large, the *chun tzu* carries these qualities of the ideal host with him through life generally. Endowed with a self-respect that generates respect for others, he approaches them with an eye, not to *"What can I get from you?,"* but rather, *"How can I accommodate you?".*

Only of such large-hearted people, Confucius thought, can civilization be built. "If there is righteousness in the heart, there will be beauty in the character. If there is beauty in the character, there will be harmony in the home. If there be harmony in the home, there will be order in the nation. If there be order in the nation, there will be peace in the world."

3. The third ideal, *li,* has two meanings. The first of these is propriety – the way things should be done. Confucius thought that people were not likely to get very far if each had to figure out for himself what behaviors are appropriate, so he collected the finest examples of exemplary living he could find. Through maxims, anecdotes, and his own example he sought to chart an entire way of life, so that no one who was familiar with it need be in doubt as to how to behave.

Propriety covers a wide range, but we can get the gist of Confucius' concerns if we look at his teachings on the Rectification of Names, the Doctrine of the Mean, the Five Constant Relationships, the Family, and Age.

Beginning with the Rectification of Names, Confucius argued that those that designate social roles should be defined normatively. When he said that nothing is more important than that a father be a father, or that a ruler be a ruler, he was saying that we should build into the very definitions of those words what fathers and rulers should be. The word "father" should mean, not merely a man who has sired a child, but one that loves the child he has sired. Comparably with "ruler," "friend," "teacher," or whatever social role is in question.

As for the Doctrine of the Mean, it charts a middle course between unworkable extremes. With "nothing in excess" as its motto, its closest Western counterpart is Aristotle's Golden Mean. Respect for it brings harmony and balance. It encourages compromise, and discourages fanaticism.

Constituting the warp and woof of social life, the Five

Constant Relationships are those between parent and child, husband and wife, elder sibling and junior sibling, elder friend and junior friend, and ruler and subject. It is vital to the health of society that these key relationships be rightly constituted. None of them are transitive; in each, different responses are appropriate in the two terms. Parents should be loving, children reverential; elder siblings gentle, younger siblings respectful; husbands good, wives "listening"; elder friends considerate, younger friends deferential; rulers benevolent, subjects loyal. That three of the Five Relationships pertain within the family is indicative of how important Confucius considered this institution to be. Within the family, it is the children's respect for their parents that holds the key; hence the concept of filial piety. *"The duty of children to their parents is the fountain from which all virtues spring."*

This regard for one's parents opens onto Respect for Age generally. Two points lock together here. On purely utilitarian grounds it would be good to have a society in which the young attend to the old, for soon the young will be old themselves and will themselves need tending. But Confucius also thought that age merits respect because of the wisdom experience confers. Years season wisdom and mellow the spirit. If these twin points were in place, a Chinese could look forward to being served more, and listened to more, with every passing year, and to some extent the terrors of aging would be offset.

In these five points we have sketched important particulars of *li* in its first meaning, which is propriety, or right conduct. The companion meaning of the word is ritual, which changes right – in the sense of what it is right to do – into rite. Or rather, it infuses the first meaning *with* the second, for when right behavior is detailed to Confucian lengths, the individual's entire life becomes choreographed; it is transformed into a sacred dance. Its steps have been indicated. There is precedence for every act.

4. The fourth ideal in the Confucian scheme is *te*. Literally this word meant power, specifically the power by which men are ruled. But what should be the nature of that power? We have watched Confucius disagree with the Realists' definition of it as brute force. What was his alternative?

No state can forcibly constrain all of its citizens all the time, Confucius thought, or even a large fraction of them a large part of the time. Rulers need the voluntary cooperation of their subjects, and this will emerge only when people believe that their leaders merit their cooperation. To merit it, leaders must be persons of character, sincerely devoted to the common good and possessed of the character that compels respect. Real *te*, therefore, is the power of moral example. In the final analysis, goodness enters society through the impress of leaders that people respect and admire. Everything turns on the head of state. If he is crafty or worthless, nothing good can accrue. But if he is a true *"king of consent"* whose sanction derives from his goodness, such a person will gather a cabinet of *"unpurchasable allies."* Their devotion to the public welfare will in turn quicken the public conscience of local leaders and seep down to inspire citizens generally. *"He who governs by te is like the north star. It keeps its place and other stars turn toward it."*

5. Finally, there is *wen*. This refers to *"the arts of peace"* as contrasted to *"the arts of war"* – to music, poetry, painting, the sum of culture in its aesthetic and spiritual mode.

Confucius valued the arts tremendously, but not art for art's sake. It was art's power to ennoble the human spirit that he admired. *"By poetry the mind is aroused; from music the finish is received. The odes quicken the mind. They induce self-contemplation. They teach the art of sensibility. They help to restrain resentment. They bring home the duty of serving one's parents and one's prince."*

This capacity of *wen* has a political dimension, for what succeeds in international relations? Ultimately, the victory goes to the state with the highest culture – the one with the finest art, the noblest philosophy, the grandest poetry. For in the end it is these that elicit the spontaneous admiration of women and men everywhere.

Above: *A water buffalo and his keeper, Sung Dynasty.* Opposite:
*Ting Dynasty cooking vessel. Confucius' emphasis on correct social
relationships puts everyday life at the center of human spirituality.*

THE CONFUCIAN PROJECT

LET US ASSUME THAT THE DELIBERATE TRA-DITION Confucius worked to establish was in place. How would life appear to a Chinese whose life was fashioned by it? It would loom as a never-ending opportunity to become more human. In the Confucian scheme, the good man or woman is one who is always trying to become better. The project is not pursued in a vacuum; this is not yogis retiring to mountain caves to discover the God within. Quite the contrary. A Confucian positions him- or herself in the center of ever-shifting, never-ending cross-currents of human relationships, and would not have it otherwise; sanctity in isolation had no meaning for Confucius. The point is not merely that human relationships are fulfilling; the Confucian claim runs deeper than this. It is, rather, that apart from human relationships

there is no self. The self is a center of relationships. It is constructed through its interactions with others and is defined by the sum of its social roles.

This concept is so different from Western individualism that it warrants another paragraph. Confucius saw the human self as a node, not an entity; it is a meeting place where lives intersect. In this it resembles a sea anemone, which is little more than a net through which tides and currents wash to form deposits that build what little substance the plant possesses. But this image, while

accurate in its way, is too passive. We will do better to exchange its sea currents for winds in the sky that an eagle rides. These winds support the eagle who controls its altitude by tilting its wings. Human beings are likewise in motion, but in our case it is human relationships that support us, and their prevailing currents are the Five Constant Relationships. The Confucian project is to adjusting one's "wings" at the angle that lets these relationships carry us to empyrean heights. Or as Confucius would have said, toward the goal of becoming more completely human. In this analogy, Confucius' Five Constant Relationships present themselves as relatively stable currents in atmospheric conditions that in other respects can fluctuate wildly. All five are asymmetrical in that (as we have seen) behavior that is appropriate to one person in each pair differs from what is appropriate for the partner. The asymmetry presupposes role differentiations and details their specifics.

The crucial question here is whether their specifics place one party in each pair above the other. In one sense they clearly do. It seemed altogether natural to Confucius that children should look up to their parents, wives to husbands, subjects to rulers, and younger friends and siblings to their older counterparts; for the latter, generally older, are more experienced and provide natural role models. But this is where wingslants must be adjusted precisely, for a hairs-breadth difference puts the

Confucian project into a nose dive. The danger is greatest for the "top" partner in each pair who could be tempted to assume that the position carries built-in perquisites rather than ones that must be earned. Confucius argued the contrary: that the perquisites must be merited. The loyalty that is due the husband from the wife is contingent on the husband's being the kind of husband who warrants – instinctively inspires – such loyalty; comparably with the other relationships. In the ruler-subject relationship, for example, the ruler retains the Mandate of Heaven – his right to rule – only insofar as he rules well. Two thousand years before Europe separated divine right from the office of kingship, the Confucians built the Right of Revolution into their political platform. *"Heaven sees as the people see; heaven wills as the people will."*

As a metaphor for the Confucian project we introduced the image of an eagle that ascends by adjusting its wings to the currents of the Five Constant Relationships. If we round off this metaphor by asking what ascent means here we find that the answer is: becoming a *chun tzu,* a fully realized human being, through expanding one's empathy indefinitely. The expansion proceeds in concentric circles that begin with oneself and spread from there to include, successively, one's family, one's face-to-face community, one's nation, and finally all humanity. In shifting the center of one's concern from oneself to one's family one transcends selfishness. The move from family to community transcends nepotism. The move from community to nation overcomes parochialism, and the move to all humanity counters chauvinistic nationalism.

This broadening process is accompanied by one that is deepening, for in saying above that the Confucian self is the sum of its roles, we should not imply that it has no subjective center. Confucius' repeated calls for self-examination show that he not only recognized an interior side of the self but considered it important. Inside and outside work together in the Confucian scheme. The inner world deepens and grows more refined as empathy expands.

Above: Small outdoor shrine. Opposite: The lotuses in this pond suggest the Confucian ideal of a community of fully realized human beings.

ETHICS OR RELIGION

IS CONFUCIANISM A RELIGION OR AN ETHIC? It definitely approaches life from an ethical angle, but this does not keep it from being a religion in its inclusive reaches. Thus far we have confined ourselves to Confucius' social teachings, but though these were his primary concern, they do not exhaust his outlook.

To understand the transcendent dimension of his thought we need to set it against the backdrop of the world view he inherited. That view divided the world into Heaven and Earth which, though distinct, were solidly joined. The terms referred less to places than to the people who inhabited the places. Thus Heaven was the abode of the ancestors, (ti), as presided over by the supreme ancestor Shang Ti; while Earth consisted of the mortals who currently walk its face. The whole was one unbroken procession in which death spelled no more than transition from the body to a more honorable estate. The two populations were in constant contact; ancestors watched over their offspring while counting on them to supply some of their needs through offerings. Of the two realms, Heaven was unquestionably the more powerful, august, and important.

Being mutually dependent, Heaven and Earth needed to keep in touch. The most concrete way by which Earth communicated to Heaven was through sacrifice. The Chinese of the day thought it not only propitious but fitting to share with their forbears the goods of this earth whose essences were carried aloft on the smoke of sacrificial offerings. Augury, for its part, was the channel through which they tapped into what the ancestors could bestow in return — most importantly their knowledge of the impending future. Collectively, the ancestors remembered the entire past, which put them in a favorable position to extrapolate what the future held. Lacking vocal

chords, they could not voice verbally what they knew, so to apprise the current generation they resorted to omens. Some of these they fed into nature: thunder, lightning, movements of stars, or the patterns of birds in flight. As a more direct way to alert someone to impending dangers, they might make his eyelids tremble, or his ears buzz. Practiced fortunetellers could actively seek out omens by throwing yarrow stalks, or interpreting the cracks that appeared when hot irons were applied to bones or tortoise shells. Whatever the occasion — a trip, a war, a birth, marriage — it was prudent to solicit Heaven's foresight.

In each of these features of early Chinese religion in its continuity with the ancestors, its sacrifices, and its augury — the emphasis was on Heaven, the more important of the two terms. To understand Confucianism as a religion, we should watch Confucius reversing that priority. He shifted China's attention from Heaven to Earth without removing Heaven from the picture.

The shift itself is easily documented. On a much debated issue of his day — which should come first, the claims of earthlings or ancestors? — he answered that though the spirits should not be neglected, people should come first. Normally (we are told) he *did not talk about spirits.* *"Recognize that you know what you know, and that you are ignorant of what you do not know,"* he advised. *"Hear much, leave to one side that which is doubtful, and speak with due caution concerning the remainder."* Invariably when he was questioned about other-worldly matters, he drew the conversation back to human beings. Asked about serving the spirits of the dead he answered, *"When you are not yet able to serve people, how can you serve the spirits?"* Asked about death he replied, *"You do not yet understand life. How can you understand death?"* In short, one world at a time. We find a concrete instance of his this-worldly empha-

sis in the way he shifted attention from ancestor worship to filial piety. In ancient China the dead were actually worshipped. Confucius did not interrupt those ancestral rites; far from denying that the spirits of the dead exist, he advised treating them *"as if they were present."* He directed his own emphasis, though, toward the living family.

In sum, though Confucius was reserved about the supernatural, he was not without it. Somewhere in the universe, he believed, there is a power that is on the side of right. It follows from this that the spread of right-eousness is a cosmic demand. He taught that the Will of Heaven is the first thing a *chun tzu* will respect, and he believed that that Will backed his mission. *"Heaven has appointed me to teach my doctrines, and until I have done so, what can the people do to me?"* Feeling neglected by his people, he consoled himself with the thought: *"There is Heaven—it knows me!"* One of the most quoted religious sayings of all times has come from his pen. *"He who offends the gods has no one to pray to."*

With these things in mind, we should add a final step to the Confucian project that was outlined on page 114. Having noted there that the task of becoming fully human involves transcending (sequentially) egoism, nepotism, parochialism, ethnocentrism and chauvinistic nationalism, we must now add a final step. It involves transcending isolating, self-sufficient humanism as well. In its fullness, humanity *"forms one body with Heaven, Earth, and the myriad things."*

Above: *Detail from the scroll* **"Life Along the River on the Eve of Ch'ing Ming Festival".**

IMPACT ON CHINA

FOR OVER TWO THOUSAND YEARS Confucius' teachings have profoundly affected a quarter of the population of this globe. Their advance reads like a success story, for the surprising upshot of Confucius' outwardly undistinguished career was the founding of a class of scholars who were to become China's ruling elite, and the emergence of Confucius himself as the most important figure in China's history. In 130 B.C. the Confucian texts became the basic discipline for the training of government officials, a pattern that continued until the Empire collapsed in 1905. In the Han Dynasty Confucianism became in effect China's state religion; in 59 A.D. sacrifices were ordered for Confucius in all urban schools, and in the seventh and eighth centuries temples were erected in every prefecture of the empire as shrines to him and his principal disciples. China's famous civil service examinations had the Confucian corpus at their heart. They helped create the Chinese Empire which, if we multiply the two thousand years that it lasted by the number of citizens it included, emerges as quantitatively the most impressive social institution that human beings have devised.

It is not easy to say what Confucius contributed to this institution because generic Chinese values accommodated themselves to his to a degree that makes it difficult to separate the two. What we shall do in the remainder of this chapter is take note of some features of the Chinese character that Confucius and his disciples reinforced where they did not originate them. Those features pretty much blanket East Asia today, for Japan, Korea, and much of Southeast Asia intentionally adopted the Confucian ethic.

We can begin with China's social emphasis – its overriding concern with social, ethical, and political matters. Historians think this may have gotten its start in China's age-old need for massive irrigation projects on the one hand, and gigantic dikes to contain her wild rivers on the other. In any case, it has produced a talent for social effectiveness – for getting things done on a large scale. The consequences have been both good and bad. On the debit side it has strengthened the hands of dictators, but it has also wrought accomplishments. Facing up to its population problem in the third quarter of this century, China halved her birthrate in a single decade, and in the thirty years from 1949 to 1979, gained the upper hand on famine, flood and epidemic disease. The *Scientific American* in its September 1980 issue, called this "a great event in history."

Directly related to the subject of this book is the way China positioned its religious traditions. In India and the West religions are exclusive if not competitive, but China considered these traits divisive and configured its religions in a way that served the needs of everyone. Traditionally every Chinese was Confucian in ethics and public

---

Opposite: *The Great Wall. Confucius reinforced the characteristic Chinese social effectiveness that has made achievements like this possible.* Above: *Scene from a "cadre school" during Mao's Cultural Revolution.*

life, Taoist in private life and hygiene, and Buddhist in matters relating to death, with a healthy dash of shamanistic folk religion thrown in for good measure. As someone has put the point: every Chinese wears a Confucian hat, Taoist robes, and Buddhist sandals. Japan added Shinto to the mix.

The importance of the family in China scarcely requires comment. Some sinologists argue that when ancestor worship and filial piety are included, the family emerges as the real religion of the Chinese people. Surnames precede given names, and the extended family survived well into the twentieth century; one hundred and fifteen prefixes (like aunt and uncle) were needed to do justice to its complex relationships. Family ties can smother, but they can also support. One thinks of low crime rates at home – the burglary rate in Japan is one percent of that in the United States – and the impressive record of East Asian immigrants in foreign lands.

The upward tilt toward the elder partner in three of Confucius' Five Constant Relationships elevated East Asia's respect for age to the point of veneration. Faced with the terrors of bodily decline, China constructed attitudes that softened their blows. We have already mentioned that with each passing year a Chinese could count on more solicitude from family and friends, and on being listened to with increasing attention and respect.

Confucius' Doctrine of the Mean continues in the Chinese preference for negotiation, mediation, and the "middle man," as against impersonal courts of law. Until recently legal action has been regarded as something of a disgrace, a confession of inability to work things out through compromises. In ratio to their populations, Japan has one lawyer for every twenty-four in the United States.

And there is wen: Confucius' conviction that learning and the arts are not mere veneer but powers that elevate societies and the human heart. China placed the scholar-bureaucrat at the top of its social scale, and soldiers at the bottom. One wonders whether anywhere other than Tibet (and Arabia during the brief years that the Caliphate was intact) there has been such an attempt to effect Plato's ideal of the philosopher king. Here and there the attempt bore fruit. There have been golden ages in China when the arts have flourished as nowhere else in their time and deep learning was achieved: calligraphy, Sung landscape painting, and the life-giving dance of *tai chi chuan* come quickly to mind. Paper was invented. Four centuries before Gutenberg, moveable type was discovered. There has been great poetry, magnificent scroll painting, and ceramics that some critics consider unrivaled.

As Confucius predicted, these cultural achievements have brought political rewards. They endowed Chinese civilization with a power of assimilation that at its peak was unrivaled. Having the most open frontier of all the great civilizations, China was subject to wave after wave of invasions by cavalried barbarians. To their gates came the Tartars whose one long-range raid inflicted a mortal wound on the Roman Empire. But what the Chinese could not fend off, they absorbed. Each wave of invaders tended to lose its identity through voluntary assimilation. They admired and emulated what they saw.

The magic did not last. In the fifteenth century Chinese civilization was still unrivaled throughout the world, but stagnation set in and the last two centuries must be discounted because the West, armed with superior military technology, snatched China's fate from its hands. There is little point in discussing Confucianism in the context of a Western instigated war that forced opium on the Chinese and divided their land into European spheres of influence. Even the twentieth century importation of Marxism must be seen as an act of desperation to regain a lost autonomy.

For Confucius' persisting influence we must look not

to politics but to the East Asian economic miracle of the latter twentieth century. Japan, Korea, Taiwan, and Singapore, all shaped by the Confucian ethic, have become the center of world economic growth – impressive witness to what can happen when scientific technology links up with social technology, if we may use this phrase for Confucius' invention. A single statistic says much. In 1982, Japanese workers took on average only 5.1 of the 12 vacation days they were entitled to. By their own accounts, "longer vacations would have imposed burdens on our colleagues." Carrying over into the courtesy for which Orientals have been famous, comes this report: "In the cyclonic mess of Kyoto traffic, two cars scrape bumpers. Both drivers leap out. Each bows, apologizing profusely for his carelessness."

These are lingering echoes of the Confucian spirit, but one must wonder if they are not fading ones. In a Westernizing world, what is the future of this religion?

No one knows. It may be that we are looking at a dying way of life. If so, it would be appropriate to close this chapter with the words Confucius applied to himself when on his deathbed his eyes rested for the last time on the majestic dome of T'ai Shan, China's sacred mountain:

> "The Sacred Mountain is falling,
> The bean is breaking.
> The wise man is withering away."

On the other hand, prophets have a way of outlasting politicians. Gandhi has outlasted Nehru, and Confucianism is back in China's public schools.

The Chinese character shou, meaning longevity.

道

CHAPTER V

TAOISM

There is a being, wonderful, perfect;

It existed before heaven and earth.

How quiet it is!

How spiritual it is!

It stands alone and it does not change.

It moves around and around,

but does not on this account suffer.

All life comes from it.

It wraps everything with its love as in a garment,

and yet it claims no honor, for it does not demand to be Lord.

I do not know its name, and so I call it Tao, the Way,

and I rejoice in its power."

Above: *Bronze mirror decorated with taoist images.* Left:
*Lonely Eminence Hill dominates the city of Guilin in the
south of China*

THE OLD MASTER

N O CIVILIZATION IS monochrome. In China the classical tones of Confucianism have been balanced not only by the spiritual shades of Buddhism but by the romantic hues of Taoism.

According to tradition, Taoism (pronounced Dowism) originated with a man named Lao Tzu who is said to have been born about 604 B.C. We know nothing for certain about him; all we have is a mosaic of legends. Some of these are fantastic, while others seem quite plausible: that he kept the archives in his native western state and lived a simple and unassertive life. The only purportedly contemporary portrait tells of Confucius who, hearing reports of the strange man, sought him out. He was impressed by Lao Tzu, we are told, and likened him to a dragon – enigmatic, larger than life, and mysterious.

The traditional portrait concludes with the report that Lao Tzu, saddened by his people's disinclination to cultivate the natural goodness he advocated and seeking greater personal solitude for his closing years, climbed on a water buffalo and rode westward towards what is now Tibet. At the Hankao Pass a gatekeeper tried to persuade him to turn back. Failing this,

he asked if Lao Tzu would not at least leave a record of his beliefs to the civilization he was abandoning. This Lao Tzu consented to do. He retired for three days and returned with a slim volume of 5000 characters titled *Tao Te Ching*, or The Way and Its Power. A testament to humanity's at-home-ness in the universe, it can be read in half an hour or a lifetime. It remains to this day the basic text of Taoist thought.

Whether this final account is fact or fiction, it is so true to Taoist attitudes that it will remain a part of Taoism forever. Scholars do not see the *Tao Te Ching* as having been written by a single hand, and doubt that it attained the form in which we have it until the second half of the third century B.C. They concede, however, that its ideas cohere to the point where we must posit the existence of someone under whose influence the book took shape, and they have no objection to our calling that someone Lao Tzu.

Above: *The ox-herding pictures used as running illustrations in this chapter, although now known in their Buddhist versions, were originally Taoist.* Center: *Landscape painting by artist Wen Cheng-ming.* Opposite: *Horse and rider, by Chao Meng-fu.*

TAOISM

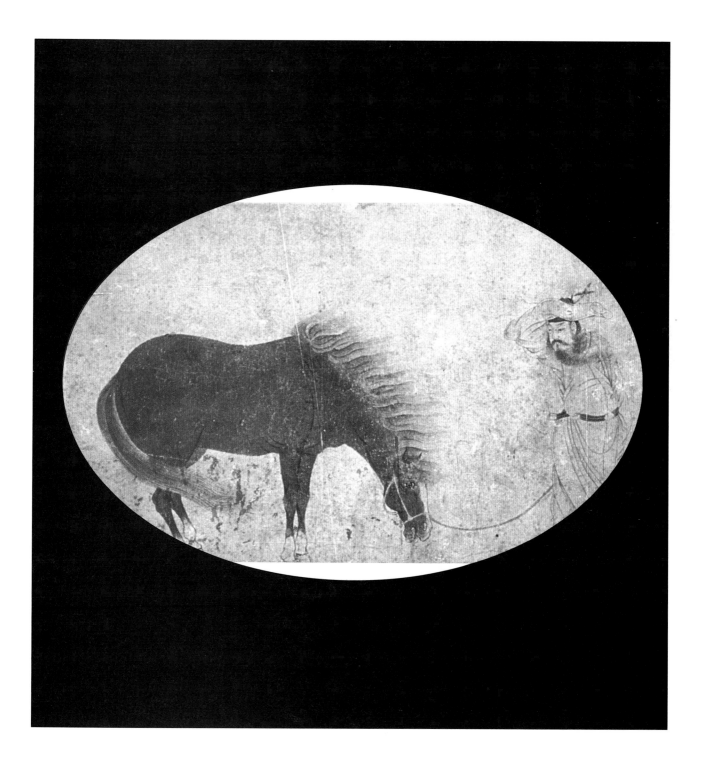

THREE MEANINGS OF TAO

O N opening Taoism's bible, the *Tao Te Ching*, we sense at once that everything revolves around the pivotal concept of *Tao* itself. Literally this word means path, or way. There are three senses, however, in which this "way" can be understood.

First, *Tao* is the *way of ultimate reality*. This Tao cannot be perceived or even clearly conceived, for it is too vast for reason to fathom. It is, all the same, the ground of everything that follows. Above all, behind all, beneath all is the Womb from which all life springs and to which it returns.

Though the *Tao* is ultimately transcendent, it is also immanent. In this second sense it is the *way of the universe*; the norm, the rhythm, and the driving power in all nature. Basically spirit rather than matter, it cannot be exhausted, for the more it is drawn upon, the more it flows. There are marks of inevitability about it, for when autumn comes "no leaf is spared because of its beauty, no flower because of its fragrance." Yet ultimately it is benign. Giving life to all things, it may be called "the Mother of the World."

In its third sense, *Tao* refers to *the way of human life* when it meshes with the *Tao* of the universe as just described. Most of what follows in this chapter will detail what the Taoists suggest that this way of life is. First, however, it is necessary to point out that there have been in China not one but three Taoisms.

THREE APPROACHES TO
POWER & THE TAOISMS THAT FOLLOW

Scenes like this have inspired Chinese painters for centuries.

*T*AO *T*E *C*HING, the title of Taoism's basic text, has been translated *The Way and Its Power*. We have seen that the first of these substantive terms, the Way, can be taken in three senses. We must now add that this is also true of the second substantive term, power. Corresponding to the three ways *te* or power can be approached, there have arisen in China three species of Taoism so dissimilar that initially they seem to have no more in common than homonyms like blew/blue or sun/son that sound alike but have different meanings. We shall find that this is not the case, but first the three species must be identified. Two have standard designations, Philosophical Taoism and Religious or Popular Taoism. The third school (which will come second in our order of presentation) is too heterogeneous to have acquired a single designation. Its population does, however, constitute an identifiable cluster by virtue of sharing a common objective. All were engaged in vitalizing programs that were intended to facilitate the power of the *Tao*, its *te*, as it flows through human beings.

EFFICIENT POWER: PHILOSOPHICAL TAOISM

*U*NLIKE RELIGIOUS TAOISM which became a full-fledged church, Philosophical Taoism and the "vitalizing Taoisms" (as we shall refer to the second group) are relatively unorganized. Philosophical Taoism is reflective and the vitalizing programs active, but neither was institutionalized. They share a second similarity in that both are self-help programs. There are teachers, but they are better regarded as coaches who train their students – philosophical teachers in what students should understand, vitalizing teachers in what they should do. In contrast to religious Taoists, those in these first two camps work primarily on themselves.

Turning to what divides the first two schools, it has to do with their respective stances toward the *Tao's* power on which life feeds. Philosophical Taoists try to conserve their te by expending it efficiently, whereas the vitalizing Taoists try to increase its available supply.

Because philosophical Taoism is essentially an attitude toward life, it is the one that has most to say to the world at large, so will receive the longest treatment. Not until the second half of this chapter, however. Here we shall only identify it to place it in its logical position before proceeding with its two sister Taoisms.

Called School Taoism in China, philosophical Taoism is associated with the names of Lao Tzu, Chuang Tzu, and the *Tao Te Ching*. We can establish its link with power by remembering that philosophy seeks knowledge and that knowledge is power, as Bacon asserted. The knowledge the Taoists sought was the kind that empowers life. We call it wisdom, and to live wisely (the Taoist philosophers argued) is to live in a way that conserves life's vitality by not expending it in useless, draining

ways, the chief of which are friction and conflict. In the second half of this chapter we shall examine Lao Tzu and Chuang Tzu's prescriptions for avoiding such dissipations, but we can anticipate a single point here. Their recommendations revolve around the concept of *wu wei*, a phrase that translates literally as inaction but in Taoism means pure effectiveness. Action in the mode of *wu wei* is action in which friction – in interpersonal relationships,

in intrapsychic conflict, and in relation to nature – is reduced to the minimum.

We turn now to the vitalizing cults as our second species of Taoism.

Opposite: *Teenage girl in a commune outside Shanghai practicing Taoist exercises.* Above: *Kindergarten children in Shanghai.*

AUGMENTED POWER:
TAOIST HYGIENE & YOGA

TAOIST ADEPTS, AS WE SHALL CALL the practitioners of this second kind of Taoism because all were engaged in training programs of some sort, were not willing to settle for the philosophers' goal of managing their allotments of the Tao efficiently. They wanted to go beyond conservation to increase; specifically, to increase the allotments of Tao that were at their disposal.

The word *ch'i* provides the proper entrance to this second school, for though it literally means breath, it actually means vital energy. The Taoists used it to refer to the power of the Tao that they experienced coursing through them – or not coursing because it was blocked. Their main object was to remove the obstacles that reduced its flow. *Ch'i* fascinated these Taoists. Blake registered their feelings precisely when he exclaimed, *"energy is delight!"* for energy is the life force and the Taoists loved life. To be alive is good; to be more alive is better; to be always alive is best. Hence Taoist immortality cults.

To accomplish their end of maximizing *ch'i,* these Taoists worked with three things: matter, movement, and their minds.

Respecting *matter,* they tried eating things – seemingly everything – to see if *ch'i* could be ingested nutritionally. This produced a remarkable pharmacopia of medicinal herbs, but the Taoists didn't stop there. They went on to seek an elixir of physical immortality. Sexual experiments were performed wherein semen was retained so *ch'i* wouldn't be spent, and breathing exercises were devised to absorb *ch'i* from the atmosphere.

These efforts to extract *ch'i* from matter in its solid, liquid, and gaseous forms were supplemented by programs of bodily *movement* such as *t'ai-chi chuan* to invite *ch'i* from the cosmos and remove blocks to its internal

flow. This last was the object of acupuncture as well.

Turning finally to the *mind,* contemplatives developed Taoist meditation. This third way of increasing *ch'i* is the most subtle, so it requires the longest treatment.

Animating meditational or yogic Taoism was a dawning fascination with the inner as opposed to the outer self. Early peoples did not distinguish these two sides of their being appreciably. Meditational Taoism arose as the advancing self-consciousness of the Chinese brought sub-

meditated. The physical postures and concentration techniques that they employed had much in common with India's *raja yoga*, but the Chinese gave the project a characteristic twist. Their social preoccupation led them to press the possibility that the *ch'i* that poured into *yogis* when their minds were emptied of self-seeking, perturbing emotions and distracting thoughts could be transmitted psychically to the community to enhance its vitality and harmonize its affairs. The power that could be thus acquired and redirected was remarkable; indeed, it *"could shift Heaven and Earth."* For in the condition of total quiescence and stillness, the heartmind was open as never before to the Tao. *"To the mind that is still, the whole universe surrenders."* Without lifting a finger, a ruler who had mastered this stillness could order an entire people with his mystical-moral power. Without being aware of what was happening, his subjects would spontaneously forego unruly ways. *"The sage relies on actionless activity. The myriad creatures are worked upon by him. He puts himself in the background, but is always there."*

The *yogis* knew they could not hope for much public understanding. Confucians ridiculed their direct, psychic approach to social harmony, likening it to impatient farmers who tug gently on their crops each night, hoping to speed their growth. Even someone who should have understood, the Taoist mystic Chuang Tzu, burlesqued their breathing exercises. *"They expel the used air with great energy to inhale more deeply the fresh air. Like bears, they climb trees in order to breathe with greater ease."* But despite such ridicule, *Taoist yoga* had an appreciable following. Some sinologists consider it the basic perspective from which the *Tao Te Ching* was written. If they are right, it testifies to the veiled language of the book, for it is usually read in the philosophical way we shall soon come to. Before we turn to that way, however, we must introduce the third major branch of Taoism which is religious.

Younger children in today's China practice more vigorous techniques, while the older generation begins its day with t'ai chi.

jective experience to full view. Novel and momentous, this world of the inner self invited exploration. Pioneers found it so interesting that matter suffered by comparison, being but shell and overlay. To be directly in view of the source of one's awareness was a momentous experience, for one then saw *"the self as it was meant to be."* One saw not merely *"things perceived,"* but *"that by which we perceive."*

It was to reach this pure perception that Taoist *yogis*

VICARIOUS POWER: RELIGIOUS TAOISM

PHILOSOPHICAL TAOISM sought to manage life's normal quotient of the *Tao* efficiently, and energizing Taoism sought to raise that quotient, but something was lacking. Reflection and health programs require time, and most Chinese lacked that commodity. Yet they too needed help; there were epidemics to be checked, marauding ghosts to be reckoned with, and rains that needed to be induced or stopped. Taoists responded to such problems. The measures they devised paralleled many of the freelance doings of psychics, shamans, faith healers, and soothsayers, who came by their powers naturally; but Taoism institutionalized those activities by founding, in the second century A.D., a

church. Its pantheon consists of Lao Tzu and two other deities, and the texts that were said to issue from them came to be accepted without question. The line of succession in this church continues down to the present in Taiwan.

Much of religious Taoism looks like crude superstition, but we must remember that we have little idea what energy is, how it proceeds, or the means by which (and extent to which) it can be augmented. In any case, the intent of the Taoist church is clear. As one historian puts it, "The Taoist priesthood made cosmic life-power available for ordinary villagers."

The texts they used are crammed with descriptions of rituals which, if exactly performed, have magical

effects, and the word magic holds the key to this priestly version of Taoism. The word has come to connote trickery and illusion, but traditionally it was everywhere respected as the means by which higher, occult powers are tapped for use in the visible world. Peter's healing of Aeneas (as reported in Acts 9:32-34) provides us with a Western instance.

Now as Peter went here and there among all the believers, he came down also to the saints living in Lydia. There he found a man named Aeneas, who had been bedridden for eight years, for he was paralyzed. Peter said to him, "Aeneas, Jesus Christ heals you; get up and make your bed!" And immediately he got up.

Note that this was not a miracle. It would have been a miracle if Christ had empowered the paralytic Aeneas to climb out of bed without Peter's help. As it was, Peter played a role in the cure, a necessary role we may assume, and we are confronted with magic. Sacred magic, as it happens, for if a demon had been invoked for malevolent purposes, sorcery would have been at work. It was under the rubric of magic as thus traditionally understood that the Taoist church — dividing the territory with freelance wizards, exorcists, and shamans — devised ways to harness higher powers for humane ends.

Opposite: *A Taoist healing ritual.* Above: *Central altar in the Bao-an Gong Temple.*

THE MINGLING OF THE POWERS

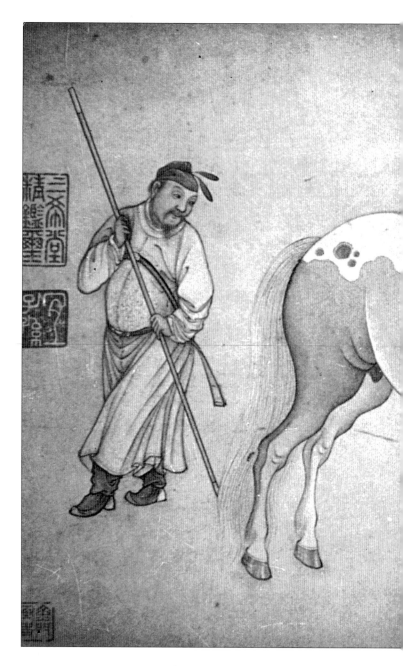

PHILOSOPHICAL TAOISM, vitalizing programs for increasing one's own *ch'i,* and the Taoist church: the three branches of Taoism which at first seemed to have little in common now show their affinities. All have the same concern – how to maximize the *Tao's* animating *te* – and the specifics of their concerns fall on a continuum. The continuum begins with interest in how life's normal allotment of *ch'i* can be deployed to best effect (Philosophical Taoism). From there it moves on to ask if that normal quotient can be increased (Taoist vitalizing programs). Finally, it asks if cosmic energies can be gathered, as if by a burning glass, and transmitted to people who need it but could not get it on their own (Religious Taoism).

The danger in this arrangement is that in the interest of clarity the lines between the three divisions have been drawn too sharply. No solid walls separate them; the three are better regarded as currents in a common river. Throughout history, each has interacted with the other two, right down to Taoism in Hong Kong and Taiwan today. It is rare to find a Taoist who is not involved to some degree with all three schools.

It is now time to return to Philosophical Taoism and give it its hearing.

The interaction between this trainer and his powerful horse suggests the principles of wu wei underlying all forms of Taoism. Painting by Leng Mei.

CREATIVE QUIETUDE

THE OBJECT OF PHILOSOPHICAL TAOISM is to align one's daily life to the *Tao,* to ride its boundless tide and delight in its flow. The basic way to do this, as was earlier noted, is to perfect a life of *wu wei.* We have seen that *wu wei* should not be translated as do-nothingness or inaction. Better renderings are pure effectiveness, or creative quietude.

Creative quietude combines two seemingly incompatible conditions – supreme activity and supreme relaxation. They can coexist because human beings are not self-enclosed entities; they ride an unbounded sea of *Tao* which supports them, as we would say, through their subliminal minds. One way to create is through following the calculated directives of the conscious mind. This smacks more of sorting and arranging than of inspiration. Genuine creation comes when the resources of the subliminal self come into play. But for this to happen, a certain dissociation from the surface self is required. The conscious mind must get out of the way, stop standing in its own light.

Wu wei is the supreme action, the precious simplicity, suppleness, and freedom that flows from us, or rather through us, when our egos and conscious efforts yield to a power not their own. How are we to describe the action that flows from such a life? Fed by a force that is infinitely subtle and intricate – the *Tao* – the life is graceful, for it lives by a vitality that has no need of abruptness, much less violence. The *Tao* flows in and flows out again, turning life into a dance that is neither feverish nor unbalanced. *Wu wei* is life lived above excess and tension.

"Keep stretching a bow, you repent of the pull,

A whetted saw grows thin and dull"

(Tao Te Ching)

It is not idle. It exhibits, rather, an effectiveness in which no motion is wasted on bickering or outward show.

"One may move so well that a footprint never shows,

Speak so well that the tongue never slips,

Reckon so well that no counter is needed"

(Tao Te Ching)

Effectiveness of this order requires an extraordinary skill, like that of the fisherman who landed enormous fish with a thread because it was made so skillfully that it had no weakest point at which to break. Skill like this is seldom noticed, for viewed from the outside *wu wei* seems effortless. This is because it seeks out empty spaces and moves through them in the way of Prince Wen Hui's cook whose cleaver never grew dull. When he cut up an ox, *"out went a hand, down went a shoulder; he planted a foot, he pressed with a knee, and the ox fell apart with a whisper."* Asked for his secret, he replied, *"There are spaces in the joints. When my thin blade finds those spaces, it has all the room it needs. So it remains sharp."* (Chuang Tzu).

Of the natural elements, it was water that impressed the Taoists most. They admired the way it supports objects and carries them effortlessly on its tide. Poor swimmers flail against it while good swimmers float motionlessly, knowing that it will support them if they don't fight it. Then again, water is unobtrusive and adaptive; it assumes the shape of its containers and seeks out the lowest places. Yet despite its accommodations, it subdues what is hard and brittle. Its currents carve canyons

from granite, and melt the hills we call eternal.

Infinitely supple, yet incomparably strong — these virtues of water are precisely those of *wu wei*. The person who embodies them "works without working." He acts without strain, persuades without argument, is eloquent without flourish, and gets results without coercing. *"A leader is best when people barely know that he exists. Of a good leader, when his work is done the people will say, 'We did this ourselves.'"* (Tao Te Ching).

A final characteristic of water that makes it an appropriate analog to *wu wei* is the clarity it attains through calmness. *"Muddy water let stand will clear."*

Above: *Portrait of Lao Tzu, legendary author of the Tao Te Ching.*
Opposite: *Tao has been called the Watercourse Way.*

OTHER TAOIST VALUES

THE TAOISTS' REJECTION of self-assertiveness and competition has already been implied in the concept of *wu wei*, but it is important enough to be mentioned in its own right. The *Tao Te Ching* warns that *"he who stands on tiptoe does not stand firm,"* and adds that *"the ax falls first on the tallest tree."* An almost reverential regard for humility led Taoists to honor hunchbacks and cripples, and they were fond of pointing out that the value of cups, windows, and doorways lies in what is not there. *"Selfless as melting ice"* is one of their images; to which they add, *"He who feels punctured must once have been a bubble."* Throughout runs a profound disinterest in the things the world prizes. Why struggle and compete? The *Tao* doesn't need to do so.

> *"Nature does not have to insist,*
> *Can blow for half a morning,*
> *Rain for half a day."*

This mention of nature leads into another feature of Taoism, its profound naturalism. Nature should not be exploited and abused, any more than people should be. It should be befriended, not conquered.

> *"Those who would take over the earth*
> *And shape it to their will*
> *Never, I notice, succeed.*
> *The earth is like a vessel so sacred*
> *That at the mere approach of the profane it is marred.*
> *They reach out their fingers and it is gone."*

This ecological stance toward nature deeply affected Taoist art, beginning with its architecture. Taoist temples do not stand out from the landscape. They are nestled against the hills, back under the trees, blending in with the environment. They teach that human beings, too, are at their best when they are in harmony with their surroundings. It is no accident that the greatest periods of Chinese art have coincided with upsurges of Taoist influence. Before reaching for their brushes, painters would go to nature and lose themselves in it, to become, say, the bamboo that they would paint. They would sit for half a day or fourteen years before making a stroke. The Chinese word for landscape painting is composed of the radicals for mountain and water, one of which suggests vastness and solitude, the other pliability, endurance, and continuous movement. Man's part in the vastness is small, so we have to look closely for human beings in the paintings if we find them at all. Usually they are climbing with their bundles, riding a buffalo, or poling a boat — the human self with its journey to make, its burden to carry, its hill to climb, while surrounded by beauty on every side.

This naturalism in art translates into naturalness in the Taoists' way of life. Formalism, show, and ceremony left them cold, and they considered pomp and extravagance downright silly. The simple, even primitive, is better, for much of civilization is artificial. Travel is pointless and prompted by idle curiosity. These attitudes, of course, separated them from the Confucianists, for they saw nothing to be gained from punctiliousness and the meticulous observance of propriety. The most those can produce is lacquered social surfaces — skin deep and brittle. The idea that life can be consciously ordered is ridiculous to begin with, for social blueprints amount to no

"Clearing Autumn Skies"; watercolor by the 11th century Chinese
painter Kuo Hsi.

more than Three in the Morning. And what is Three in the Morning? Once in the state of Sung, hard times forced a keeper of monkeys to reduce their rations. *"From now on,"* he announced, *"it will be three in the morning and four in the evening."* Faced with howls of rebellion, the keeper agreed to negotiate and eventually accepted his monkeys' demand that they be given four in the morning and three in the evening. The monkeys gloried in their triumph. Another Taoist postulate is the relativity of all values and, as its correlate, the identity of opposites. Here Taoism tied in with the traditional Chinese *yin/yang* symbol which is pictured on this page. The polarity in this symbol sums up all of life's basic oppositions: day and night, life and death, male and female, and the rest. The terms in each pair are not flatly opposed, for they complement each other. Each invades the other's hemisphere and takes up its abode in the deepest recess of its domain. And in the end, both are resolved by the circumference that envelops them, the Tao in its eternal wholeness.

True to this symbol, Taoism eschews sharp dichotomies. All values and concepts are relative to the mind that entertains them. When it was suggested to the wren and the cicada that there are birds that fly hundreds of miles without alighting, both quickly agreed that such a thing was impossible. *"You and I know very well,"* they nodded, *"that the furthest one can ever get, even by the most tremendous effort, is to that elm tree over there, and even this one cannot be sure of reaching every time. All these stories about flying hundreds of miles at a stretch are sheer nonsense."*

Even good and evil are not (in Taoist perspective) the opposites they seem, as the story of "The Farmer whose Horse Ran Away" illustrates. On hearing of the misfortune, the farmer's neighbor arrived to commiserate, but all he got from the farmer was, *"Who knows what's good or bad?"* This proved to be true, for the next day the horse returned, bringing with it a drove of wild horses in its train. This time the neighbor arrived with congratulations, only to receive the same response. This too was so, for the next day the farmer's son tried to mount one of the wild horses and broke a leg. More commiserations from the neighbor, with the same response which was again validated, for soldiers soon came around commandeering for the army, and the son was spared because of his injury.

Even regarding death, the Taoists held to their principle of relativity, seeing it as life's natural complement. When Chuang Tzu's wife died, a friend who had come to express condolences found him sitting on the ground with his legs spread wide apart, singing away and whacking out a tune on the back of a wooden bowl. The friend was shocked. *"After all,"* he said, *"she lived with you devotedly all these years, watched your eldest son grow to manhood, and grew old along with you. For you not to have shed a tear over her remains would have been bad enough, but singing and drumming away on a bowl — this is just too much!"*

Left: *Painting by Chao Yuna. Good and evil are relative values in the Taoist world view, as illustrated by the story of "The Farmer Whose Horse Ran Away." Above: Yin/yang symbol on lacquered box.*

"You misjudge me," said Chuang Tzu. *"When my wife died, of course I was in despair. But then I reasoned that before she was born she had no body, and it became clear to me that the same process of change that brought her to birth eventually brought her to death. She whom I have lost has lain down to sleep for awhile in the chamber between heaven and earth. To wail and groan while my wife is sleeping would be to deny nature's sovereign law."*

Given its aversion to violence, it is not surprising to find Taoism inclining toward pacifism. *"One who would guide a leader in the use of life will warn him against the use of arms. An army's harvest is a waste of thorns. Conduct your triumph as a funeral."* If it was Confucius that placed the scholar-bureaucrat at the top of China's social scale, it was Lao Tzu who placed the soldier at the bottom. *"The way for a true man to go is not the way of a soldier. Heaven arms with compassion those whom she would not see destroyed."*

War is a somber matter, and Taoism addresses life's serious issues. Yet it always retains a quality of lightness that verges on gaiety. There is a sophistication, urbanity, and charm about the perspective which is infectious. Nowhere is this more apparent than in anecdotes in which Taoists cast Confucians in the role of foils. In one of these, Chuang Tzu is taking a stroll with the Confucian, Hui Tzu. Coming to a bridge, Chuang Tzu leans over and remarks, *"Look at those minnows darting here and there. How free and pleasurable is the life of a fish."*

"You are not a fish," Hui Tzu counters contentiously. *"How do you know what gives pleasure to fish?"*

"You are not I," says Chuang Tzu. *"How do you know that I don't know what gives pleasure to a fish?"*

Horsemen from a 10th century scroll. Confucius brought the order and grace of tradition into an unsettled and restless world.

CONCLUSION

Circling each other like yin and yang themselves, Taoism and Confucianism represent the two indigenous poles of the Chinese character. Confucius represents the classical, Lao Tzu the romantic. Confucius advocates calculated behavior, Lao Tzu praises spontaneity and naturalness. Confucius' focus is on the human; Lao Tzu connects the human to what transcends it. As the Chinese themselves say, Confucius roams within society, Lao Tzu wanders beyond. Something in life reaches out in each of these directions, and Chinese civilization would have been poorer if either had not appeared.

There are books whose first reading casts a spell that is never quite undone, the reason being that they speak to the deepest "me" in the reader. For all who quicken at the thought that always, everywhere, the *Tao* is within us, the *Tao Te Ching* is such a book. Though never practiced to perfection, its lessons of simplicity, openness, and wisdom have been for millions of Chinese a joyful guide.

> *"There is a being, wonderful, perfect;*
> *It existed before heaven and earth.*
> *How quiet it is!*
> *How spiritual it is!*
> *It stands alone and it does not change.*
> *It moves around and around, but does not*
> *on this account suffer.*
> *All life comes from it.*
> *It wraps everything with its love as in a garment, and yet*
> *it claims no honor, for it does not demand to be Lord.*
> *I do not know its name, and so I call it Tao, the Way,*
> *and I rejoice in its power."*

CHAPTER VI

ISLAM

There is a means of polishing all things
whereby rust may be removed.
That which polishes the heart
is the invocation of Allah.

The Taj Mahal, masterpiece of Islamic architecture.

BACKGROUND

*T*HE WORD ISLAM DERIVES from *salam* which means primarily "peace" but in a secondary sense "surrender." Its full connotation, therefore, is the peace that comes from surrendering one's life to God. Those who adhere to Islam are known as Muslims.

If we ask how Islam arose, the outside answer looks for socio-religious currents that were playing over Arabia in Muhammad's day, but the Muslims' answer is different. In their eyes Islam begins not with Muhammad in sixth century Arabia, but with God. "In the beginning God...," the Book of Genesis tells us. The Koran agrees while using the word *Allah*, which means literally "the God." Not *a* god, for there is only one. *The* God.

God created the world, and after it human beings. The name of the first man was Adam. The descendants of Adam and Eve led to Noah, who had a son named Shem from which the word Semite derives. The descendants of Shem led to Abraham who married Sarah. Sarah had no son, so Abraham took Hagar for his second wife. Hagar bore him a son, Ishmael, whereupon Sarah conceived and likewise had a son, named Isaac. Sarah then demanded that Abraham banish Ishmael and Hagar from the tribe. Up to this point the Koran follows the Bible, but here the accounts diverge, for according to the Koran, Ishmael went to the place where Mecca was to rise. His descendants, flourishing in Arabia, became Muslims whereas those of Isaac, who remained in Palestine, gave rise to the Hebrews who were later called Jews.

Muslim worshippers overflow from a crowded mosque into the streets of Zanzibar in Africa.

THE SEAL OF THE PROPHETS

FOLLOWING ISHMAEL'S LINE IN ARABIA we come eventually in the latter half of the sixth century A.D. to Muhammad, the prophet through whom Islam reached its definitive form, Muslims believe. There had been authentic prophets of God before him, but he was their culmination, so he is called *The Seal of the Prophets*. No legitimate prophets will succeed him.

The world into which Muhammad was born is described by subsequent Muslims as ignorant. Life under the conditions of the desert had never been serene. Scarcity of material goods made brigandage a regional institution and the proof of virility. In the sixth century, however, political deadlock and the collapse of the magistrate in the leading city, Mecca, aggravated this generally chaotic situation. The prevailing religion – best described as animistic polytheism – provided no check. Conditions could

hardly have been better calculated to produce a smoldering undercurrent which erupted in sudden affrays and blood feuds, some of which extended for half a century. The times called for a deliverer.

He was born into the leading tribe of Mecca, the Koreish, in approximately 570 A.D., and was named Muhammad, "highly praised." Both his parents died while he was small, but an uncle adopted him and raised him

affectionately. The angels of God, we are told, opened Muhammad's heart and filled it with light. The description epitomizes his early character as this comes down to us by tradition. Pure-hearted and beloved in his circle, he was, it is said, of sweet and gentle disposition. His bereavements having made him sensitive to human suffering in every form, he was always ready to help others, especially the weak and the poor. From most of his contemporaries, though, he felt removed. Their lawless strife, and the general immorality and cynicism of his day produced in the prophet-to-be a reaction of dismay. Silently, broodingly, his thoughts turned inward.

Upon reaching maturity he took up the caravan business and at the age of twenty-five entered the service of a wealthy widow named Khadija. His prudence and integrity impressed her greatly, and gradually their relation deepened into affection, then love. They were married, though she was fifteen years his senior, and the match proved happy in every respect. *"God comforted him through her,"* we are told, *"for she made his burden light."*

Following his marriage, there were fifteen years of preparation before his ministry began. A mountain on the outskirts of Mecca contained a cave, and Muhammad, seeking solitude, began to frequent it. Peering into the mysteries of good and evil, unable to accept the super-

stition and fratricide that were accepted as normal, "this great fiery heart" was reaching out for God.

The desert *jinn* were irrelevant to his quest, but one deity was not. Named Allah, he was worshipped by the Meccans not as the only God but as an impressive one nonetheless. Through vigils, often lasting the entire night, Muhammad became convinced that Allah was far greater than his countrymen supposed. This God was surely not a god or even the greatest of gods. He was, as his name asserted, *the* God – One and only, One without rival. Soon from this mountain cave was to sound the greatest phrase of the Arabic language; the deep, electrifying cry which was to rally a people and explode their power to the limits of the known world: *La ilaha illa 'llah!* There is no god but God!

But first the prophet must receive, around 610 A.D., his commission. On the Night of Power the Book was opened to a ready soul. As Muhammad lay on the floor of the cave there came to him an angel in the form of a man who said to him, *"Proclaim!"* Muhammad protested that he was not a proclaimer, but the angel persisted, saying: *"Proclaim in the name of your Lord who created man from blood coagulated! Proclaim: your Lord is wondrous kind, Who teaches by the pen, Things men knew not, being blind"* (Koran 96:1-3).

Opposite: *A 14th century Turkish painting showing the infant Muhammad in his mother's arms.* Above: *An angel visits Muhammad to urge him to proclaim the truth he has seen.*

Arousing from his trance, Muhammad felt as if the words he had heard had been branded on his soul. Terrified, he rushed home and told Khadija that he had become either a prophet or a madman. At first she resisted this disjunction, but on hearing his full story she became his first convert.

The voice returned repeatedly, and its command was always the same – to proclaim. Muhammad's life was no more his own. From that time forth it was given to God and to humanity, preaching with unswerving purpose the words that God was to transmit for twenty-three years. What those words proclaimed will be reserved for later sections. Here we need only speak of the response it drew and note that its appeal was to human reason as vectored by religious discernment.

In an age charged with supernaturalism, when miracles were accepted as the stock-in-trade of the most ordinary saint, Muhammad refused to pander to human credulity. Allah, he insisted, had not sent him to work wonders. If signs be sought, let them be not of Muhammad's greatness but of God's, and for these one need only open one's eyes to the wonders of nature. The only miracle that Muhammad claimed was that of the Koran itself. That he with his own resources could have produced such truth – this was the one naturalistic hypothesis he could not accept.

As for the reaction to his message, it was (for all but a few) violently hostile. The reasons for the hostility can be reduced to three: its uncompromising monotheism threatened polytheistic beliefs and the considerable revenue that was coming to Mecca from pilgrimages to its 360 shrines (one for each day of the lunar year); its moral teachings demanded an end to the licentiousness that citizens clung to; and its social content challenged an unjust order.

As such teachings suited neither their tastes nor their privileges, the Meccan leaders were determined to have none of it. They began their attack with ridicule, but when this proved ineffective, they turned to threats and then to open persecution. To no avail; persecution only steeled the will of the new Prophet and his converts. Muhammad set the pattern for their fidelity. He continued to throw heart and soul into his preaching, adjuring listeners on every side to abandon their evil ways and prepare for the day of reckoning.

The odds were so against him that in the first three years he made fewer than forty converts. His enemies, though, could not seal the hearts of the Meccans against his words forever. Slowly but steadily, people of energy, talent, and worth became convinced of the truth of his message, until by the end of a decade several hundred families were acclaiming him as Allah's authentic spokesman. By this time the Meccan nobility were alarmed, and determined to rid themselves of the troublemaker for good.

Above: *Muhammad consecrating the Black Stone of Ka'ba.* Opposite: *Muhammad surrounded by his disciples, preaching to the people of Medina.*

THE MIGRATION THAT LED TO VICTORY

S HE FACED THIS SEVEREST CRISIS of his career, Muhammad was suddenly waited on by a delegation of the leading citizens of Yathrib, a city two hundred and eighty miles to Mecca's north. Through pilgrims and other visitors to Mecca, Muhammad's teachings had won a firm hold there. The city was facing internal rivalries that put it in need of a strong impartial leader, and Muhammad looked like the man. After receiving a delegation's pledge that they would worship Allah only and observe the precepts of Islam, Muham-

mad accepted the charge. When the Meccan leaders got wind of his intended exodus they did everything in their power to prevent his going, but together with a companion he eluded their watch and set out for Yathrib. The Meccans followed in hot pursuit, but the two managed to reach their destination. The year was 622 A.D.

The migration, known in Arabic as the *hijra,* is regarded by Muslims as the turning point in world history and is the year from which they reckon their calendar. Yathrib soon came to be known as Medinat al-Nabi, the City of the Prophet, and then by contraction as Medina, "the city."

From the moment of his arrival at Medina, Muhammad assumed a different role: from prophecy he was pressed into administration. His manner remained as unassuming as ever; he lived in an ordinary clay house, milked his own goats, and was accessible night and day. But as a statesman he was, by all accounts, brilliant. He exercised the justice necessary for order, but when the injury was toward himself he was gentle and merciful, even to his enemies. In all, the Medinese found him a master whom it was as difficult not to love as not to obey.

For the remaining ten years of his life his personal history merged with that of the Medinese commonwealth. He welded the five heterogeneous and conflicting tribes of the city, two of them Jewish, into an orderly confederation and awakened in its citizens a spirit of cooperation unknown in the city's history. His reputation spread, and people began to flock from every part of Arabia to see the man who had wrought this miracle.

There followed a struggle with the Meccans for the mind of Arabia as a whole. The Meccans attacked Medina, and for several years victories changed hands, but then turned permanently in Muhammad's favor. Eight years after his Migration from Mecca, he who had left that city as a fugitive returned as conqueror. Characteristically, Muhammad forgave his former oppressors. Making his way to the Ka'ba, a cubical temple (said to have been built by Abraham) which he rededicated to Allah and consecrated as Islam's geographical center, he accepted the city's mass conversion.

Muhammad himself returned to Medina. Two years later, in 632 A.D., he died with virtually all of Arabia under his control. Before the century closed, his followers had conquered Armenia, Persia, Syria, Palestine,

Iraq, North Africa and Spain, and had crossed the Pyrenees into France. In a brief lifetime he had called forth, from unpromising material in a land that had been only a geographical expression, a nation and had established a religion which today claims a fifth of the world's population.

Opposite: *Illuminated pages from an 11th century copy of the Koran.* Above: *The Ka'ba, geographical center of Islam.*

THE STANDING MIRACLE

*T*HE BLEND OF ADMIRATION, respect, and affection that Muslims feel for Muhammad is an impressive fact of history; they never mention his name without adding, *"blessings and peace be upon him."* Even so, they never mistake him for the earthly center of their faith. That place is reserved for the bible of Islam, the Koran.

Literally the Arabic word *qur'an* means recitation. So great was Muhammad's regard for its contents that (as we have seen) he considered it the only miracle God worked through him – God's "standing miracle," he called it. That he could himself have produced a book that provides the ground plan of all knowledge and at the same time is grammatically perfect and without poetic peer – this, Muhammad, and with him all Muslims are convinced, defies belief.

Muslims tend to read the Koran literally. They consider it the earthly facsimile of an Uncreated Koran in almost exactly the way that Christians consider Jesus to have been the human incarnation of God. Not that there are two Korans, of course. Rather, the created Koran is the material crystallization of the infinite reality of the Uncreated Koran. When the created Koran is said to be a miracle, the miracle referred to is the presence of the Uncreated Koran within the letters and sounds of its created (and therefore necessarily in certain ways circumscribed) counterpart.

The words of the Koran came to Muhammad in manageable segments over twenty-three years through voices that sounded at first like reverberating bells, but gradually condensed into a single voice that identified itself as Gabriel's. Muhammad had no control over when Gabriel would speak. When he did, Muhammad's state would visibly change. He reported that the words assaulted him as if they were solid and heavy. Once they arrived while he was riding a camel; by the time they had ceased, its belly was pressed against the earth with its legs splayed out. The words that Muhammad exclaimed in these often trance-like states were memorized by his followers and recorded on bones, bark, leaves, and scraps of parchment with God preserving their accuracy throughout.

The Koran continues God's revelations to the Jews and Christians and presents itself as their culmination. However, it judges the Old and New Testaments as having two defects from which it, itself, is free. For circumstantial reasons, the Hebrew and Christian Bibles record only portions of Truth. Second, they were partially corrupted in transmission, which explains the occasional discrepancies that occur between their accounts and parallel ones in the Koran. Exemption from these two limitations makes the Koran the final and infallible revelation of God's will.

From the outside this book, which for Muslims is Allah's verbal incarnation, presents obstacles – Carlyle called it the most toilsome reading he ever undertook. How are we to account for the discrepancy between the Koran as read from within and from without?

The language in which it was proclaimed provides an initial clue, for no other language seems able to play on human emotions the way Arabic can. But language is not the only barrier the Koran presents, for its contents too are like no other religious text. Unlike the Upanishads, it is not explicitly metaphysical. It does not ground its theology in dramatic narratives as the Indian epics do, nor in historical ones as do the Hebrew scriptures. Nor is God revealed in human form as in the Gospels and the *Bhagavad-Gita.* Confining ourselves to the Semitic scriptures, we can say that whereas the Old and New Testaments are directly historical and indirectly doctrinal, the Koran is directly doctrinal and indirectly historical.

This page and overleaf: These finely illustrated Persian manuscripts are typical of the extraordinary flowering of art and literature in the early centuries of Islam.

Because the overwhelming thrust of the Koran is to proclaim the unity, omnipotence, omniscience and mercy of God — and correlatively the total dependence of human life upon Him — historical facts are in its case merely reference points that have scarcely any interest in themselves. When the Lord-servant relationship is the essential point, all else is commentary and allusion.

Perhaps we shall be less inclined to fault the Koran for the opaque face it presents to foreigners if we note that foreign scriptures present their own problems to Muslims.

To speak only of the Old and New Testaments, Muslims express disappointment in finding that they do not take the form of Divine speech and merely report things that happened. In the Koran, God speaks in the first person; he describes himself and makes known his laws. The Muslim is therefore inclined to consider each individual sentence of the Holy Book as a separate revelation and to experience the words themselves, even their sounds, as a means of grace.

Putting comparisons behind us, it is impossible to overemphasize the central position of the Koran in Islamic life.

With large portions memorized in childhood, it regulates every decision and interprets every event. It is a memorandum for the faithful, a reminder for daily doings, and a repository of revealed truth. It is a manual of definitions and guarantees, and at the same time a road map for the will.

Finally, it is a collection of maxims to meditate on in private, deepening one's sense of the divine glory. *"Perfect is the Word of your Lord in truth and justice"* (6:115).

BASIC THEOLOGICAL CONCEPTS

WITH A FEW STRIKING EXCEPTIONS that will be noted, the basic theological concepts of Islam are virtually identical with those of Judaism and Christianity, its forerunners. We shall confine our attention in this section to four that are the most important: God, Creation, the Human Self, and the Day of Judgment.

As in the other historical religions, everything in Islam centers on its religious Ultimate, God. God is immaterial and therefore invisible. For the Arabs this casts no doubt on his reality, for as desert dwellers, the notion of invisible hands that drove the blasts that swept the desert and formed deceptive mirages was always with them. The Koran did not introduce the Arabs to the unseen world or even to monotheism, for a few solitary seekers, called *hanifs,* had moved to that position already. Its innovation was to rid the scene of Allah's rivals.

We must immediately add that Muslims see monotheism as Islam's contribution not simply to the Arabs but to religion in its entirety. Hinduism's prolific images are taken as proof that it never arrived at the worship of the single God. Judaism was correctly instructed, but its teachings were confined to the people of Israel. Christians, for their part, compromised their monotheism by deifying Christ. The Koran honors Jesus as a prophet and accepts his virgin birth, but it draws the line at the doctrine of the Incarnation and the Trinity, seeing these as blurring the Divine/human distinction.

Turning to the Koranic depiction of God's nature, the first thing that strikes us is his awe-inspiring power. Unlimited power inspires fear, and it is fair to say that Muslims fear Allah. Theirs is not, however, a cringing fear in the face of a capricious tyrant. It is, rather (they

argue) the only realistic emotion when people face up to the magnitude of the consequences that follow from being on the right or wrong side of an uncompromisingly moral universe. If nihilism is the dissipation of difference, a leveling-out of life through moral entropy, Allah's universe is its exact opposite.

Good and evil matter, and choices have consequences. The other side of fear of the Lord, however, is that when it has been dealt with, other, lesser fears subside. The second, supporting root of the word *islam* is peace.

It is important to remember this last point because the holy dread that Allah inspires is more than outweighed by his love for his creatures. Allah's compassion and mercy are cited 192 times in the Koran as against 17 references to his wrath and vengeance. He who is Lord of the worlds is also the Deliverer from affliction, the Friend of the bereaved, and the Consoler whose love is more tender than that of the mother-bird for her young.

From God we can turn to Creation as our second theological concept. The Koran does not present the world as oozing from the infinite by some vague process of emanation. Allah deliberately created it. This fact carries two important consequences.

First, the world of matter is completely real. (Herein lies one of the sources of Islamic science, which during Europe's Dark Ages flourished as nowhere else on earth.) Second, having been fashioned by a Craftsman that is perfect, matter must be – not perfect, for there cannot be two perfections – but overwhelmingly good.

Conjoined, these two points inspire a respect for the material sides of life that the other two Semitic religions, Judaism and Christianity, likewise affirm.

Foremost among God's creations is the human self, whose nature, Koranically defined, is our third doctrinal subject. That nature is unequivocally good; it has been stained by no catastrophic fall. The closest Islam comes to the Christian doctrine of original sin is in its concept of forgetting. People do forget their divine origin, but their fundamental nature is irrevocably good, so they are entitled to self-respect and a healthy self-image.

With life acknowledged as a gift from its Creator we can turn to its obligations, which are two. The first of these is gratitude for life received. The Arabic word for infidel is shaded more toward one who lacks thankfulness than one who disbelieves. The second human obligation calls us back to the name of this religion. Islam, we recall, means surrender. We must now attend to this attribute explicitly.

Thoughts of surrender are so freighted with military connotations that it requires conscious effort to notice that the word also tokens self-giving, in which mode no religion is without it. William James speaks so insightfully to this point that his words are worth quoting.

"When all is said and done, we are in the end absolutely dependent on the universe; and into sacrifices and surrenders of some sort, deliberately looked at and accepted, we are drawn and pressed as into our only permanent positions of repose. Now in those states of mind which fall short of religion, the surrender is submitted to as an imposition of necessity, and the sacrifice is undergone at the very best without complaint. In the religious life, on the contrary, surrender and sacrifice are positively espoused: even unnecessary givings-up are added in order that the happiness may increase. Religion thus makes easy and felicitous what in any case is necessary."

To this account of surrender's virtues we can add in Islamic parlance that to be a slave to Allah is to be freed from other, degrading forms of slavery – to greed, say, or anxiety, or ambition. Also, the "slavery" referred to here is voluntary, for the human soul is a free agent. Several passages in the Koran seem to imply predestination, but they do not finally do so, for *"whoever gets to himself a sin, gets it solely on his own responsibility"* (4:111).

Nowhere is the soul's freedom more conspicuous than on the Day of Judgment, our concluding theological concept. The Koran presents life as a brief but immensely precious opportunity, offering a once-and-for-all choice. Hence the urgency that informs the entire Book. The chance to return to life for even a single day to make good use of their opportunities is something "the losers," facing their Reckoning, would treasure beyond anything they desired while they were yet alive.

Depending on how it fares in its Reckoning, the soul will repair to either the Heavens or the Hells, which in the Koran are described in vivid, concrete, and sensual imagery. The Koran allows these images to be read either literally or allegorically, for *"some of the signs are firm and others are figurative"* (3:5). Underlying their differences of interpretation, all Muslims believe that each soul will be held accountable for its actions on earth, with its future thereafter dependent upon how well it has observed God's commands.

As a final point: if all this talk of judgment still seems to cast God too much in the role of punisher, we can resort to verses in the Koran that exempt Allah from direct involvement altogether. In those verses souls judge themselves. What death burns away is self-serving defenses, forcing one to see with total objectivity how one has lived one's life. In the uncompromising light of that vision where no dark corners are allowed, it is one's own actions that rise up to accuse or confirm. Once the self is extracted from the realm of lies, the falsities by

which it armored itself become like flames, and the life it there led like a shirt of Nessus.

God, Creation, the Human Self, and the Day of Judgment – these are the chief theological pegs on which the Koran's teachings hang. In spite of their importance, however, the Koran is a book that emphasizes deeds rather than ideas. It is to those that we turn in the next two sections.

Meditation in a mosque in Asuan, Egypt.

THE FIVE PILLARS OF ISLAM

IF A MUSLIM WERE ASKED to summarize the way Islam counsels people to live, his answer might be: It teaches them to walk the straight path. The phrase comes from the opening surah (chapter) of the Koran which includes the supplication, *"Guide us in the straight path, the path of those on whom Thou hast poured forth Thy grace."*

Why *"the straight path"*? To the obvious answer (a straight path is not crooked or corrupt) there is another which is distinctive to Islam. A straight path is one that is straightforward; it is direct and explicit. More than other religions, Islam claims to detail the way of life it proposes, spelling it out in explicit directives. Every major type of action is classified on a sliding scale from the forbidden, through the indifferent, to the obligatory. Muslims consider this to be one of their religion's strengths. God's revelation to humankind, they say, has proceeded through four great stages. To Abraham, God revealed the truth of monotheism; to Moses, the Ten Commandments; and to Jesus, the Golden Rule. There remained the question of what the Golden Rule requires – how it is to be put into practice. Once life becomes complicated, guidelines are needed and the Koran provides them.

What are these guidelines? We shall divide our presentation into two parts. In this section we shall consider the Five Pillars of Islam, the principles that regulate the private lives of Muslims in their dealings with God. In the next section we shall consider the Koran's social teachings.

The first of the Five Pillars is Islam's creed, or confession of faith known as the *shahadah*. It consists of a single sentence: *"There is no god but Allah, and Muhammad is His Prophet."* The first half of the proclamation announces the cardinal principle of monotheism, that there is no god but *the* God. The second affirmation – that Muhammad is God's prophet – registers the Muslim's faith in the authenticity of Muhammad and the validity of his revelation. At least once during his or her lifetime a Muslim must say the *shahadah* correctly, slowly, thoughtfully, aloud, with full understanding, and with heartfelt conviction. In actuality, Muslims pronounce it often, especially its first half, *La ilaha illa 'llah.* In every crisis and at every moment when the world threatens to overwhelm them, not excepting the approach of death, *"There is no god but God"* will spring from Muslims' lips. A pious man, seized by rage, will be stopped in his tracks by this phrase which distances him from his emotion. A woman, screaming in childbirth, will fall silent as she remembers. A student, bowed over his test in an examination hall, will raise his head and

Above: *Painted dish shows an image from an esoteric tradition in Islam that speaks of "awakening the lataif," or the five organs of spiritual perception.* Right: ***"The Ascent of the Prophet Muhammad"*** *from a 16th century Indian manuscript.*

utter the phrase, and a barely audible sigh of relief will pass through the entire assembly. The *shahadah* is the ultimate answer to all questions.

The second pillar of Islam is canonical prayer. An obvious reason to pray is to give voice to the gratitude one feels for life itself, but a deeper reason is to keep human life in perspective. The Koran considers this the most difficult lesson people must learn, and directs itself entirely (one can almost say) to making things clear on this front. Not having created themselves, human beings are derivative; but they can't seem to get this straight and keep placing themselves at the centers of their worlds, living as if they were laws unto themselves. Wherewith, havoc. In prayer, Muslims acknowledge their creatureliness before the Creator, and take thereby the first step toward orienting their wills *(islam)* toward him.

How often each day should Muslims pray? There is an endearing account in the Koran which has Allah originally setting the number at fifty, which Moses (when he heard of it during Muhammad's Night Journey through the heavens) pronounced ridiculous.

Through the negotiations that Moses insisted be instigated, Muhammad was able to reduce the number to five. Even this Moses considered too many — "*I know those people,*" he told Muhammad. But Muhammad refused to press the matter further and the number was fixed at five. The times of the five prayers are likewise stipulated: on arising, when the sun is overhead, in mid-afternoon, at sunset, and before retiring. Congregational worship is not an Islamic emphasis, nor is any day of the week considered especially holy; but Muslims are expected to pray in mosques when they can, and are especially encouraged to do so Friday noon. Muslims began by facing Jerusalem (where Muhammad began his Night Journey through the heavens) when they prayed, but a Koranic revelation then instructed them to pray in the direction of Mecca. Ablutions precede canonical prayers, which begin while standing but reach their climax in the foetal position with forehead touching the floor. In content, the prayers stress praise and gratitude while including supplication.

The third pillar of Islam is charity. Those who are comfortable should share with the unfortunate. Again the Koran is explicit; annually, two and one-half percent of one's holdings should be distributed to the poor. Recipients of charity, too, are named. They are to be persons in immediate need, slaves in the process of buying their

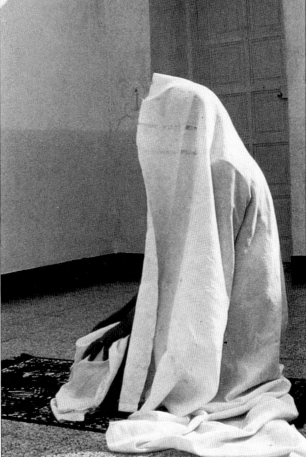

freedom, debtors who are unable to meet their obligations, strangers and wayfarers, and those who collect and distribute the donations.

The fourth pillar of Islam is the observance of ramadan. Ramadan is the holy month in the Islamic calendar, because during it the Koranic revelation commenced and (ten years later) Muhammad effected his migration from Mecca. To commemorate these two great occasions, able-bodied Muslims (who are not ill or involved in crises like war or unavoidable journeys) fast during Ramadan. From the first moment of dawn to the setting of the sun, neither food nor drink nor smoke passes their lips; nor are they sexually active. As the Muslim calendar is lunar, Ramadan rotates around the year. What is the significance of this fast? For one thing, it makes one reflect. (Why am I performing this unnatural act?) It teaches self-discipline. It reminds one of one's frailty and dependence. And it fosters compassion, for only the hungry know what hunger means.

Islam's fifth pillar is pilgrimage. Once during his or her lifetime, every Muslim who is physically and economically able to do so is expected to journey to Mecca where God's climactic revelation first descended. The basic purpose of the journey is to heighten the pilgrim's commitment to God and his revealed will, but the practice carries fringe benefits. It is, for one thing, a reminder of human equality, for upon reaching Mecca, pilgrims exchange their clothes (which are status-ridden) for two simple sheet-like garments. The gathering also promotes international understanding. In bringing together people from multiple countries, it demonstrates that they share a loyalty that transcends national and ethnic barriers. Pilgrims pick up information about other lands and peoples, and return to their homes knowing more about the world.

The Five Pillars of Islam consist of things Muslims do to support the house of Islam. There are also things they should not do. Gambling, thieving, lying, eating pork, drinking intoxicants, and being sexually promiscuous are some of these. Even Muslims who transgress these rulings acknowledge that they are normative. With the exception of charity, the precepts we have considered in this section pertain to the Muslim's personal life. We turn now to the social teachings of Islam.

Above: *Muslim woman in prayer.* Opposite: *Man praying inside a mosque.*

SOCIAL TEACHINGS

THE DIFFERENCE BETWEEN PRE- AND POST-Islamic Arabia raises the question of whether history has ever witnessed a comparable moral advance among so many people in so short a time. Before Muhammad there was virtually no restraint on inter-tribal violence. Glaring inequities in wealth were accepted as the natural order of things. Women were regarded more as possessions than as human beings, and infanticide, especially of girls, was commonplace. Drunkenness and gambling have already been mentioned. Within a half century a remarkable change in the moral climate was effected on all of these counts. In accomplishing this near-miracle, Islam was helped by a feature of the religion that has already been alluded to, namely its explicitness. For in addition to being a spiritual guide, the Koran is a legal compendium. It joins faith and politics, religion and society, inseparably.

Islamic law is of enormous scope. It will be enough for our purposes if we summarize its provisions in four areas of collective life.

Above: *Mosque in Baghdad.* Right: *Islamic laws broke the barriers of economic caste and improved the status of women in the Arab world.*

1. Economics.

Islam is acutely aware of life's material supports, and moved in on this area with laws that broke the barriers of economic caste and enormously reduced the injustices of special interest groups.

A comparison with the body's circulatory system can suggest how those laws proceed. Health requires that the body's blood flow freely and vigorously; sluggishness can induce disease, and blood clots occasion death. It is not different with the body politic where wealth takes the place of blood as the life-giving substance. As long as this analogy is honored and laws are in place to insure that wealth is in vigorous circulation, Islam does not object to the profit motive, economic competition, or entrepreneurial initiatives. So freely are these allowed, in fact, that the Koran has been characterized as "a manual for businessmen." It insists, though, that acquisitiveness and competition be balanced by the fair play that  "keeps arteries open," and by compassion that is strong enough to pump life-giving blood — material resources — into its smallest capillaries. These "capillaries" are fed by the Poor Due which (as has been noted) stipulates that annually a portion of one's holdings be distributed to the poor. As for the way to prevent "clotting," the Koran went after the severest economic curse of the day — primogeniture — and outlawed it. It requires that inheritance be shared by all heirs, daughters included.

One verse in the Koran prohibits the taking of interest. At the time this was appropriate, for loans were then used to tide the unfortunate over in times of disaster. Now that loans provide venture capital, Muslims accommodate by involving lenders as partners in the venture and entitled thereby to a share of its profits. When capitalism is approached in this manner, Muslims consider it compatible with Koranic principles. Its excesses are another matter. The equalizing provisos of the Koran would, if duly applied, offset them.

2. The status of women.

Chiefly because it permits a plurality of wives, Islam has been accused of degrading women.

If we approach the issue historically, comparing the status of Arabian women before and after Muhammad, the charge is patently false. Addressing conditions in which the very birth of a daughter was regarded as a calamity, the Koranic reforms improved woman's status incalculably. They forbade infanticide. They required that daughters be included in inheritance – not equally it is true, but to half the proportion of sons, which seems just, considering the fact that unlike sons, daughters would not assume financial responsibility for their households. In her rights as citizen – education, suffrage, and vocation – the Koran leaves open the possibility of woman's full equality with man, an equality that is being approximated as the customs of Muslim nations become modernized. If in another century women under Islam do not attain the social position of their Western sisters, a position to which the latter have been brought by industrialism and democracy rather than religion, it will then be time (Muslims say) to hold Islam accountable.

It was in the institution of marriage, however, that Islam made its greatest contribution to women. It sanctified marriage, first, by making it the sole lawful locus of the sexual act. Second, the Koran required that a woman give her free consent before she may be wed. Third, it tightened the wedding bond enormously. The Koran does not forbid divorce, but it countenances it only as a last resort. At the time of marriage, husbands are required to provide the wife with a sum on which

both agree and which she retains in its entirety should a divorce ensue. Wives as well as husbands can instigate divorce should it prove necessary.

There remains, however, the issue of polygamy, or more precisely polygyny. It is true that the Koran permits a man to have up to four wives simultaneously, but there is a growing consensus that a careful reading of its regulations point toward monogamy as the ideal. Supporting this view is the Koran's statement that "*if you cannot deal equitably and justly with [more than one wife], you shall marry only one.*" This leads many jurists to argue that the Koran virtually enjoins monogamy, for it is almost impossible to distribute affection and regard with exact equality.

This having been said, the fact remains that the Koran does permit polygyny, and after Khadija's death, Muhammad had multiple wives. Muslims take both items as instances of Islam's versatility in addressing diverse circumstances. There are occasions, they argue, when polygyny is morally preferable to its alternative. A war that decimated the male population could provide an example, forcing (as this would) the option between polygyny and depriving a large proportion of women of motherhood and a nuclear family, and encouraging prostitution. Pressing their case, Muslims point out that multiple marriages are at least as common in the West, the

difference being that they are successive. Is "serial polygyny" manifestly superior to its coeval form as long as women have the right to opt out of the arrangement (through divorce) if they want to?

Finally, Muslims, though they consider the wife's sexual satisfaction to be a marital obligation, do not skirt the volatile question of whether the male sexual drive is stronger than the female's. If it is, rather than allowing the male's sensuality to run riot, Islam establishes a polygynous framework that provides a modicum of control. Multiple wives are allowed, but not gratification exempt from responsibilities.

As for the veiling of women and their seclusion generally, the Koranic injunction is restrained. It says only to "*Tell your wives and your daughters and the women of the believers to draw their cloaks closely round them when they go abroad*" (33:59). Extremes that have evolved from this ruling are matters of local custom and are not religiously binding.

Opposite: *Muslim women must give their consent to marriage, and have the right to instigate divorce under Islamic law.* Above: *A West African mosque.*

3. Race Relations.

Islam stresses racial equality and has achieved a remarkable degree of interracial coexistence. The ultimate test in this area is willingness to intermarry, and Muslims see Abraham as modeling this willingness in marrying Hagar who was black. Malcolm X's discovery (during his 1964 pilgrimage to Mecca) that racism had no place in Islam changed his own attitudes on the subject dramatically. Muslims like to recall that the first *muezzin,* Bilal, was an Ethiopian who prayed regularly for the conversion of the Koreish – "whites" who were persecuting the early believers, many of whom were black.

4. The Use of Force.

Muslims report that the most inflexible image of Islam that they encounter in the West is that of a militant religion that has spread primarily by the sword. They see this as a prejudice, born of the thirteen hundred years in which Islam and Europe have shared common borders and much of the time fought over them. It is a stereotype, forged by people who have seen Islam as their enemy.

Grant, Muslims say, that the Koran does not counsel turning the other cheek, or pacifism. It teaches forgiveness and the return of good for evil when circumstances warrant, but these do not add up to not resisting evil. The Koran allows punishment of wanton wrongdoers to the full extent of the injury done. Extend this principle to collective life and you have the principle of a just or holy war, which the Koran also endorses. But these do not warrant the charge of militancy.

As an outstanding general, Muhammad left many traditions regarding the decent conduct of war. Agreements are to be honored and treachery avoided; the wounded are not to be mutilated, nor the dead disfigured. Women, children, and the old are to be spared, as are orchards, crops, and sacred objects. The towering question, though, is when war is justified. The Koran's definition of a Holy War is virtually identical with that of a Just War in the Canon Law of Catholicism. It must be either defensive or to right an horrendous wrong.

Moving from theory to practice, Muslims claim that in one instance the two coincided. Muhammad adhered meticulously to the charter he forged for Medina, which – grounded as it was in the Koranic injunction, *"Let there be no compulsion in religion"* (2:257) – is arguably the first mandate for religious tolerance in human history. Muslims admit that this exemplary beginning was not sustained, but as no histories are exemplary, the question reduces to whether Islam's has been more militant than that of other religions. As the charge that it has been has come primarily from Christianity, its history will serve here as the point of reference.

In favor of Islam are the long centuries during which in India, Spain, and the Near East, Christians, Jews, and Hindus lived quietly and in freedom under Muslim rule. Even under the worst rulers, Christians and Jews held positions of influence and in general retained their religious freedom. It was Christians, not Muslims (we are reminded) who in the fifteenth century expelled the Jews from Spain where under Islamic rule they had enjoyed one of their golden ages. To press this example: Spain and Anatolia changed hands at about the same time – Christians expelled the Moors from Spain while Muslims conquered what is now Turkey. Every Muslim was driven from Spain, or put to the sword, or forced to convert, whereas the seat of the Eastern Orthodox Church remains in Istanbul to this day. Indeed, if comparisons are the issue, Muslims consider Christianity's record to be the darker of the two. Who was it, they ask, who preached the Crusades in the name of the Prince of Peace? Who instituted the Inquisition, invented the rack and the stake as instruments of religion, and plunged Europe into its devastating wars of religion?

The safest generalization on which this discussion can end comes from the historians. Islam's record on the use of force is no darker than that of Christianity.

Opposite: *Celebrative atmosphere outside the Jama Masjid mosque in Delhi.* Above: *A mosque in the Fuji Islands.*

SUFISM

WE HAVE BEEN TREATING Islam as if it were monolithic, which of course it is not. Like every religious tradition it divides. We shall pass over its main historical division – between the Sunnis and the Shi'ites who disagreed as to who should succeed Muhammad – and focus instead on a division that is of more general interest. It is the division between the mystics of Islam, called Sufis, and the remaining majority of the faith, who are equally good Muslims but are not mystics.

A century or two after Muhammad's death, a number of Muslims who were especially attached to the spiritual teachings of the Koran began to wear coarse woolen garments – from which the name Sufi, for *suf* means wool – to protest the silks and satins of sultans and califs.

Alarmed by the worldliness they saw overtaking Islam, they wanted to purify it from within. Externals should yield to internals, matter to meaning. *"Love the pitcher less,"* they cried, *"and the water more."*

These Sufis were drawn to the Koranic disclosure that there is an inward as well as an outward side to the divine nature. God's relatively obvious aspects might suffice for the majority of Muslims, but the Sufis wanted to plumb Allah's depths. And they wanted to experience him now, in this very lifetime, and not wait until the afterlife.

This called for special methods, and to effect them the Sufis gathered around the gifted in their number whom they called *shaikhs,* or masters. In the twelfth century these communities crystallized into orders, whose members were known as *faqirs* – poor in the sense of poor to the world while being rich in God. In ways they constituted a spiritual elite, aspiring higher than other Muslims and willing to assume the heavier disciplines their extravagant goals imposed. They were not cloistered; most of them were married and engaged in normal occupations. They would repair to their gathering places in off hours to sing, dance, pray, recite their rosaries in concert, and listen to the discourses of their Masters. They pointed out that someone who was ignorant of fire could learn of it by degrees: first by hearing of it, then by seeing it, and finally by being burned by it. The Sufis wanted decisive knowledge. They wanted to be burned by God.

This required drawing close to Him, and the Sufis developed three overlapping but distinguishable routes. We shall call these the mysticisms of love, of ecstasy, and of intuitive discernment.

To begin with the first of these, Sufi love poetry is world renowned. A remarkable eighth-century woman saint, Rabi'a, discovered in her solitary vigils, often lasting all night, that God's love was at the core of the universe. Not to steep oneself in that love and reflect it to others was to forfeit life's supreme beatitude. Because love is never more evident than when its object is absent, that being the time when the beloved cannot be taken for granted, Persian poets in particular dwelt on the pangs of separation to deepen their love of God and draw close to him. The Persian poet Rumi used the plaintive sound of the reed flute to embellish this theme.

> *Listen to the story told by the reed,*
> *of being separated.*
> *Since I was cut from the reedbed,*
> *I have made this crying sound.*
> *Anyone separated from the one he loves*
> *understands what I say.*
> *Anyone pulled from a source longs to go back.*

Rabi'a celebrates the overcoming of separation in her famous night prayer:

> *"My God and my Lord:*
> *eyes are at rest, the stars are setting,*
> *hushed are the movements of birds in their nests,*
> *of monsters in the deep.*
> *And you are the Just who knows no change,*
> *the Equity that does not swerve,*
> *the Everlasting that never passes away.*
> *The doors of kings are locked*
> *and guarded by their henchmen.*
> *But your door is open to those who call upon you.*
> *My Lord, each lover is now alone with his beloved.*
> *And I am alone with Thee."*

Opposite: The sacred dance of the dervishes, practiced among those belonging to the mystic part of Islam known as Sufis. Overleaf: Boy at prayer in a small neighborhood mosque in Zanzibar.

We are calling the second Sufic approach to the divine presence ecstatic (literally, to stand outside oneself) because it turned on experiences that differ, not just in degree but in kind, from usual ones. At times the content of what ecstatics experienced engrossed them so completely that it left no margin for awareness of themselves. They lost consciousness of who they were, where they were, and what was happening to them, and were in this sense en-tranced.

Sufis honor their ecstatics, but in calling them *"drunken"* they serve notice that they must return to sobriety, bringing the substance of their visions back with them. In plain language, transcendence must be made immanent; the God who is encountered in isolation from the world must also be encountered within it. This latter does not require ecstasy as its preliminary, and the direct route to cultivating it carries us to the third Sufi approach: the way of intuitive discernment.

Like the other two methods this one brings knowledge, but of a distinct sort. If love mysticism yields "heart knowledge," and ecstasy yields "visual or visionary knowledge" because extraterrestrial realities are seen imagistically, we can say that intuitive mysticism brings "mental knowledge" provided that we keep in mind that an exceptionally deep level of mind is being referred to. At this level of knowledge no images are needed; but neither are thoughts, which is what distinguishes it from ordinary mentation. In the directness of its discernment it resembles sensory knowledge, but in this case the objects that it directly apprehends are immaterial; they are spiritual objects. Knowledge of this sort does not eclipse the world in the way the visions of ecstatic Sufis do. Instead, it clothes that world in celestial light. Or to rephrase the point, it recognizes the world's objects as garments that God must assume if there is to be a world in the first place. These garments become progressively transparent as discernment gains strength. One sees through them as guises in which God has bedecked, and thereby veiled, himself.

The principal method the Sufis employ for penetrating God's veils is symbolism. In using visible objects to speak of invisible things, symbolism is the language of religion in the way numbers are the language of science. Mystics, however, employ it to an exceptional degree; for instead of stopping with the first spiritual object a symbol points to, they use that object as a stepping stone to yet another that is more exalted. Every verse of the Koran conceals a minimum of seven hidden significations and the number can reach to seventy.

To illustrate this point: For all Muslims, removing one's shoes before stepping into a mosque is a mark of reverence. The Sufi begins with this symbolism, but goes on to see in the act the additional meaning of removing everything that separates the soul from God. Or the act of asking forgiveness: All Muslims pray to be forgiven for specific transgressions, but in addition to this the Sufi asks to be forgiven for his separate existence. This sounds strange, and indeed, exoteric Muslims find it unintelligible. The Sufis, though, see it as an extension of Rabi'a's teaching that *"your existence is a sin with which no other can be compared."* Because existence is a standing out from something, which in this case is God, existence involves separation. To avoid separating themselves from Allah, the Sufis developed their doctrine of *fana,* or extinction. Not that their consciousness was to be extinguished; it was their *self*-consciousness – their consciousness of themselves as separate selves replete with private personal agendas – that was to be terminated. If the termination was complete, when they looked inside the dry shells of their now-emptied selves they would find nothing of themselves. Only God.

As a final example of the Sufis' extravagant use of symbolism we can note the way they tightened the creedal assertion *"There is no god but God"* to read, *"There is nothing but God."* To exoteric Muslims this again sounded silly if not blasphemous, but the Sufis' intent was to challenge the independence that people normally ascribe to things. Monotheism to them meant more than the theoretical point that there are not two Gods; that they considered obvious. Picking up on the existential meaning of theism – God is that to which we give (or should give) ourselves – they agreed that the initial meaning of "no god but God" is that we should give ourselves to nothing but God. But we do not catch the full significance of the phrase, they argued, until we see that we do give ourselves to other things when we let them engage us as objects in their own right; objects that have

heart is the invocation of Allah." Remembrance of God is at the same time a forgetting of self, so Sufis consider the repetition of Allah's Name the best way of directing their attention Godward.

The foregoing paragraphs sketch what Sufism is, but they do not explain why this section opened by associating it with a division within Islam. The reason is that Muslims are of two minds about Sufism, and the reason for that is that Sufis take certain liberties that exoteric Muslims cannot in conscience condone. Having seen the sky through the skylight of Islamic orthodoxy, Sufis become persuaded that there is more sky than the aperture allows. When Rumi asserted, *"I am neither Muslim nor Christian, Jew nor Zoroastrian; I am neither of the earth nor of the heavens, I am neither body nor soul,"* we can understand the exoterics' fear that orthodoxy was being strained beyond permissible limits. Mysticism breaks through the boundaries that protect the faith of the typical believer. In doing so, it moves into unconfined regions that, though fulfilling for some, carry dangers for those who are unprepared for their teachings.

Sufis have their rights, but — if we may venture the verdict of Islam as a whole — so have ordinary believers whose faith in unambiguous principles, fully adequate for salvation, could be undermined by teachings that seem to tamper with them. For this reason many spiritual Masters have been discreet in their teachings. This is also why exoteric authorities have regarded Sufism with understandable suspicion. Control has been exercised, partly by public opinion and partly by means of a kind of dynamic tension between the exoteric religious authorities, on the one hand, and Sufi *shaikhs* on the other. Together they have achieved, on the whole, a healthy balance for the faith.

the power to interest or repel us by being simply what they are. To think of light as caused by electricity — by electricity only and sufficiently, without asking where electricity comes from — is idolatrous, for only God is self-sufficient.

Symbolism, though powerful, works somewhat abstractly, so the Sufis supplement it with the practice of remembering Allah by repeating His Name. *"There is a means of polishing all things whereby rust may be removed,"* Muhammad said, while adding, *"That which polishes the*

The minaret of the mosque towers above this Berber village in Morocco near the Tizi-n-Tichka Pass of the Atlas Mountains.

WHITHER ISLAM?

FOR LONG PERIODS since the Koran announced God's oneness, Muslims have wandered from its spirit. Their leaders are the first to admit that time and again, practice has been replaced by mere profession, and that fervor has waned.

Viewed as a whole, however, Islam unrolls before us one of the most remarkable panoramas history affords. We have spoken of its early greatness. Had we pursued its history there would have been sections on the Muslim empire which, a century after Muhammad's death, stretched from the Atlantic to the Indus and the frontiers of China, from the Aral Sea to the upper Nile. More important would have been the sections describing the spread of Muslim ideas: the development of a fabulous culture, the rise of literature, science, medicine, art and architecture; the glory of Damascus, Baghdad and Egypt, and the splendor of Spain under the Moors. There would have been the story of how during Europe's Dark Ages Muslim philosophers and scientists kept the lamp of learning kindled, ready to spark the Western mind when it roused from its long sleep.

Nor would the story have been entirely confined to the past, for there are indications that Islam is emerging from several centuries of stagnation which colonization no doubt abetted. It faces enormous problems: how to

distinguish modern industrialism (which on balance it welcomes), from Westernization (which on balance it doesn't); how to realize the unity that is latent in Islam when the forces of nationalism work powerfully against it; how to hold on to Truth in a pluralistic, relativizing age. But having thrown off the colonial yoke, Islam is stirring with some of the vigor of its former youth. From Morocco on the Atlantic, eastward across North Africa, through the Indian sub-continent (which includes Pakistan and Bangladesh) on to the near-tip of Indonesia, Islam is a vital force in the contemporary world. As there are some 900 million Muslims in the global population of five billion, one person out of every five or six belongs today to this religion which guides human thought and practice in unparalleled detail. And the proportion is increasing. Read these words at any hour of day or night and somewhere from a minaret (or now by radio) a *muezzin* will be calling the faithful to prayer, announcing:

> *God is most great.*
> *God is most great.*
> *I testify that there is no god but God.*
> *I testify that Muhammad is the Prophet of God.*
> *Come to prayer. Come to salvation.*
> *God is most great.*
> *God is most great.*
> *There is no god but God.*

Opposite: *A spiral-shaped minaret soars into the sky in Samarra.* Above: *After several centuries of suffering under colonialism, Islam is emerging today as a vital force in the contemporary world.*

CHAPTER VII

JUDAISM

Hear O Israel,
the Lord our God,
the Lord is One.

Above: *The so-called* **"Stone of Moses"** *or Ka-Ka-Bal, on which Moses is said to have demonstrated his magical skills. Left: A covering for the Torah, 18th century.*

IT HAS BEEN ESTIMATED that one-third of Western civilization bears the marks of its Jewish ancestry. We feel its force in the names we give to our children (Abraham Lincoln), in our art (Michaelangelo's "*David*"), and our national life in sayings that feed our souls. ("*Proclaim liberty throughout the land*" as inscribed on the Liberty Bell). The real impact of the ancient Jews, however, lies in the extent to which Western civilization took over their perspective on the deepest questions life poses.

When, mindful of this impact, we go back to the land, the people, and the history that made this impact, we are in for a surprise. We might expect these to be as impressive as their influence, but they are not. Chronologically, the Hebrews were latecomers on the stage of history. When they finally settled down, the land they chose was equally unimpressive. One hundred and fifty miles in length, about fifty miles in breadth, Canaan was a postage stamp of a country, about one-eighth the size of Illinois. Even Jewish history, when viewed from without, amounts to little. It is not dull, but by external standards it is very much like the histories of countless other little peoples. Compared with the histories of the great powers of the time, Jewish history is strictly minor league.

If the key to the achievement of the Jews lies neither in their antiquity nor in the proportions of their land and history, where does it lie? The lead that we shall follow is this: What lifted the Jews from obscurity to greatness was their passion for meaning.

Silver scroll containing the Book of Esther, from the Hebrew Museum in Prague.

MEANING IN GOD

IN THE BEGINNING GOD...." From beginning to end, the Jewish quest for meaning was rooted in their understanding of the Supreme Being. Whatever a people's philosophy, it must take account of the Other. There are two reasons for this. First, no human being is self-created, from which it follows that humankind has issued from something other than itself. Second, everyone at some point finds his or her power limited. Add therefore to the Other as that from which one has issued, a second meaning. At certain points it exceeds our control.

Faced with this ineluctable Other, people wonder if it is meaningful. Four characteristics could keep it from being so; if it were prosaic, chaotic, amoral, or hostile. The glory of the Hebrew search for meaning lies in its refusal to give in to any of these alternatives.

The Jews resisted the prosaic by personifying the Other. In this they were at one with their ancient contemporaries. The concept of the world as comprised mainly of lifeless matter is a late invention. The early world was alive and sentient, through and through.

Underlying the poetry of biblical descriptions of God lay the claim that ultimately Reality – the Other – is more like a person than like a thing. Of this claim two things are to be said. First, evidence against it is so lacking that as knowledgeable a philosopher-scientist as Alfred North Whitehead could embrace it in the twentieth century. Second, the claim is nobler than its alternative. The Jews were reaching out for the most exalted concept of the Other that they could conceive, and people had more depth and mystery than other analogical starting points.

Where the Hebrews differed from their neighbors was in focusing the personal traits of the Other in a single, nature-transcending will. For other Mediterranean peoples, each major power of nature was a distinct deity; whereas in the Bible, nature in its entirety was created by, and under the sovereignty of the Lord of all being.

Other gods are mentioned in the Hebrew scriptures, but – being both derivative from Yahweh (wrongly rendered as Jehovah in early English translations) and mortal, they are not on his plane.

The significance of the monotheism the Jews arrived at precociously lies in the focus it affords life. If God is that to which one gives oneself completely, to have more than one God is to live a divided life. A consistent way that leads to human fulfillment calls for constancy – singleness – in the Other that supports it. That this singleness existed was the bedrock of Hebrew belief. *"Hear, O Israel, the Lord our God, the Lord is One"* (Deut 6:4).

There remains the question of whether the Other, now seen as personal and one, was either amoral or hostile. If it were either, meaning would again be compromised, for if this is not a moral universe, goodness cannot in the long run prevail. The odds against it are insuperable.

We come here to the supreme achievement of Jewish theology, which lay not in its monotheism but the character it ascribed to its single God. Two traits characterized the gods of the Jews' contemporaries. First, they tended to be amoral. Second, they had no concern for human beings. The Jews reversed both these points. While the gods of Olympus pursued beautiful women, the God of Sinai watched over widows and orphans. While Mesopotamia's Anu and Canaan's El remained aloof, Yahweh spoke the name of Abraham and lifted his people from anonymity.

Such, then, was the Hebrews' conception of the Other that confronts human beings. It was not prosaic, for at its center was a Being of awesome majesty. It was not chaotic, for it coalesced in a divine unity. It was neither amoral nor indifferent, for its goodness was *"from everlasting to everlasting."* There were solid grounds for the Jews' exultation as they exclaimed rhetorically, *"Who is like you among the gods, O Yahweh?"* *"What great nation has a God like the Lord?"*

MEANING IN CREATION

*I*N "THE BROTHERS KARAMAZOV" Dostoyevsky has Ivan blurt out: *"I don't accept this world of God's, and although I know it exists, I don't accept it at all. It's not that I don't accept God, you must understand, it's the world created by Him I don't and cannot accept."*

Ivan is not alone in finding God, perhaps, good, but the world not; entire philosophies have done the same. The Jews, on the other hand, affirmed the world. The account of creation in the opening chapter of Genesis concludes with Yahweh surveying his handiwork and finding it *"very good."*

That judgment, which the scribe put in the mouth of Yahweh, may be the most important one the human spirit can register. Everyone at times finds him- or herself asking whether life is worthwhile, which amounts to asking whether, when the going gets rough, it makes sense to continue to live.

There is a passage in T. S. Eliot's *The Cocktail Party* that addresses this point. Celia, who has been not just disappointed but disillusioned in love, goes to a psychiatrist for help and begins her first session with this unusual statement:

"I must tell you
that I should really like to think there's something wrong with me

Because, if there isn't, then there's something wrong with the world itself — and that's much more frightening!

That would be terrible.

So I'd rather believe
there is something wrong with me, that could be put right."

An illuminated Old Testament manuscript in Hebrew.

Celia puts the point in a nutshell. When things grow difficult, what are we to conclude? That the fault is in the stars, dear Brutus, or that it lies closer at hand, in ourselves? Neither answer can be objectively verified, but there is no doubt as to which elicits the more creative response. In the one case we can do something about problems; in the other we are helpless pawns. Seen in this light, the Jewish affirmation of the world's goodness equipped them with a constructive starting point. However desperate their lot, however deep the valley of the shadow of death, they never despaired of life itself. Meaning was always waiting to be won. The opportunity to respond creatively was never absent.

Thus far we have been speaking of the Jewish estimate of creation as a whole, but one element in the Biblical account deserves special attention: its regard for the physical, material component of existence.

Much of Greek thought takes a dim view of matter. Likewise Indian philosophy, which considers matter a barbarian, spoiling everything it touches. Salvation in such contexts involves freeing the soul from its material container. The Hebrew Bible presents things differently. Opening with the words, *"In the beginning God created the heavens and the earth,"* it closes its first chapter with God reviewing *"everything that he had made,"* earth included, *"and behold, it was very good."* The emphasis, *"very,"* gives

a lilt to the entire Jewish, and subsequently Western, view of the natural world. Pressing for meaning in every direction, the Jews refused to abandon the physical aspects of existence as illusory, defective, or unimportant. The abundance of food made the Promised Land *"a good land."* Sex also was good. An occasional splinter group (such as the Essenes) might disagree, but Jews as a whole hold marriage in high esteem. The prophets' denunciation of the inequalities of wealth was premised on the conviction that possessions are good – so good that no one should be without them. Even in death the Jews would not renounce the body; hence their belief (which Christians and Muslims would continue) in bodily resurrection.

Unlike India, East Asia prizes nature; but to be appreciated and conformed to, not (as the Jews were to add) worked with. When, after registering earth's goodness, Yahweh goes on to commission his children to *"have dominion"* over it (Gen. 1:26), a new note was struck. The combined thesis that nature is good and a field for importantly constructive endeavor, was novel for its day. It was a combination that (as we know) was destined to bear fruit, for it is no accident that modern science first emerged in the Western world.

The Jewish view of the material world as "very good" was a radical departure from the ancient Greek and Indian philosophies.

MEANING IN HUMAN EXISTENCE

*T*HE MOST CRUCIAL ELEMENT in a people's outlook is their self-image, and here too the Jews looked for meaning. The anthropological question interested them deeply, but not for theoretical reasons. They wanted to understand human nature so they would not miss its highest registers.

That the human self is limited they knew intimately. Compared with the majesty of the heavens, people are *"dust."* The powers of nature can crush them *"like moths."* Their earthly span is brief *"as grass,"* and troubled *"like a sigh"* (Ps 8:4). There were times when the Jews wondered why God should give people a second thought.

The remarkable feature of their anthropology, though, was that without losing sight of human weakness they saw concomitantly its unspeakable grandeur. The word "unspeakable" is exact here, for the translators of the King James Version of the Bible refused to follow the Psalmist who positioned human beings only *"a little lower than God"* (Ps 8:5). That claim struck the translators as presumptuous, so they toned it down to read *"a little lower than the angels."* The one charge that has never been leveled against the Bible is that its characters are not completely human. Even its greatest heroes like David are presented in so unvarnished a fashion that the Book of Samuel has been called the most honest historical writing of the ancient world. Yet no amount of realism could dampen Jewish aspiration. The same creatures who on occasion deserve the epithets *"maggot and worm"* (Job 25:6) are also the beings whom God has *"crowned with glory and honor"* (Ps 8:6).

On the realistic side of this ledger we have cited physical weakness, but moral weakness weighed heavier for the Jews. *"I was born guilty, a sinner when my mother conceived me"* (Ps 51:5). It is altogether wrong to conclude from this verse that the Jews thought that human nature is depraved and that sex is evil. The verse does, however, contribute something of importance to Jewish anthropology. The word sin comes from a root meaning "to miss the mark," and this people repeatedly do. Their missteps, though, are not fore-ordained, for the Jews never questioned human freedom. People forge their destinies through freely chosen decisions. *"I have set before you life and death. Therefore choose life"* (Deut 30:19).

Finally, it followed from the Jewish concept of their God as a loving God that people are God's beloved children. In one of the tenderest metaphors of the entire Bible, Hosea pictures God yearning over people as though they were toddling infants:

> *It was I who taught Ephraim to walk,*
> *I took them up in my arms;*
> *I led them with cords of human kindness,*
> *with bands of love.*
> (Hos 11:3)

What are the ingredients of the most creatively meaningful image of human existence that the mind can conceive? Remove human frailty, and the estimate lacks realism. Remove grandeur, and aspiration recedes. Remove sin, and sentimentality threatens. Remove freedom, and responsibility goes by the board. Remove, finally, divine love, and life becomes estranged. With all that has been discovered about human life in the intervening 2500 years, it is difficult to fault the Jewish assessment.

MEANING IN HISTORY

WHAT IS AT STAKE when we ask if there is meaning in history? Nothing less than our entire attitude toward the social order and collective life within it. If we decide that history is meaningless it follows that the social, political, and cultural contexts of life should not concern us. Our task would be to rise above them if possible, and weather them if not.

The Jewish estimate of history was the opposite of this attitude of indifference; they saw history as of towering significance. It was important, first, because they were convinced that the context in which life is lived affects that life in every conceivable way, positioning its problems, delineating its opportunities, and conditioning its outcomes. Second, if contexts are important, so is collective action; social action as we usually call it. There are times when the only way to change things is by working together – planning, organizing, and acting in concert. Third, history was important as a field of opportunity. Being governed by God, nothing within it happened accidentally. Yahweh's hand was at work in every event, fashioning it into lessons for those who have the wit to learn. Finally, history was important because the opportunities it offers are not on a par. All are important, but some – Abraham's call and the Exodus come to mind immediately – were decisive. History needed to be heeded, for lost opportunities would not return.

This last point – the uniqueness of events and decisiveness of some – was epitomized in the Hebrew notions (a) of God's direct intervention in history at certain critical points, and (b) of a chosen people as recipients of his unique commissions. Both are illustrated in the epic of Abraham. Noting history's deterioration, God was not inactive. He told Abraham to go to a new land and found a new people. It was a watershed moment. Because Abraham answered Yahweh's call he became the first Hebrew, the first of a "chosen people."

We shall return to this "chosen people" theme, but for the present we must ask what gave the Jews their insight into history's significance. We have noted the *kind* of meaning they found in history. What enabled them to see history as *embodying* this meaning?

For India, human destiny lies outside history altogether. Israel's neighbors, for their part, kept destiny within history, but in history as currently constituted, for they thought that the social order was as unalterable as the laws of nature. The Israelites' historical outlook differed from both these views because they had a different idea of God. God would not have created nature were it unimportant; at the same time, as nature's creator he could not be reduced to it. The consequence of distinguishing clearly between God and his handiwork was momentous, for it meant that the "ought" could not be assimilated to the "is." God's will transcended (and often differed from) what was happening in history.

By this double stroke of planting man solidly in nature – and in history as nature's human stratum – but not confining him to it (because God's will constitutes a different order from nature's claims), the Jews established history as both important and subject to review. For the Jews, history was always in tension between Yahweh's intentions and man's failure to cooperate with those intentions. As a consequence, Judaism laid the groundwork for the social conscience that has been a hallmark of Western civilization. When things are not as they should be, change is required. The prophets set the pattern. Protected by religious sanctions, the Hebrew prophets were a reforming political force which history has never surpassed, and perhaps never again equaled.

A cover for the Torah, from a 19th century Spanish synagogue.

MEANING IN MORALITY

HUMAN BEINGS ARE SOCIAL CREATURES. Without other people they fail to become human; yet with other people they often act barbarically. The need for morality stems from this double fact. Nobody likes rules any more than they like stop lights, but without constraints, human relations would become as snarled as traffic jams. The Jews compiled their law to stipulate the constraints they thought life requires. Rabbinic Law contains 613 commandments, but four will suffice for our purposes. The four ethical precepts of the Ten Commandments, they were enacted to control the four principal danger zones in human relationships, which are force, wealth, sex, and speech.

What the Ten Commandments prescribe in these areas are the minimum standards that make collective life possible. Regarding force they say in effect: you can bicker and fight, but killing within the in-group will not be tolerated, for it instigates blood feuds that rip the community apart. *"Thou shalt not murder."* Similarly with sex. You can be flirtatious, even promiscuous, and though we may not approve, we will not take action unless the parties are married. Then we will step in, for infidelities there rouse passions the community can't stand. *"Thou shalt not commit adultery."* As for possessions, you may make your pile as large as you please and be shrewd and cunning in the enterprise, but direct pilfering off someone else's pile is taboo; for this violates the sense of fair play and generates animosities that get out of hand. *"Thou shalt not steal."* Finally, regarding the spoken word you may dissemble and equivocate, but there is one time when we require that you tell the truth. If a dispute reaches such proportions as to be brought before a tribunal, its judges must know what

happened. If you lie then, while under oath, the penalty will be severe. *"Thou shalt not bear false witness."*

The importance of the Ten Commandments in their ethical dimensions lies not in their uniqueness but in their universality. They do not speak the final word on the topics they address. They speak the words that must be spoken if other words are to follow.

A page from an 18th century Moravian copy of the Haggadah, the traditional order of service for Passover based on the story of the Exodus from Egypt.

MEANING IN JUSTICE

*I*T IS TO A REMARKABLE GROUP OF MEN whom we call the Prophets more than to any others that Western civilization owes its convictions (1) that individuals are responsible not only for their face-to-face dealings, but for the social structures of their society; and (2) that the future of any people depends in large part on the justice of its social order.

Etymologically, a prophet is someone who speaks for, or on the authority of, another. In the biblical period it was used to refer to a distinctive group of persons who spoke for God.

A review of the prophetic movement shows it not to have been a single phenomenon. Moses stands in a class by himself, but the prophetic movement passed through three stages in each of which Yahweh worked differently.

The first was the stage of the Prophetic Guilds. Here we do not encounter individual prophets, for prophecy was a field phenomenon; a form of collective, self-induced ecstasy. With the help of music and dancing, itinerant prophetic bands would work themselves into fever-pitches of possession. Its members would lose their self-consciousness in a collective sea of divine intoxication.

Ethics was of no concern at this stage; it was only the ecstatic states of consciousness that came over these prophets that made them assume (along with the people among whom they moved) that they were divinely inspired. Ethics arrived with the second stage of the prophetic movement, that of the Individual Pre-Writing Prophets. At this stage the prophetic guilds launched individuals like rockets from their midst – Elijah, Elisha, Nathan, and others – but as prophecy was still in its pre-writing stage, no books are attributed to them. They stayed in touch with their support groups while being less dependent upon them. Divine visitations could come to them while they were alone, and Yahweh voiced his concerns through them.

The story of Naboth shows how prominently justice figured in those concerns. Because Naboth refused to turn over his family vineyard to King Ahab he was framed on false charges of blasphemy and stoned; blasphemy being a capital crime, his property would then revert to the throne. When news of the incident reached Elijah, the word of the Lord came to him, saying, *"Go down to meet Ahab king of Israel. Say to him, 'Thus says the Lord. You have killed and taken possession. In the place where dogs licked up the blood of Naboth, dogs will also lick up your blood.'"*

The story carries revolutionary significance for human history, for it is the story of how someone without official position took the side of a wronged man and denounced a king to his face on grounds of injustice. One searches history in vain for its parallel. Elijah was not a priest. He had no formal authority for the terrible judgment he delivered. The normal pattern of the day would have called for him to be struck down by bodyguards on the spot. But the fact that he was "speaking for" an authority not his own was so transparent that the king accepted his verdict as divinely decreed.

The third and climactic phase of the prophetic movement arrived with the great Writing Prophets: Amos, Hosea, Jeremiah, Isaiah, and others. They continued to be ecstatics, and the ethical note that the Pre-Writing Prophets struck was likewise retained, but with an important addition. Whereas Elijah registered God's displeasure over an individual act – King Ahab's – the Writing Prophets discerned Yahweh's disapproval of injustices that were embedded in the social fabric.

The Writing Prophets found themselves in a time that was shot through with inequities, special privilege, and injustices of the most flagrant sort. These threatened the internal stability of the Jewish nation, but the Writing Prophets saw them as threatening the international standing of the Jews as well. Israel's corruption, they heard Yahweh telling them, would result in attack by Assyria, Egypt, Syria or Phoenicia, its mighty neighbors.

We could easily miss the originality of the prophetic perception here, so it will be well to state it explicitly. The standard view of the time saw international relations as governed by might — if not the might of the states themselves, then the might of the gods that backed them. For the Jews, though, gods and nations were pieces on Yahweh's game board. Victory would go to the nation that conformed to God's unthwartable intent, which was to see that *"justice rolled down like waters, and righteousness like a mighty stream."* Here again we find the Jews opting for the position that induced the most creative response. If the fate of peoples turns solely on power politics, there is little a small nation can do. But where others saw only power plays, the prophets heard God's warning to shape up or suffer the consequences. Clean up your national act or be destroyed.

In abstract terms the Prophetic Principle comes to this: The prerequisite of political stability is social justice, for it is in the nature of things that injustice will not endure. Stated theologically, the point reads: God has high standards. Divinity will not put up forever with exploitation, corruption, and mediocrity.

The prophets of Israel and Judah are one of the most amazing groups of individuals in all history. In the midst of the moral desert in which they found themselves, they spoke words the world has never been able to forget. They came from all classes. Some were sophisticated, others as plain and natural as the hillsides where they lived. Yet one thing was common to them all: the conviction that every human being, simply by virtue of his or her humanity, is a child of God and therefore in possession of rights that even kings must respect. The prophets lived in a vaster world than their compatriots, a world wherein kings seem small and the power of the mighty is as nothing compared with purity, justice, and mercy. So it is, that wherever men and women have gone to history for encouragement and inspiration in the age-long struggle for justice, they have found it most pointedly in the proclamations of the prophets.

Left: *"The Prophet Jeremiah,"* by Marc Chagall. The prophets of Israel and Judah brought a passion for social justice into a world where only might had ruled before.

MEANING IN SUFFERING

FROM THE EIGHTH TO THE SIXTH CENTURIES B.C. during which Israel and Judah tottered before the aggressive power of Syria, Assyria, Egypt, and Babylon, the prophets found meaning in their predicament by seeing God as serious in demanding that the Jews be just. *"Because they sell the righteous for silver, and the needy for a pair of sandals, your strongholds shall be plundered"* (Amos). To see things this way required moral energy, for it would have been easier to give up in defeat or assume that God would stage a last minute rescue. The climax, though, is yet to come. Defeat was not averted. In 721 B.C. Assyria wiped the Northern Kingdom from the map forever; and in 586 Judah, the Southern Kingdom, was likewise conquered, though her leaders survived and were taken captive to Babylonia. If ever there was a time when meaning seemed to be exhausted, this was it. The Jews had had their chance and had bungled it. Surely now the prophets might be expected to cap their people's downfall with a self-serving "I told you so." This retort, though, was not in the prophets' vocabulary. The most staggering fact in the Jewish quest for meaning is the way in which, when meaning had been exhausted at the deepest strata of experience they had thus far plumbed, the prophets dug deeper to uncover an entirely new vein. Not to have done so would have amounted to accepting the prevailing view that the victors' god was stronger than the god of the defeated, a logic that would have ended the biblical faith and the Jewish people along with it.

The rejection of that logic rescued the Jewish future. A prophet who wrote in sixth century Babylonia where his people were captives argued that Yahweh had not been worsted by the Babylonian god Marduk; history was still Yahweh's province. This meant that there must have been a point in Israel's defeat, and the challenge was again to see it. The point that Second Isaiah saw was not this time punishment. The Israelites needed to *learn* something from their defeat, but their experience would also be *redemptive* for the world.

On the learning side, there are lessons and insights that suffering illumines as nothing else can. In this case the experience of defeat and exile was teaching the Israelites the true worth of freedom which they had taken too lightly. Lines have come down to us that disclose the spiritual agony of the Israelites as displaced persons — how heavily they felt the yoke of captivity, how fervently they longed for their homeland. *"By the rivers of Babylon — there we sat down, and there we wept when we remembered Zion."* But what the Jews might themselves learn from their captivity was not the only meaning of their ordeal. God was at the same time using them to introduce into history insights that all peoples need, but to which they are blinded by complacency. Specifically, Yahweh was burning into the Jews

---

Above: *Detail of a silver platter showing the oppression of the Jews in Egypt.* Right: *Star of David painted in the surrealist manner, marked by symbols central to the Jewish faith.*

through their suffering a passion for freedom and justice that would spread to all humankind.

> I have given you as a light to the nations,
>
> to open the eyes that are blind,
>
> to bring out the prisoners from the dungeon,
>
> from the prison those who sit in darkness.

(Isa 42:6-7)

Stated abstractly, the deepest meaning the Jews found in their Exile was that of vicarious suffering: meaning that enters the lives of those that are willing to endure pain that others might be spared it.

An Ethiopian Jew reads the scriptures. In Judaism, holiness and history are inseparable.

MEANING IN MESSIANISM

*T*HOUGH THE JEWS were able to find their suffering meaningful, meaning climaxed for them in Messianism.

We can work our way into this concept by way of a striking fact. Historical progress is a Western idea — other peoples have now assimilated·it, but it originated in the West. There is an explanation for this. The outlooks of other civilizations were forged by ruling classes who tend to be satisfied with the way things are, whereas during most of their formative period the Jews were either oppressed or displaced. They were underdogs, and underdogs have only one direction to look: up. This upward tilt of Jewish hopes and imaginings impregnated the Western mind. A better tomorrow is possible, if not assured.

Hope has more purchase on the human heart when it is concretized, so the Jews personified their hope in the figure of a coming Messiah, or Chosen One. During the Babylonian Exile they looked to this Messiah to effect the "ingathering of the exiles" to their native homeland. After the second destruction of the Temple in 70 A.D., the Messiah was expected to reverse the diaspora that ensued.

Thereafter the concept grew complex. Always fired by hope, the Messianic idea came to have two sides: a politico-national side (which foresaw the triumph of the Jews over their enemies and their elevation to a position of importance in world affairs), and a spiritual-universal side (in which their political triumph would be attended by a moral advance of universal proportions). Different scenarios were scripted in which hope fluctuated between these two versions.

A second difference concerned the way the Messianic age would arrive. Some expected an actual Messiah, while others foresaw God dispensing with a human agent and intervening directly to institute an age of universal harmony.

A third tension reflected the restorative and utopian impulses in Judaism. Restorative Messianism looked for the re-creation of past conditions, typically the Davidic monarchy as idealized. But Messianism also accommodated Judaism's forward looking impulse by envisioning the Messianic Age as a state of things that never before existed.

Finally, Messianists differed concerning whether the new order would be continuous with previous history or would shake the world to its foundations and replace it (in the End of Days) with an aeon that was supernaturally different in kind. As the power of the Jews dwindled in the face of a rising Europe, apocalypticism overtook hopes for military victory and they banked increasingly on a miraculous redemption. The Messianic Age would break in at any moment, abruptly and cataclysmically.

In all four of these polarities the alternatives were deeply intertwined while being contradictory in nature. The Messianic idea crystallized (and retained its vitality) out of the tensions created by its ingredient opposites. The vitality of the idea proved to be infectious. Christianity reshaped it into the Second Coming of Christ; seventeenth century Europe into the idea of historical progress; and Marx into his dream of a coming classless society.

But whether we read the Messianic idea in its Jewish, its Christian, its secular, or its heretical version, the underlying theme is the same. There's going to be a great day!

THE HALLOWING OF LIFE

UP TO THIS POINT we have been dealing with ideas that the Jews developed to make sense of their experience, but we have come to the point where we must turn to their practices. For Judaism is less an orthodoxy than an orthopraxis. It has no official creed, but ceremonies and rituals (such as the circumcision of males and the Sabbath supper) are decisive.

Before turning to Jewish ritual it will be well to speak briefly of ritual in general, for this book has not thus far addressed it. From a narrowly rational or utilitarian point of view, ritual is a waste of time and money, yet it serves functions that nothing can replace. For one thing, it eases us through unfamiliar situations. Some of these are trivial, like the handshake and scripted *"Pleased to meet you,"* that eases the awkwardness of meeting a stranger. From such simple beginnings, however, ritual extends to death. Stunned by a tragic bereavement, we would flounder if we were thrown on our own and had to think our way through the ordeal. Ritual scripts our actions and directs our responses. And it sets a particular death in perspective, fitting it into a larger framework. *"Ashes to ashes, dust to dust"* – the words don't say whose ashes, for this is everybody; all of us. Ritual also summons courage: *"The Lord giveth and the Lord taketh away; blessed be the name of the Lord!"* As for happy times, rituals can turn these into celebrations – weddings, birthdays, and most simply, a family's evening meal. Here, in this best meal of the day when perhaps for the first time the family is relaxed and together, a blessing can be more than the starting line for a food race. It can hallow the occasion.

Moving from these general observations to ritual's place in Judaism, its function is to hallow life – in principle the whole of life. This happens when the Jew sees the world as reflecting the source of all holiness, namely Yahweh. The route to such seeing is piety. The opposite of piety is to accept the good things of life, most of which come to us quite apart from our own efforts, as if they were matters of course, without relating them to God. In the Talmud, to eat or drink without first making a blessing over the meal is compared to robbing God of his property. Jewish law sanctions the good things of life – eating, marriage, children, nature – but on condition that they be hallowed. It teaches that people should eat; that they should prepare their tables in the presence of the Lord. It teaches that people should drink; that they should use wine to consecrate the Sabbath. It teaches that people should be merry, that they should dance around the Torah.

If we ask how this sense of the sacred can withstand the suction of life's monotony, Jews answer: by grounding life in tradition. Without attention, the human sense of wonder and the holy will stir occasionally; but to become a steady flame it must be tended. One of the best ways to do this is to steep oneself in a history that cries aloud of God's providential acts and mercy in every generation. The most historically minded of all the religions, Judaism finds holiness and history inseparable. In sinking the roots of their lives deep into the past, Jews draw nourishment from events in which God's acts were clearly visible. The Sabbath eve with its candles and cup of sanctification, the Passover feast with its many symbols, the austere solemnity of the Day of Atonement, the ram's horn sounding the New Year, the scroll of the Torah adorned with breastplate and crown – the Jew finds nothing less than the meaning of life in these things, a meaning that spans the centuries in affirming God's great goodness to his people.

Above: *A table set for the Sabbath. Jewish law sanctions the good things of life such as eating, marriage, and nature, but on condition that they be hallowed.*

REVELATION

WE HAVE FOLLOWED THE JEWS in their interpretation of the major areas of human experience and found them arriving at a profounder grasp of meaning than any of their Mediterranean neighbors. This raises the question: What produced this achievement? The Jews answer with a disclaimer: they were not its source. The truths were revealed to them.

Revelation means disclosure; as a theological concept, it means divine disclosure. The Jews recorded Yahweh's disclosures to them in a book, the Torah, and commentaries on it. This, though, puts the cart before the horse, for the scriptures chronicle actions, and it was through those actions that God initially revealed himself. The most decisive of these actions was the Exodus, an incredible event in which God liberated an unorganized, enslaved people from the mightiest power of the age. This event not only launched the Israelites as a nation. It was, in addition, the first clear act by which Yahweh's character was disclosed to them.

That God was a direct party to their escape from Pharaoh, the Jews did not doubt. By every known sociological law, they should never have become a people, let alone survived. Yet here was the fact: A tiny, loosely-related group of people who had no real collective identity and were in servitude to the great power of the day had succeeded in making their getaway, eluding the chariots of their pursuers. It seemed impossible to the Jews that their liberation was their own doing. It was a miracle. *"I am the Eternal your God who brought you out of the land of Egypt"* (Ex 20:2).

Vividly cognizant of God's saving power in the Exodus, the Jews proceeded to read their earlier history in the light of this divine intervention. As their libera-

tion had obviously been engineered by God, what of the sequence that led up to it? The Jews saw God's initiative at work in every step of their journey. It was no vagabond impulse that prompted Abraham to leave his home in Ur and assume the long, uncharted trek toward Canaan. Yahweh had called him to father a people of destiny. So it had been throughout. Isaac and Jacob had been providentially protected, and Joseph exalted in Egypt, for the express purpose of preserving God's people from famine. From the perspective of the Exodus everything fell into place. From the beginning God had been leading, protecting, and shaping his people for the decisive Exodus event that made of the Israelites a nation.

And what was the nature of the God that the Exile disclosed? First, Yahweh was powerful – able to outdo the mightiest power of the time and whatever gods might be backing it. But equally, a God of goodness and love. Though this might be less obvious to outsiders, it was overwhelmingly evident to the Jews who were its direct recipients. Repeatedly their gratitude burst forth in song: *"Happy are you, O Israel. Who is like you – a people saved by Yahweh"* (Deut. 33:29). Had they themselves done

The offering of the first fruits of the harvest being carried to the Temple of Jerusalem.

anything to deserve this miraculous release? Not as far as they could see. Freedom had come to them as an act of sheer, gratuitous grace, a clear instance of Yahweh's unanticipated and astonishing love for them.

Besides God's power and love, the Exodus disclosed a God who was intensely concerned with human affairs. Whereas the surrounding gods were primarily nature deities, the Israelites' God had come to them not through sun or storm or fertility but in an historical event. That realization changed Israel's agenda forever. No longer would they be party to cajoling the forces of nature. They would attend to Yahweh's will and try to obey it. Given these three basic disclosures of the Exodus – of God's power, goodness, and concern for history – the Jews' other insights into God's nature followed readily. From his goodness it followed that he would want people to be good as well; hence Mount Sinai, where the Ten Commandments were established as the Exodus's immediate corollary. The prophets' demand for justice extended God's requirements for virtue to the social sphere – institutional structures, too, are accountable. Finally, suffering must carry significance because it was unthinkable that a God who had miraculously saved his people would abandon them completely.

We entered this chapter via the Jewish passion for meaning, but as our understanding of the religion deepens this needs to be recast. Meaning was secured, but not (from the Jewish perspective) because they sought it exceptionally. It was revealed to them. But why was it revealed to the Jews? Their own answer has been: because we were chosen. This raises a problem. The Jews had begun by thinking of Yahweh as exclusively their God, but in time they came to see him as the God of all peoples. Why, then, did he direct his revelation to them, and seemingly them only?

THE CHOSEN PEOPLE

THE JEWISH DOCTRINE of their election begins in a conventional mode – almost all peoples consider themselves special – but it soon surprises us. For unlike other peoples, the Jews singled themselves out for responsibilities rather than privileges. They were chosen to serve, and to suffer the trials that service would often exact. By requiring that they *do and obey all that the Lord hath spoken,"* their election imposed on them a far more demanding morality than was exacted of their peers. Nor was this all. We have seen that Second Isaiah's doctrine of vicarious suffering meant that the Jews were elected to shoulder a suffering that would otherwise have had to be distributed more widely. Still, the problem is not resolved. For grant that God called the Jews to heroic ordeal, not sinecure; the fact that they were singled out for a special role in the redemption of the world still looks like favoritism.

This rankles. Flying as it does in the face of democratic sentiments, it has provoked a special theological phrase to accommodate it: "the scandal of particularity." It is the doctrine that God's doings can focus like a burning glass on particular times, places, and peoples – in the interest, to be sure, of intentions that embrace human beings universally. We shall not be able to validate this doctrine, but we can understand what led the Jews to accept it, and what it did for them.

Our search for what led the Jews to believe that they were chosen will carry us past an obvious possibility – national arrogance – to the facts of their history that have already been rehearsed. Israel came into being as a nation through an extraordinary occurrence in which a milling band of slaves broke the shackles of the tyrannical power of their day and were lifted to the status of a free and self-respecting people. Almost immediately this brought an understanding of God that was immeasurably above that of their neighbors, and standards of morality and justice that still challenge the world. Through the three thousand years that have followed they have continued their existence in the face of unbelievable odds and adversity, and have contributed to civilization out of all proportion to their numbers. Even objective assessments must grant that the Jews have been unique. Their rise as much as their continuance, historians generally agree, is rationally inexplicable.

If that is the case, there are two possibilities. Either the credit belongs to the Jews themselves, or it belongs to God. Given this alternative, the Jews instinctively turned the credit Godward. One of the striking features of this people has been their persistent refusal to see anything innately special about themselves as human beings. So the specialness of the Jewish experience must have derived from God. Chosenness, a concept that appears at first to be arrogant, turns out to be the humblest interpretation the Jews could give to the facts of their origin, survival, and exceptional contributions to civilization.

It is possible, of course, to resent particularism even here, but one must ask whether in doing so we would not be resenting the kind of world we have. For like it or not, this is a world of particulars, and human beings are saddled with them. Nothing registers on human attention until it obtrudes from its background. What follows from this fact for theology? God probably blesses us as much through the air we breathe as through other gifts, but if piety had had to wait for people to infer God's goodness from the availability of oxygen, it would have been long in coming.

The same holds for history. If relief from oppression were routine, the Jews would have taken their liberation for granted. Chalk it up to human obtuseness – the fact remains that divine favors could envelop humanity as the sea envelops fish; were they automatic, people would consider them routine. Perhaps it was only by acting exceptionally – uniquely – that Yahweh could get humanity's attention.

Today Jewish opinion is divided on the doctrine of the election. Some Jews believe that it has outgrown whatever usefulness or objective validity it may have had in Biblical times. Other Jews believe that until the world's redemption is complete, God continues to need people who are set apart; peculiar in the sense of being God's task force in history.

Opposite: *Traditional wedding plate. This page, top: Celebrants at a Bar Mitzvah, initiation ceremony for young men in the Jewish faith.* Bottom: *The western wall of the Temple of Jerusalem.*

ISRAEL

THUS FAR WE HAVE BEEN DEALING WITH THE BIBLICAL PERIOD, but of course Judaism didn't end there. In 70 A.D. the Romans destroyed the Temple in Jerusalem that the Jews had rebuilt on returning from their Babylonian exile, and the focus of Judaism shifted from the sacrificial rite of the Temple to the study of the Torah and its accompanying oral tradition in academies and synagogues. Thenceforth it was not the priests but the rabbis (literally teachers) who held Judaism together. Rabbinic Judaism grounded itself in the commandment to make the study of the Torah a lifelong endeavor, and through it Judaism acquired a distinctly intellectual flavor. The rabbinic accomplishment of keeping Judaism alive for the two thousand years of its diaspora is one of the wonders of history, but having taken note of it we shall jump two millennia to close this chapter with a look at the twentieth century.

Judaism is the faith of a people. As such it contains, as one of its features, faith in a people – in the significance of the role the Jews have played and will continue to play in human history. During the biblical period the Jews needed their identity (to keep the truths that were coming to them from being compromised by neighboring polytheisms). And in their long European ghetto period a continuing identity was forced on them. But with their emancipation by the French Revolution, the need for a continuing Jewish identity ceased to be self-evident.

Arguments for its continuation differ. Some Jews adhere to the religious thesis of the preceding section: as God has chosen Israel to be a unique instrument for good, the shape and edge of that instrument should be retained. Other Jews argue that cultural diversity enriches societies. Underlying both rationales is the question, what constitutes Jewish identity?

Not doctrine, for there is nothing one has to believe to be a Jew. Judaism is like a circle that is whole but divisible into sections that converge in a common center. No individual section is required, but the more sections one embodies, the more Jewish one will be.

Four sections are preeminent: faith, observance, culture, and nation. Most of this chapter has been given to the content of Hebraic faith. Jews approach that content from intellectual angles that range from fundamentalism to ultra-liberalism, but the direction in which their faith looks is much the same. This can also be said of ritualistic observance. Jews vary in their interpretation of the Sabbath, dietary laws, and daily prayer, and in the extent to which they observe such rituals. The intent of observance, though, is the same: to hallow life. As this too has been described, what remains is to say a few words about culture and nation.

Culture includes mores, art forms, styles of humor, philosophy, a literature, and much else. Here we must limit ourselves to three ingredients: language, lore, and affinity for a land.

Jewish lore is apparent, for Biblical names and stories lace Western culture throughout. To these, Jews add the Talmud, a vast compendium of history, law, folklore, and commentary that is the basis of post-biblical Judaism. This in turn is supplemented by the *Midrashim,* an almost equal collection of legend, exegesis, and homily which began to develop before the biblical canon was fixed and reached its completion in the late Middle Ages. The whole provides an inexhaustible mine for scholarship, anecdote, and cultural identity.

As for language and land, these are Hebrew and Israel. As it was in Hebrew and the Holy Land that Revelation came to the Jews, both are sacred for their associations. Jews conduct all or part of their prayers in Hebrew, and consciousness of the Holy Land enlivens their reading of the Torah and their study of rabbinic literature. But to speak of Israel is to enter the fourth component of total Judaism, its nation. For we live in a century when, for the first time since their compulsory dispersion in 70 A.D., Palestine has been restored to the Jews.

The reasons leading to the establishment of the modern state of Israel in 1948 are complex. Beyond the powerful religious pull toward return, the chief contributing motifs were four.

1 The argument from security. The 1938-1945 Nazi-instigated Holocaust convinced many that Jews could not hope for security in Europe.

2 The psychological argument. Some were convinced that it was psychologically unhealthy for the Jews to be everywhere in minority status.

3 The cultural argument. The substance of Judaism was running thin and its tradition was bleeding to death. Somewhere in the world there needed to be a land where Judaism was the dominant ethos.

4 The social, utopian argument. Somewhere in the world there should be a nation dedicated to the historical realization of prophetic ideals and ethics. Long before the Holocaust, a small but determined number of Jewish dreamers made their way to Palestine to forge a life in which they would be free to ordain all aspects of their existence.

Whatever the reasons that have gone into its creation, Israel is here. Its achievements have been impressive. Its land reclamation, its hospitality to Jewish immigrants, its provisions for the laboring class, its new patterns of group living, its intellectual and cultural vitality – all have combined to make Israel an exciting social experiment.

But the twentieth century has also brought two agonizing problems for the Jews. The first relates to the Holocaust. What meaning can the concept of a Chosen People have in the face of a God who permitted this enormity? The other problem relates to the idealistic argument for the state of Israel that was mentioned. Having all but scripted the ideals of freedom and justice for Western civilization if not for the entire world, Jews now find themselves withholding these rights – forced for security reasons to withhold them, many Jews believe – from Palestinians whose territories they occupy as a result of the 1967 war.

Without presuming to answer these problems, we can appreciate the burdens they place on the conscience of this exceptionally conscientious people. Facing their gravity, they take courage in the fact that at least they are now politically free to confront their problems. As the Star of David waves over their spiritual homeland, the dominant thought in the minds of the Jews is: *Am Yisrael chai*, Israel lives! How wonderful to be living when all this is happening.

Opposite: From Bohemia, a crown for the Torah.

CHAPTER VIII

CHRISTIANITY

"For God so loved the world,
that he gave His only begotten Son..."

Above: *This Bodhisattva, depicted as the good shepherd, suggests*
that the similarity between Christianity and Buddhism may be closer
than it at first appears. Left: **"The Trinity"** *by Russian artist*
Andrej Rubliev, c. 15th century.

THE HISTORICAL JESUS

OF ALL THE GREAT RELIGIONS, CHRISTIANITY IS THE MOST WIDESPREAD and has the largest number of adherents. From its often bewildering complexity it will be our task to indicate, first the central strands that unite this religion, and then its three major divisions: Roman Catholicism, Eastern Orthodoxy, and Protestantism.

Christianity centers in the life of Jesus of Nazareth. The biographical details that we have are meager. He was born in Palestine, probably around 4 B.C., and grew up in Nazareth. He was baptized by a prophet, John, who was electrifying the region with his proclamation of God's coming judgment. In his early thirties he had a teaching-healing career that lasted between one and three years. In time he incurred the hostility of some of his own compatriots and the suspicion of Rome, which led to his crucifixion. What was the life that was lived within the framework of these meager facts?

Minimally stated, Jesus was a charismatic wonder-worker who stood in a tradition that stretched back to the beginnings of Hebrew history. The prophets and seers that comprised that tradition mediated between the everyday world, on the one hand, and a Spirit world that enveloped it. From the latter they drew power which they used both to help people and to challenge their ways. We shall consider this Spirit world and how Jesus drew upon it to alleviate suffering and seek a new social order.

a) "The Spirit of the Lord is upon me."

According to Luke, Jesus opened his ministry by quoting this statement from Isaiah and adding, *"Today this scripture has been fulfilled."*

The spiritual order dominated the biblical tradition in which Jesus stood. It included angels and other invisible beings, but it centered in Yahweh. To stress its superiority Jews pictured the spiritual order as residing above the earth, but this was imagery only; the two were not spatially separate, and were in continuous interaction. Spirit could be known. Periodically Yahweh spoke through prophets, but human beings could also take the initiative in contacting it. Fasting and solitude were important means for doing this. During their vigils, seekers literally immersed themselves in Spirit, and on returning to the world often gave proof of having done so.

The most important fact for the understanding of Jesus' historical career is that he stood squarely in the tradition of these Spirit-filled mediators. John, who had baptized him, was his immediate predecessor in this tradition, and it is a testament to John's spiritual power that in baptizing Jesus he opened his spiritual eye, which enabled him to see "the heavens opened and the Spirit descending upon him like a dove." Having descended, the Spirit drove Jesus into the wilderness where, during forty days of prayer and fasting, he consolidated the Spirit that had entered him. He then returned to the world, empowered.

b) "By the Spirit of God I cast out demons."

The Jews accepted without question the supremacy of Spirit over nature. The Spirit-filled personages of the Bible have power. To say that they were charismatic is to say they had power to attract people's attention, but the reason they attracted notice was the exceptional power they possessed *vis-à-vis* nature. They "had something," as we say — something ordinary mortals lack. That something was Spirit. The Bible repeatedly depicts them as *"filled with the power of the Spirit."* They healed diseases, cast out demons, and occasionally quelled storms, parted waters, and caused the dead to return to life. The Gospels attribute these powers to Jesus.

But Jesus could have been a healer and exorcist without attracting more than local attention. What made him outlive his time and place was the way he used Spirit not just to heal individuals but – this was his hope – to heal humanity, beginning with his own people.

c). *"Thy kingdom come, on earth."*

Politically, the position of the Jews in Jesus' time was desperate. They had been in servitude to Rome for the better part of a century and, along with their loss of freedom, were being taxed almost beyond endurance. Existing responses to their predicament were four. The relatively well off Sadducees favored making the best of a bad situation and accommodated themselves to Hellenistic culture and Roman rule. The other three positions hoped for change. Two of them were renewal movements. The Essenes considered the world too corrupt to allow for faith's reflowering, so they withdrew into property-sharing communes and devoted themselves to piety. The Pharisees on the other hand remained within society and sought to revitalize Judaism through adhering strictly to the Mosaic law, especially its holiness code. Representatives of the fourth position thought that change could come only through armed rebellion. Their catastrophic revolt of 66-70 A.D. led to the second destruction of the Temple in Jerusalem.

Into this political cauldron Jesus introduced a fifth option. Unlike the Sadducees he wanted change. Unlike the Essenes, he stayed in the world. Unlike the advocates of armed revolt, he extolled peacemaking and urged that even enemies be loved. It was the Pharisees that Jesus stood closest to, for the difference between them was one of emphasis only. The Pharisees stressed Yahweh's

Right: *John the Baptist preaching in the desert; his own head rests on the platter at his feet. A 15th century Greek icon painted on wood.*

holiness while Jesus stressed Yahweh's compassion. The difference appears at first to be small, but in actuality it proved to be too big for a single religion to accommodate.

The Pharisaic platform was essentially this: being majestically holy himself, Yahweh wanted to hallow the world as well; and to accomplish this aim he had selected the Jews to plant for him a beachhead of holiness in history. It was laxity in the observance of the holiness code, delivered to Moses on Mount Sinai, that had reduced the Jews to their degraded state, and only the wholehearted return to it would reverse their fate.

Jesus subscribed to much of this, but he could not accept the lines that the holiness program drew between people. Beginning by categorizing acts and things as clean or unclean (foods and their preparation, for example) it went on to categorize people according to whether they respected those distinctions. The result was a social structure that divided people who were clean and unclean, pure and defiled, sacred and profane, Jew and Gentile, righteous and sinner. Jesus saw social barriers as an affront to Yahweh's compassion, and he disregarded them. This made him a social prophet, challenging the boundaries of the existing order and advocating an alternative vision of the human community.

It is important to emphasize that the issue was not God's compassion; it was whether the social system that the holiness code structured was compassionate. Jesus' conviction that it was not put him at odds with the Pharisees. His protest did not prevail, but it did attract enough attention to alarm the Roman authorities, which led to Jesus' arrest and execution on charges of treason. Thereafter the future of the "Jesus people" lay with the wider world.

Opposite: *Jesus overturning the tables of the money-changers; El Greco.* Above: *Illumination from an 11th century manuscript showing the miracles of Jesus.*

THE CHRIST OF FAITH

HOW DOES ONE MOVE FROM THE JESUS of history to the Christ whom his followers came quickly to believe had been God in human form? They did not reach that conclusion before Jesus' death, but even in his lifetime we find momentum building in its direction. Having tried to describe Jesus' life objectively, we turn now to the way he appeared to his disciples – what they saw him do, what they heard him say, and what they sensed him to be, beginning with what he did.

a) *"He went about doing good."*

The Gospels are filled with accounts of Jesus' miracles, but it would be a mistake to place our emphasis there. For one thing, Jesus did not himself emphasize them; almost all of them were performed quietly, apart from the crowd, and as demonstrations of the power of faith. We get a better perspective on Jesus' activities if we place the emphasis where one of his disciples did. Once, in addressing a group, Peter found it necessary to epitomize Jesus' life, and said, *"He went about doing good."* Moving easily and without affectation among ordinary people and social misfits, healing them, counseling them, Jesus went about doing good. He did so with such single-minded effectiveness, that those who were with him constantly found their estimate of him modulating to a new key. They found themselves thinking that if divine goodness were to manifest itself in human form, this is how it would behave.

This panel from the Sistine Chapel shows the Sermon on the Mount (left) and the miracle of Jesus healing the leper.

b) *"Never spoke man thus."*

It was not only what Jesus did, however, that made his contemporaries place him in a new category. It was also what he said.

Taken separately, all of Jesus' teachings have counterparts in the Old Testament or Talmud; but taken as a whole, they have a vividness, urgency, and absence of second-rate material that makes them startlingly new. The language Jesus uses is fascinating in itself. It is compact and invariably cuts to the quick; but in addition it is extravagant to a degree that wise men, feeling it necessary to weigh their assertions, can't manage. If your hand offends you, cut if off. If your eye stands between you and the best, gouge it out. Jesus talks of camels that hump through needles' eyes, of people who fastidiously strain gnats from their drinks while oblivious of the camels that caravan down their gullets. He talks of people whose outer lives are stately mausoleums while their inner lives stink of decaying corpses. This is not language tooled for rhetorical effect. The language is integral to the message – prompted by its driving urgency.

So what did Jesus use such language to say? Quantitatively, not a great deal, yet his teachings may be the most repeated in history. *"Love your neighbor as yourself. What you would like people to do to you, do to them. Come unto me, all you that labor and are heavy laden, and I will give you rest. You shall know the truth, and the truth shall make you free."* Most of the time, though, he told stories: of buried treasure, of sowers who went out to sow, of pearl merchants, of a good Samaritan. People who heard these stories were moved to exclaim, *"This man speaks with authority. Never spoke man thus!"*

They were astonished, as we would be if we could recover their original impact. For they are "hard sayings" in presenting a scheme of values that is at radical odds with the usual. We are told that we are not to resist evil

but to turn the other cheek. The world assumes that evil must be resisted by every means available. We are told to love our enemies and bless those who curse us. The world assumes that friends are to be loved and enemies hated. We are told that the sun rises on the just and the unjust alike. The world considers this undiscriminating. We are told that outcasts and harlots enter the kingdom of God before many who are perfunctorily righteous. Again unfair; the world assumes that respectable people should lead the way. We are told that the gate to salvation is narrow. The world would prefer it to be broad.

We are told to be as carefree as birds and flowers. The world counsels prudence. We are told that it is more difficult for the rich to enter the Kingdom than for a camel to pass through a needle's eye. The world admires wealth. We are told that the happy people are those who are meek, who weep, who are merciful and pure in heart. The world assumes that it is the rich, the well-positioned, and the powerful who are happy. A wind of freedom blows through these teachings that makes the world want to postpone them, saying, not yet, not yet!

The only way to make sense of Jesus' extraordinary admonitions is to see them as cut from his understanding of the God who loves human beings absolutely, without pausing to calculate their worth or due. Why are we to give the needy our cloak as well as our coat? Because God has ministered far more importantly to our needs. Why should we go with others the second mile? Because we know — deeply, overwhelmingly — that God has borne with us for far longer stretches. Why should we love not only our friends but our enemies? Because God lets the evilhearted in on his sunshine. To us, Jesus' summons to unstinting love seems unrealistic, but he would have said that that is because we do not perceive — or better, truly experience — the constant, unstinting love that God directs toward us. If we did experience it, we would still face difficult choices for which Jesus offered no rulebook. Because circumstances affect these, he confined his teachings to the stance from which concrete problems should be considered.

We have spoken of what Jesus did and what he said, but what finally edged his disciples toward the conclusion that he was divine was the person they found him to be.

c) *"We have seen his glory."*

The most impressive thing about the teachings of Jesus is not that he taught them but that he appears to have lived them. From the accounts that we have, his entire life was one of humility, self-giving, and love that sought not its own. The supreme evidence of his humility is that it is impossible to discover precisely what Jesus thought of himself. He wasn't concerned with that. He was concerned with what people thought of God.

Through the pages of the Gospels Jesus emerges as a man who bore about him (as someone has said) no strangeness at all except the strangeness of perfection. He loved people and they loved him in turn — intensely and in great numbers. He stands by the Sea of Galilee and they press so hard that he has to speak to them from a boat. He sets out for the day and a crowd of several thousand accumulates, missing their lunch, staying on until suddenly they discover that they are famished. This response from Jesus' contemporaries was the returning echo of his response to them. We have seen that he ignored the barriers that mores erected between people. He loved children. He hated injustice, and perhaps hated hypocrisy even more because it hid people from themselves and precluded the authenticity he sought to build into relationships.

In the end it seemed to those who knew him best that here was a man in whom the human ego had disappeared, leaving his life so completely under the will of God that it was transparent to that will. It came to the point where they felt that as they looked at Jesus they were looking at something resembling God in human form. It is this that evoked the lyric cry of the early Church: *"We have seen his glory, full of grace and truth."*

Opposite: *Portrait of Jesus from a fresco in Novgorod, Russia.*

THE END & THE BEGINNING

AFTER MINGLING WITH HIS PEOPLE and teaching them for a number of months, Jesus was crucified. But his followers were soon preaching the gospel of their Risen Lord.

We are given too few details to know exactly what happened after the crucifixion. Jesus' close associates reported that he appeared to them in a new way, but it is not possible to determine exactly what that way was. Certain accounts suggest corporeality – eating, and Thomas's touching the wound in his side – while others are more visionary, reporting him as passing through closed doors. Thus he seems not to have resumed his former body; resurrection was not resuscitation. Instead, it was entry into another mode of being that was sometimes visible but usually was not. What is clear is that Jesus' followers began to experience him in a new way, namely as having the qualities of God. He could now be known anywhere, not just in physical proximity.

Faith in Jesus' resurrection produced the Church and its Christology. To grasp its power to do this we must see that it concerned more than the fate of a worthy man. Its claim extended to the status of goodness in the universe, contending that it was omnipotent. The resurrection reversed the cosmic position in which the cross had placed Jesus' goodness. Instead of being fragile, the love the disciples had encountered in him was victorious over everything, including death.

"Jacob's Ladder" by Marc Chagall.

THE GOOD NEWS

THE CONVICTION THAT JESUS CONTINUED TO LIVE transformed a dozen or so disconsolate followers of a slain and discredited leader into one of the most dynamic groups in human history. We read that tongues of fire descended upon them. People who were not speakers became eloquent. They exploded across the Greco-Roman world, preaching what has come to be called the Gospel but is literally the Good News. Starting in an upper room in Jerusalem, they spread their message with such fervor that in their own generation it took root in every major city of the region.

A symbol can introduce what their Good News was. Early on, Christians began to scratch on walls, or the ground, the outline of a fish, its head pointing to the place where their persecuted sect held its underground meetings. They chose the fish for their logo because the Greek letters for fish are also the first letters of the Greek words for "*Jesus Christ, Son of God, Savior.*" That phrase contained the essence of the Good News the Christians were on fire with. To grasp its import we will do well to look first at the way it affected its proclaimers, and proceed from there to what produced that effect.

The people who first listened to Jesus' disciples proclaiming the Good News were as impressed by what they saw as by what they heard. They saw lives that had been transformed – men and women who had changed overnight by finding, so it seemed, the secret of living. Specifically, there seemed to be two qualities that informed them. The first of these was mutual regard: "*See how these Christians love one another*" is one of the earliest observations we have from outsiders. Integral to this regard was a total absence of social distance. Here were men and women who not only said that everyone was equal in the sight of God, but who lived as though they meant it. The second quality they exhibited was joy. The opposite of numerous, powerful, and wealthy, they were persecuted; yet in the midst of their trials they had found an inner peace that surfaced in happiness. Life was no longer something to cope with. It was glory discerned.

What produced their joy and love? The New Testament record shows that three intolerable burdens had been lifted from their shoulders. The first of these was fear, including the fear of death. The second was guilt. The third was the cramping confines of self-centeredness.

It is not difficult to see how release from these three burdens could bring new life, but this only pushes our question back a step. What freed the Christians of these liabilities? And what did a man named Jesus, now gone, have to do with the process that they should credit it as his doing?

The only power that can effect transformations of the order we have described is love. Post-Freudian psychology is beginning to suspect that the deepest impulse in the human self is to be lovingly related to people. The impulse must be activated, however; typically through the mother's initiating love for her infant. The process begins when the mother's loving smile awakens love in her baby and (as coordination develops) elicits its smile in return. The process continues into childhood. A loving human being is not produced by exhortations, rules, and threats. Love only emerges in children when it is poured into them, normally by nurturing parents.

If human beings find their latent love triggered by the love of others for them – or to reword the point, if the love that builds in them is the love that comes to them, assimilated and then reflected back onto the world – all that needs to be added to this rendering of the matter is the question of degree. If the normal quotient of human love derives from being bombarded by finite human love, how much more love might the early Christians have acquired by sensing, flowing toward each of them, a love of infinite proportions – God's love. Imagination may fail us here, but logic need not. If we too felt ourselves to be loved, not abstractly or in principle but vividly and personally, by one who unites all power and perfection, that experience could reduce our fear, guilt, and self-obsession to zero.

God's love is precisely what the first Christians did feel. They had experienced Jesus' love directly, and had become convinced that he was God incarnate. Once love of this proportion reached them it could not be stopped. Melting the barriers of fear, guilt, and self, it coursed through them as if they were sluice gates, augmenting their previous love for others to the point where a difference in degree became a difference in kind, and a new quality, Christian love, was born. Conventional love is evoked by lovable qualities in the beloved, but the love that emanated from Christ embraced sinners and outcasts, Samaritans and enemies. It gave, not prudentially in order to receive, but because giving was its nature. Paul's famous account of Christian love should not be read as adding some pointers to an energy the world was already familiar with. His words point to the attribute of a specific person, Jesus Christ. They should be read as defining a novel capacity which, as it had been fully realized only in Christ, Paul was describing for the first time.

"Love is patient; love is kind; love is not envious or arrogant or rude. It does not insist on its own way; it is not irritable or resentful; it does not rejoice in wrongdoing, but rejoices in the truth. It bears all things, believes all things, hopes all things, endures all things. Love never ends." (I Cor 13:4-8)

THE MYSTICAL BODY OF CHRIST

*T*HE CHRISTIANS WHO SPREAD THE GOOD NEWS throughout the Mediterranean world did not feel themselves to be alone. They were not even alone together, for they believed that Jesus was in their midst as a concrete, energizing power. Convinced of this, the disciples went out to possess a world they believed God had already given them.

To vivify the intense corporate identity they felt, they used a metaphor that Jesus had bequeathed them: *"I am the vine, you are the branches."* A spiritual substance – the Holy Spirit, Christ's deputy in the world from which he had departed – was flowing through them as palpably as sap flows through a vine.

Saint Paul added the human body as a second metaphor for the emerging Church and, being closer to home, it became definitive. Though the talents and offices of individual Christians might differ as much as eyes and feet, all were animated by a single life-giving substance, the Holy Spirit. This described the early Christian experience exactly. The Church was the Mystical Body of Christ. Mystical meant supernatural and mysterious, but not unreal. Christ had dropped his human body, but in order to exchange it for a new physical body – the Church – through which he would complete his mission. This mystical physical body was born in the "upper room" in Jerusalem at Pentecost.

Continuing the richness of this metaphor: If Christ was the head of his corporate body and the Holy Spirit its soul, individual Christians were its cells. The aim of Christian worship was to say those words and do those things that sustained the Mystical Body and, reciprocally, infused the cells – individual Christians – with the Body's vitality. The transaction literally "incorporated" Christians into Christ's person, for Christ now in an important sense *was* the Church. In any given Christian the divine life might be flowing fully, sluggishly, or not at all according to whether his or her faith was vital, perfunctory, or apostate, the latter condition being comparable to paralysis. Some cells might even grow cancerous and turn on their host – these were Christians who brought disrepute on the Church through scandal. But to the degree that members were in Christian health, the pulse of the Holy Spirit coursed through them. This bound Christians to one another and at the same time placed them in the closest conceivable relation to Christ himself.

Building upon this original conception, Christians came to think of the Church as having a double aspect. Insofar as it consisted of Christ and the Holy Spirit dwelling in people and suffusing them with grace and love – the Invisible Church – it was perfect. Insofar as it consisted of fallible human members – the Visible Church – it inevitably fell short of perfection and needed to be criticized.

Christians differ on whether salvation is possible outside the Body of Christ. Liberals think it is. At the other extreme are fundamentalists who insist that no one but those who are knowingly and formally Christians will be saved. Between these extremes are Christians who answer by way of the distinction that was just introduced, between the Visible and Invisible Church. Pope Pius IX spoke for them when he rejected membership in the Visible Church as requisite for salvation, while including in the Invisible Church all human beings who live honorably, uprightly and by their best lights. Eternal life is for them, too.

THE MIND OF THE CHURCH

W E HAVE SEEN THAT IT WAS NOT THE DISCIPLES' MINDS that were first drawn to Jesus. Rather, it was the experience of living in the presence of someone in whom love, joy, and power intersected in a way his disciples came to believe was divine. In time, however, Christians felt the need to understand this phenomenon, and Christian theology was born. So what is theology?

Religion always includes an ethic, but that is never its entire story. Ethics springs from a vision of reality that sets it in motion. And that vision, in turn, is born of experience. Because religious experience is of things that are invisible, it gives rise to symbols as the mind tries to think about invisible realities. Symbols are ambiguous, however, so eventually the mind introduces thoughts to resolve the ambiguities of symbols and systematize their deliverances. Reading this sequence backwards, we can define theology as the systematization of thoughts about the symbols that religious experience gives rise to. The Christian Creeds are the bedrock of Christian theology for being the earliest attempts by Christians to understand systematically the events that had transformed their lives.

We may begin with the doctrine of the Incarnation. Holding as it does that in Christ God assumed a human body, it affirms that Christ was both God and man. Not half God and half man, but fully both. This sounds contradictory; but many of the findings of quantum mechanics are equally so – that matter is both wave and particle, for example – so the discussion needn't stop here.

The doctrine of the Incarnation claims something about both God and Jesus. First, about Jesus.

In identifying Jesus with God, one of the things the Church was saying was that his life provides the perfect

model for us, for the existential meaning of *"God"* is that to which one gives oneself without reservation. This much is obvious. But as we delve deeper into the Incarnation surprises await us.

To begin with, though the Christian announcement of a God-man was as startling in its day as it is ours, the shock attaches to opposite poles. Because it is difficult to believe that a human being can be divine, *we* find the shocking feature of the Incarnation to be what it says about Jesus: that he was God. In its own world, however, the dividing line between the human and the divine was so faint – emperors routinely claimed to be divine – that a struggling sect's claim that its founder was divine raised few eyebrows. What else is new?

The Christians insisted that there was something new about their God-man. His originality lay in the kind of God he disclosed; specifically, a God who was willing to assume the limitations of a human life. That willingness, together with the character of the life God had willingly assumed – Jesus' life – added up to a different understanding of divinity than the Mediterranean world had known. The Christian God was *concerned* about humanity; concerned enough to suffer in its behalf. This was unheard of, to the point where it prompted not just disbelief but alarm. In the eyes of threatened conservatives, such blasphemy, coupled as it was with the Christians' radically egalitarian social views, needed to be silenced. Persecutions were instituted, and catacombs built to escape them.

"Mary Magdalene anointing the feet of Jesus."; *by 14th century Milanese painter Giovanni.*

As for what the Incarnation asserts about Christ, here too there are surprises. For instead of wasting many words on Jesus' divinity, the Creeds took it as their first task to insure his humanity. The vagueness of the divine/human distinction in Greco-Roman understanding made this necessary. The gods of Olympus were quasi-human and quasi-divine, and Christ didn't fit that pattern for wedding categorical opposites, for he was absolutely both.

Belief in Christ's divinity was secure, for that conviction escalated rapidly. It was his humanity that was in trouble, so the Church used its first Creed – the Apostles' – to lock it in place.

"*I believe in God the Father Almighty, Maker of heaven and earth; and in Jesus Christ our Lord, who was conceived by the Holy Ghost, born of the Virgin Mary, suffered under Pontius Pilate, was crucified, died, and buried...*".

After acknowledging God, the Apostle's Creed moves immediately to its overriding concern: to establish that the man part of the God-man splice was human in every respect. Jesus *really was* born, it says; he really did suffer, he really died and was buried. These incidents were not episodes in which God feigned contact with the human estate. They were as real for Christ as they are for us.

It is not difficult to see why (at the cost of immense logical awkwardness) the Church felt that it needed to retain Christ's humanity. A bridge must touch both banks, and Christ was the bridge that joined humanity to God. "*God became man that man might become God,*" was a Church Father's way of putting the matter. To have said that Christ was man but not God would have been to deny that his life was fully *normative*. To have said that he was God but not man would have been to deny that his example was fully *relevant;* it might be a realistic standard for God but not for human beings. Had the Apos-

tles relaxed either claim they would have betrayed their core experience.

Turning to the doctrine of the Atonement, its root meaning is reconciliation, the recovery of wholeness or at-one-ment. Christians were convinced that Christ's life and death had effected an unparalleled *rapprochement* between God and humanity. Two metaphors have dominated the Church's understanding of this realignment. The legalistic one assumes that disobedience – depicted by the eating of forbidden fruit in Eden – estranged humanity from God. The sin was of infinite proportion for having been directed against an infinite God, so only an infinite initiative could heal the damage done. This Christ accomplished through his vicarious death on the cross.

At times, notably in the Middle Ages, this reading has carried weight, but Christendom's presiding metaphor for the Atonement has been release from bondage. As the bondage Christ released humanity from was sin, we begin with that topic.

Typically it is broached in the plural: sins are spoken of, which suggests specific acts. The deeper meaning of the word is singular. Sin is disconnectedness, or estrangement from God. It is the heart's misplacement; a disalignment of its affections. Where there is wholehearted love for the All, for the universal good as we might say, the will *wants* that good, and rules are superfluous. Normally, though, self-love pulls against our love for others.

Thus the bondage that imprisons us is self-love. Put the other way around, it is estrangement from participation in the divine life which is premised on the wellbeing of all. This estrangement doesn't feel good. Paul admitted this: "*I feel awful,*" he said. Prisoners always do. Part of their wretchedness springs from their helplessness, so Paul continues, "*I do not do what I want, but I do*

the very thing I hate." His entrapment leads to his cry of despair: "*Who will rescue me from this body of death?*" Alcoholics know that cry well. If there is to be a rescue it must come from without, or better, from above, from a higher power. That higher power came to the Christians through Christ, so it was he that they credited for their restoration to — and At-one-ment with — unbounded life.

The third key Christian doctrine that we shall consider is the Trinity. It holds that while God is fully one, God is also three. The latter half of this claim leads Jews and Muslims to wonder if Christians are truly monotheists, but Christians are confident that they are. The differences between water, steam, and ice do not cancel the underlying identity of H_2O.

What prompted the Christians to the curious view that God is Three-in-One? Again, the notion had an experiential base. As full-fledged Jews, Jesus' disciples affirmed Yahweh unquestioningly. But as they came to see Christ as Yahweh's extension in the world, and as his life and mission gained in clarity, they began to assimilate him to the divine. This meant that they could now apprehend God either directly or through his Son, though in fact the two were so closely joined that the apprehension was the same.

Then came Pentecost, and a third visitation. While the disciples were together, suddenly from heaven there came a sound like the rush of a violent wind, and it filled the entire house where they were sitting. Divided tongues, as of fire, appeared among them, and a tongue rested on each of them. All of them were filled with the Holy Spirit.

The secular mind would say that the disciples first reified this experience, turning it into a thing — the Holy Spirit — and then personified that reification, thereby generating the third Person of the Trinity. The disciples would have rejected this explanation. They viewed the event as the dramatic arrival of a third party to the divine assembly.

Titian's view of the Pentecost, the event in Christian history which gave birth to the idea of the Trinity.

ROMAN CATHOLICISM

WHEN WE TURN FROM EARLY CHRISTIANITY to Christendom today, we find the Church divided into three great branches: Roman Catholicism, Eastern Orthodoxy, and Protestantism.

Up to 313 A.D. the Church struggled in the face of official Roman persecution. In that year it became legally recognized and enjoyed equal rights with other religions of the empire. Before the century was out, in 380, it became the official religion of the Roman Empire. With a few minor splinterings, it continued as a single institution up to 1054. Then, however, it divided into the Eastern Orthodox Church and the Roman Catholic Church. The next great division occurred in the Western Church with the Protestant Reformation in the sixteenth century. With these minimum facts before us, we shall try to understand the central perspectives of Christendom's three great branches. Beginning with the Roman Catholic Church, we shall consider it as *Teaching Authority* and *Sacramental Agent*.

The concept of the Church as Teaching Authority begins with the premise that God came to earth in the person of Jesus Christ to teach people how to live in this world so as to inherit eternal life. If this is true, it is important that his teachings continue in the world. The Gospels do not suffice for this purpose because they contain ambiguities. Bible study, individually pursued, does not resolve these ambiguities because individuals come up with different interpretations. Is divorce permissible? Was Christ born of a virgin? Did his body ascend after death? Is the fourth Gospel authentic? Without a sure court of appeal, moral and theological disintegration seem inevitable. It is to avert such disintegration that the

Church stands as the "supreme court," so to speak, to adjudicate between truth and error on important matters.

This idea of the church as Teaching Authority leads in the end to the doctrine of papal infallibility. Every nation has its ruler, be he prime minister, king, or president. The earthly head of the Church is the Pope, successor to St. Peter in the bishopric of Rome. The doctrine of papal infallibility asserts that when the Pope speaks officially on matters of faith and morals, God protects him from error.

This doctrine is so often misunderstood that it must be emphasized that infallibility is a strictly limited gift. It does not assert that the Pope is endowed with extraordinary intelligence. It does not mean that God helps him to know the answer to every conceivable question. Emphatically it does not mean that Catholics have to accept the Pope's view on politics. The Pope can make mistakes. He can fall into sin. The scientific or historical opinions he holds may be mistaken. He may write books that contain errors. Only in two limited spheres, faith and morals, is he infallible, and in these only when he has consulted widely and speaks officially as the supreme legislator of the Church, defining doctrines that should be held by all its members.

The second central idea in Catholicism is that of the Church as Sacramental Agent. This supplements the idea of the Church as Teaching Authority, for it is one thing to know what we should do, and quite another to be able to do it. The Sacraments help with this second obligation.

Two scenes from the life of Enea Piccolomini, as Cardinal (opposite) and as Pope Pius II (left.).

Christ called his followers to lives of charity and service that are supernatural in the literal sense of pulling against natural, selfish impulses. A project as demanding as this requires help, and the Church was instituted to provide it. Its means for doing so are the Sacraments.

Above: *Harvest altar at St. Sampson's Church in Cornwall.*
Opposite: *Ruins of the Chapel of St. Rose of Lima in New Mexico.*

Since the twelfth century the number of Sacraments in the Roman Church has been fixed at seven. They parallel the great moments and needs of human life. People are born, they come of age, they marry or dedicate themselves unreservedly to a life-purpose, and they die. Meanwhile they acquire a vocation, and need to be reconciled to society when they stray. The Sacraments mark these archetypal moments. By planting God's first special grace into the infant's soul, *Baptism* "delivers" that soul into the supernatural order. When the child reaches the age of reason and needs to be strengthened for responsibility and reflection, it is *Confirmed*. Usually there comes a solemn moment at which an adult is joined to a human companion in *Holy Matrimony*, or dedicates its entire life to God in *Holy Orders*. At life's close, the *Sacrament of the Sick* (extreme unction) closes earthly eyes and prepares the soul for its last passage.

Meanwhile two sacraments need to be repeated frequently. One of these is *Reconciliation* (confession), following transgressions. The other, the Church's central Sacrament, is the *Mass,* known also as the Holy Eucharist or Communion.

It is false to the Catholic concept of this Sacrament to think of it as merely commemorating Christ's life and death, for what it accomplishes is a literal transfusion of energy from God to the human soul. For the Catholic Church teaches that when the eucharistic elements are consecrated, they become Christ's body and blood. Their appearance does not change, and laboratory analysis would register no chemical alterations. All the same, the Eucharist conveys grace in the way a boat conveys its passengers, whereas, with the exception of Baptism, the other six sacraments convey grace as a letter conveys meaning. Intelligence is required for letters to be meaningful, whereas the Mass infuses grace regardless. It is exactly as important for Christians' souls to feast on the eucharistic elements as it is for their bodies to be nourished by food.

CHRISTIANITY

EASTERN ORTHODOXY

THE EASTERN ORTHODOX CHURCH broke officially with the Roman Church in 1054 A.D., each charging the other with responsibility for the schism. Having been together for more than half of their histories, the two share far more than they differ over. They honor the same Sacraments, and share the same intent regarding the Teaching Authority though here two differences arise. The first of these is numerical; the Eastern Church sees fewer issues on which unanimity is called for. Only ones that are mentioned in scripture can qualify, and only seven times – in the Seven Ecumenical Councils, all before 787 – has there been need to interpret what scripture says about them. Thus, while the Roman Catholic Church looks positively on its subsequent pronouncements (on purgatory, indulgences, the Immaculate Conception, the bodily assumption of Mary, and the like), regarding them as "developments" of doctrine, the Eastern Church looks on them as "additions" which Christians may, but need not, endorse.

In addition to how many dogmas are appropriate, the two Churches differ on how they are arrived at. We have seen that the Roman Church holds that in the final analysis they are delivered through the Pope. Having no Pope, the Eastern Church holds that God's truth is disclosed through "the conscience of the Church," a phrase that refers to Christian consensus. This consensus needs to be focused, and councils serve that need. Seven times – all of them before the East/West split – the bishops of the entire Church assembled in Ecumenical Council where the Holy Spirit preserved their collective judgments from error. But from the Eastern perspective, it was (in the last analysis) the thinking of Christians generally that the Holy Spirit preserved from error, for the bishops merely reported to the councils the views of their constituents.

We detect here an exceptionally corporate view of the Church, and this indeed has been an Eastern emphasis. Belonging as they do to the mystical body of Christ, all Christians consider themselves to be "members of one another," but it is the Eastern Church that has taken this notion most seriously. Each Christian is working, not to save his or her individual soul, but to attain salvation with and through the rest of the Church. The saying, *"One can be damned alone but saved only with others,"* comes from Russia, and Orthodoxy as a whole carries this to its logical limit by picking up on Paul's theme of the entire universe as *"groaning and in travail"* as it awaits redemption. Not only is the destiny of the individual bound up with the entire Church; individuals are responsible for helping to sanctify the worlds of nature and history. The welfare of everything in creation is affected to some degree by what each individual contributes to or detracts from it.

Though the chief consequence of this corporate emphasis is the spiritual one just stated, it has practical offshoots as well. That Church dogmas reflect the consciences of Christians generally is one of these, and the principle holds in practical matters as well. The laity in each congregation elect their own clergy, for in administration as elsewhere, divine guidance is thought to suffuse the entire Church. The clergy has its irrefrangible domain – the administration of the sacraments – but beyond these the line that separates clergy from laity is thin. Priests need not remain celibate. Even the titular head of the Eastern Church, the Patriarch of Constantinople, is no more than "first among equals," and the laity is known as a "royal priesthood."

In presenting the religions of Asia it was suggested that union has counted for more there, and individuality less, than in the West. If this is roughly correct, it helps to explain why it is the easternmost branch of Christendom that has most emphasized the Church's corporate nature – both the ecclesiastical equality of its members (as against Catholicism), and their solidarity (as against Protestantism, as we are about to see). It may also bear on the remaining emphasis of Orthodoxy that we shall mention: its mysticism.

Like all of the historical religions, Christianity believes that reality contains two realms, the natural and the supernatural. Following death, human life moves to the supernatural domain, but even in the present life it is not insulated from it. This much all Christendom teaches. The differences come in the extent to which Christians try to partake of the supernatural life while on earth. Roman Catholicism holds that the Trinity dwells in every Christian soul, but its presence is not normally felt.

Prayer and penance can *dispose* the soul to receive exceptional infusions of supernatural grace, but strictly speaking, souls have no *right* to mystical states in this life; they arrive (when they do) as free dispensations. The Eastern Church actively encourages its members to take the initiative toward the mystical life. From very early times when the deserts near Antioch and Alexandria were filled with hermits seeking illumination, the mystical enterprise has occupied a more prominent place in its life. As the supernatural world intersects the world of sense throughout, it should be a part of Christian life in general to develop the capacity to experience ecstatically the glories of God's indwelling.

The Eastern Church does not have a Pope but holds that God's truth is revealed through the "conscience of the Church," or the consensus of its members.

PROTESTANTISM

THE causes that led to the sixteenth century break between Roman Catholicism and what came to be known as Protestantism are complex and still in dispute. Political economy, nationalism, Renaissance individualism, and a rising concern over ecclesiastical abuses all figured, but the basic cause was a new conception of Christianity that emerged. Its two central features are Justification by Faith and the Protestant Principle.

Faith in the Protestant conception is not simply a matter of belief. It is a response of the entire self, which includes a movement of the *mind* (in believing certain things), a movement of the *heart* (in loving and trusting those things), and a movement of the *will* (in doing things that are prompted by that love). When Protestants say that human beings are justified – meaning, restored to right relationship with other people and the ground of their being – by faith, they are saying that it is a movement of the self on all three of its fronts that effects the change.

To grasp the distinctiveness of this notion of faith we need to see it as a critique of religious perfunctoriness. Creeds have their place, but unless the doctrines one professes reach one's heart and change the way life feels, they are mere mouthings. Comparably with rituals: prayer, churchgoing, and the like. These too are important; but once again, unless they awaken the actual experience of God's love – which in the end is what activates one's love for God – they too do not suffice. As for good works, Protestants reposition them. They are faith's consequence, more than its prelude. Where faith is genuine, people want to help others; which led Augustine to say, *"love God and do what you please."* The reverse

doesn't follow; for no number of good deeds, performed out of a sense of duty or as a means of getting to heaven, can be counted on to change the way the agent experiences life in the present.

The other controlling perspective in Protestantism has come to be called the Protestant Principle. Stated philosophically, it warns against absolutizing the relative. Theologically, it warns against idolatry.

Idolatry is not limited to its stereotype, idol-worship. It is giving one's life first and foremost to something in the finite world. The trouble with doing this is that everything finite is limited, which translates into saying that idols cannot deliver on unlimited investments in them. This is obvious when stated abstractly, but that doesn't protect people from being veritable "idol factories," as Luther called them. In Biblical times the factories produced golden calves and graven images, but now the idols the factories produce are more likely to be sex or success; oneself or an ideology; one's ethnic group or one's nation.

Religions are not immune to idolatry. Protestants consider the dogma of papal infallibility as idolatrous for removing from criticism opinions which, having been channeled through human minds, can never escape the risk of partial limitations and error. Lapses occur in the

Protestant camp as well. The chief Protestant idolatry has been bibliolatry. To believe that God speaks to people through the Bible as in no other way can be argued, but to exempt the Bible as a book from criticism, insisting that every word and letter was dictated by God and hence can contain no historical, scientific, or other inaccuracies, is again to forget that in entering the world, God's word speaks through human hearts.

A second instance of idolatry in Protestantism has been its deification of private religious experience. Protestant insistence that faith must be a living experience has at times led its constituents to assume that any vital experience must be the working of the Holy Spirit. Perhaps so; but again, what is experienced is not Spirit only. The Spirit must assume the shape of the human receptacle. Psychotics who think they are Christ provide the obvious warnings here.

The first two syllables in "protestant" dominate the word, and Protestants do protest many things, idolatry chief among them. But as the preceding chapter noted, the Greek and Hebrew roots of the word are positive; a prophet is one who speaks for someone or something. We have listened to Protestantism speaking for its distinctive version of faith. Before closing we should listen to it speaking up for the Bible, for the reason Bibliolatry is such a temptation for Protestants is because they hold the Bible in such high esteem.

In its account of God's workings through Israel, through Christ, and through the early Church, the Bible presents Protestants with their clearest picture of God's goodness and the way human beings can connect with it. In this sense the Bible is, for Protestant Christians, ultimate. It is ultimate in the sense that they believe that the most reliable way they can enter the divine life is by reading this record of God's grace with total openness and divine intent.

Protestants admit that to place the individual's encounter with God's word at the center of their religion and accept it as their final authority is risky. Added to the danger of misconstruing the Bible is the prospect that people will derive different truths from their encounters. The splintering of Protestantism into innumerable denominations is living proof of the precariousness of its position. Many Protestants are worried about the extent to which Christ's body has been broken by their approach, and an ecumenical movement has emerged to try to reverse the process. But though to some extent things have gotten out of hand, it is important to realize that Protestants do not consider diversity, as such, to be bad. People differ, and historical circumstances, too, introduce differences that need to find places in the divine economy. Life and history are too fluid to allow God's redeeming Word to be enclosed in a single form, be it doctrinal *or* institutional.

So Protestants accept the dangers in their position because, risk for risk, they prefer their precarious freedom to the security of doctrines or institutions which, even while looking toward God, remain fallible. Asked where he would stand if the Church excommunicated him, Luther replied, *"Under the sky."*

Opposite: *Mennonites forced to worship in secret in a boat. This page,* top: *John Calvin, and* below: *Martin Luther.*

THE ILLUSTRATED WORLD'S RELIGIONS

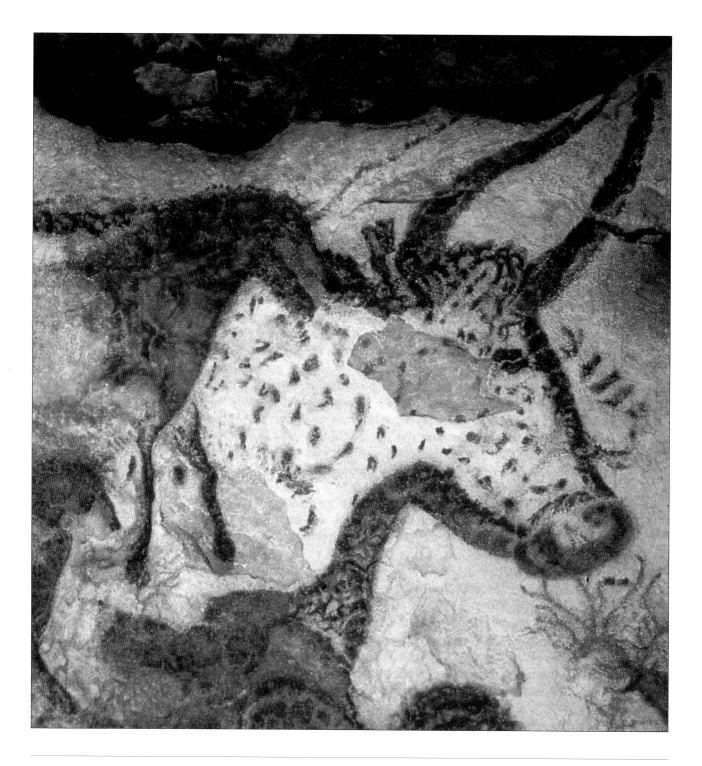

CHAPTER IX

THE PRIMAL RELIGIONS

They had what the world has lost: the ancient,

lost reverence and passion for human personality joined with the ancient,

lost reverence and passion for the earth and its web of life.

Since before the Stone Age

they have tended that passion as a central, sacred fire.

It should be our long hope to renew it in us all.

Detail of cave paintings in Lascaux.

THE AUSTRALIAN EXPERIENCE

*T*HIS BOOK HAS DEALT WITH THE MAJOR HISTORICAL RELIGIONS, which have sacred texts and a cumulative tradition that unfolds. These religions now pretty much blanket the earth, but chronologically they form only the tip of the religious iceberg, for they span a scant four thousand years as compared with the three million years or so of the religions that preceded them. During that immense time span, people lived their religion in an importantly different mode which must have shaped their sensibilities significantly. We shall call that mode *primal* because it came first; but alternately we shall refer to it as *tribal* because its groupings were invariably small, and *oral* because writing was foreign to them. This mode of religion continues in Africa, Australia, Southeast Asia, the Pacific Islands, Siberia, and among the Indians of North and South America.

We can begin by putting behind us the nineteenth century prejudice that later means better, a view that holds for technology, but not for religion. If God does not evolve, neither (it seems) does *homo religiosus;* not in any important respect. Everything that we find flowering in the historical religions, monotheism for example, is prefigured in the primal ones in faint but discernible outlines. One of the things that is prefigured is the distinction between the sacred and the profane. It is important to note this at the outset, for as this chapter unfolds we shall find that it will be difficult to put one's finger on what is specifically religious in tribal life because religion tends to blanket everything. Even so, the distinction between sacred and profane is detectable, and the Australian aborigines are the ideal group for demonstrating this fact, for in ways they are the "oldest" inhabitants on our planet. This is because Australia is the only continent that did not undergo the Neolithic experience which elsewhere began around 10,000 B.C. and witnessed the invention of farming and tooled stone implements. The division between the sacred and the profane appears among aborigines in their notion of "the Dreaming," which they contrast with ordinary life. Ordinary life is measured out in time; the seasons cycle, and generations come and go.

Meanwhile, the backdrop for this unending procession is stable. Time does not touch it, for it is "everywhen." Legendary figures people this backdrop. They are not gods; they are much like human beings, while at the same time being larger than life. What gives them their exceptional stature is that they instituted the paradigmatic acts of which daily life is woven. They molded and modeled life's essential structures – male and female; human, bird, fish, and the like – and its essential activities such as hunting, gathering, war, and love.

We are inclined to say that when the Arunta go hunting they mime the exploits of the first and archetypal hunter, but this distinguishes them from their archetype too sharply. It is more accurate to say that they fit so completely into the mold of their archetypes that each *becomes* the First Hunter; no residue remains. Similarly with other activities, from basket weaving to lovemaking. Only while they are conforming their actions to the model of some archetypal hero do the Arunta feel that they are truly alive, for in those roles they are immortal. When they fall from those roles their lives become meaningless, for time devours their doings and reduces them to nothing. Aboriginal religion turns not on worship but on identification; the participation in, and acting out of, archetypal paradigms. There are no priests or congregations; only the Dreaming and conformance thereto.

Having singled out the aborigines to establish that even in the relative undifferentiation of primal societies the sacred can be spotted, we shall hereafter refer to individual tribes only to illustrate characteristics that all tribes possess – ones that serve to set them apart from the historical religions.

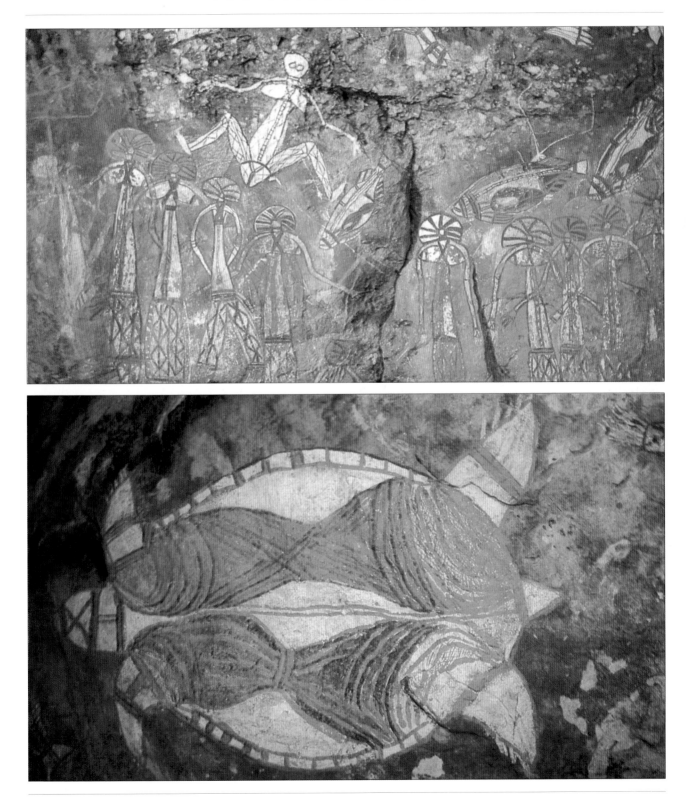

ORALITY, PLACE, AND TIME

O RALITY.
LITERACY IS UNKNOWN TO THE PRIMAL RELIGIONS where it has not been introduced from without, for tribal peoples regard writing, not as a supplement to speaking, but as a threat to the virtues of exclusive orality.

To understand why they do so we can begin with speech's vitality. Speech is alive – literally alive – because speaking *is* the speaker. It is not the whole of the speaker, but it is the speaker in one of his or her living modes. This shows speech to be alive by definition, as we see when we realize that it cannot exist – as can writing – disjoined from the speaker. It possesses *in principle* life's qualities, for its very nature is to change, adapt, and invent. Indissolubly contextual, speaking adapts itself to speaker, listener, and situation alike. This gives it an immediacy, range, and versatility that is, well, miraculous. Original wording breathes new life into familiar themes. Rhythm can enter (together with intonations, pauses, and accentuations) until speaking phases into chanting and storytelling becomes a high art. Dialect and delivery add their contributions, and when animal postures and gaits are mimed and their noises simulated, theater is born.

These virtues are obvious, but the overriding advantage of speech over writing is what it does for memory. Having libraries to fall back on, literate peoples grow slack in recall. To provide a glimpse of what life without writing would be like, we might try visualizing our forebears as bands of blind Homers who gather each evening around their fires. Everything that their ancestors learned with difficulty, from healing herbs to stirring legends, is now stored in their collective memory, and there only. Would they not revere and rehearse their heritage endlessly, each supplementing and correcting the accounts of others.

What is important for us to understand is the impact of this ongoing, empowering seminar on its participants. Everyone feeds the living reservoir of knowledge while receiving from it its answering flow of information that stocks and shapes their lives. If exclusive orality protects human memory, it also guards three other endowments. The first of these is the capacity to experience the sacred through non-verbal channels. Because writing traffics in explicit meanings, historical religions look to their texts for God's clearest (if not exclusive) revelations. This marginalizes other windows to the divine. Oral traditions do not do this. The invisibility of their texts – which is to say their myths – leaves their eyes free to notice other sacred conduits, virgin nature and sacred art being the chief of these.

Second, because writing has no limits it can proliferate to the point where trees obscure the woods. Minds are swamped by information and have difficulty seeing what is important.

This danger doesn't beset tribal peoples. They remember what is important and forget the rest.

Finally, orality safeguards community. It is impossible to be lonely in societies where there are no newspapers to hide behind, no computer screens to be glued to, no teledramas to watch by oneself in lonely, isolated apartments. Tribally speaking, language means people and interacting with them.

PLACE VERSUS SPACE.

A second distinguishing feature of primal religion is its embeddedness in place. Place is not space. Space is abstract, whereas place is concrete. A cubic yard of space is identical wherever we imagine it, but no two places are alike.

Historical religions have sacred sites, to be sure, but none of them are embedded in place per se to the extent that tribal religions are. An anecdote from the Onondaga tribe in upstate New York illustrates this.

Oren Lyons was the first Onondagan to go to college. On returning to his reservation for his first vacation, his uncle took him canoeing on their lake where he set out to interrogate him. *"Well, Oren,"* he said. *"You've been to college; you must be pretty smart. Let me ask you a question. Who are you?"* Taken aback, Oren fumbled for an answer. *"What do you mean, who am I? Why, I'm Oren Lyons. You know that."* Unimpressed, his uncle repeated his question. Successively, this nephew proposed that he was an Onondagan, a human being, a man, a young man — to no avail. When he had been reduced to silence and asked to be told who he was, his uncle said, *"You see that bluff over there? Oren, you are that bluff. And that huge pine on the other shore? You are that pine. And this water that supports our canoe? Oren, you are this water."*

Generalizing from this anecdote, when the Australian Kurnai go on walkabouts, it is likewise specific, concrete items that interest them. The springs and major trees and rocks that they encounter are not interchangeable with others of their kind; each triggers memories of the legendary events they were a part of. It would be wrong to confuse this investment in individual things with disinterest in the big picture. In fashioning their dwellings to the world's shape, the Navajos draw the entire world

into their homes. The pillars that support their roofs are named for, and thus identified with, the deities that support the entire cosmos: Earth, Mountain Woman, Water Woman, and Corn Woman.

ETERNAL TIME.

Primal time is not linear, as in the messianically forward-looking religions of the West. It is not even cyclical as the Asian religions tend to image it, revolving in

Page 233: Aboriginal rock paintings in Australia. Top: *A scene from a traditional legend.* Below: *Painting of a sea turtle. This page above:* Corn Mother. *Native American tribes of the southwestern United States often use such figures to represent the nurturing, female spirit of the Earth.*

the way the world turns and seasons cycle. Primal time is atemporal; an eternal now. To speak of a temporal or timeless time is paradoxical, but the paradox can be relieved if we see that primal time focuses on causal rather than chronological sequence. For primal peoples, "past" means preeminently, closer to the originating source of things. That that source precedes the present is of secondary importance.

The word source refers here to the gods who, where they did not actually create the world, ordered it and gave it its viable structure. Those gods continue to exist, but that does not shift interest to the present, for the past continues to be considered the Golden Age. Before creation suffered ravages of time and mismanagement, the world was as it should be. That is no longer the case, for a certain enfeeblement has occurred which requires that steps be taken to restore the world to its original condition. These steps are rites of renewal, which primal religions regularly enact. The annual Sun Dance of the Plains Indians, for example, is called the Dance for World and Life Renewal.

If we stopped here we would have said nothing distinctive about the primal view of time, for historical religions have rites of renewal as well. They all have solstice festivals of some sort to reverse the winter's darkness, and "easters" to abet nature's rebirth. For a feature of the primal view of time that the historical religions have largely abandoned we can turn to the way proximity to the divine source tends, in tribal eyes, to be a badge of worth. Thus animals are frequently venerated for having been created before humans, and among animals the otter's relative stupidity leads the Winnebagos to infer that it was created last. This principle applies to the human species as well. Its pioneers are more celebrated than their descendants who are regarded as something of epigones. Primal peoples respect their elders enormously.

We turn now to other features of primal religion that are embedded in its worldview.

Mt. Taylor, sacred mountain to the Navajos.

THE PRIMAL WORLD

A FITTING PLACE TO ENTER the primal world is with the embeddedness of primal peoples in that world. This starts with their tribe, apart from which they sense little independent identity. To be separated from the tribe threatens them with death, not only physically but psychologically as well. The tribe, in turn, is embedded in nature so solidly that the line between the two is not easy to establish. In the case of totemism it cannot really be said to exist. Totemism binds a human tribe to an animal species in a common life. The totem animal guards the tribe which, in return, respects it and refuses to injure it, for they are "of one flesh."

Totemism itself is not universal among tribal peoples, but they all share its nonchalance concerning the animal/human division. Animals and birds are frequently referred to as "peoples," and in certain circumstances animals and humans can exchange forms and convert to their opposite numbers. The division between animal and vegetable is equally tenuous, for plants have spirits like the rest of us. This drift reaches its logical term when we note that even the line between animate and "inanimate" is perforated. Rocks are alive. Under certain conditions they are believed to be able to talk, and at times they are considered divine.

Turning from the world's structure to human activities, we are again struck by the relative absence of compartmentalizations between them. In American Indian languages there is no word for art because everything is art. Equally, everything is (in its way) religion. A hunter, for example, does not set out simply to forestall his tribe's hunger. He launches on a sequence of meditative acts, all of which — whether preparatory prayer and purification, pursuit of the quarry, or the sacramental manner by which the animal is slain and subsequently treated — are sacred.

The final absence of sharp divisions that we shall note is the most telling. Nothing in the primal world separates it from a categorically different Other with which it is contrasted, be that Other God (as distinct from his creation), Nirvana (as distinct from samsara), or whatever. The primal world is a single cosmos that sustains its embryos like a living womb. Because those embryos assume that the womb exists to nurture them, they have no disposition to challenge it, refashion it, or escape from it. It is not a place of exile or pilgrimage, though pilgrimages take place within it. Its space is not homogeneous; the home has a number of rooms, we might say, some of which are normally invisible. But together they constitute a single domicile. Primal peoples are concerned with maintaining personal, social, and cosmic harmony, and with attaining specific goods — rain, harvest, children, health — as people always are. But the overriding goal of salvation that dominates the historical religions is virtually absent from them, and life after death tends to be a shadowy semi-existence in some vaguely designated place in their single domicile.

Left: *Niniganni, the python goddess of the Baga tribe in Guinea.* Right: *Detail of a cave painting in Spain.*

Australian Aboriginal painting.

THE SYMBOLIC MIND

OUR SKETCH OF THE PRIMAL WORLD up to this point has shown its internal divisions to be muted and with no transcendent reality that relativizes it. All of this, however, would amount to a string of zeros without a digit to bestow value on them were we not to introduce the divine source from which the world is believed to issue; or in other versions, divine arrangers who bring order out of chaos. The presence of these divinities raises the question of theism.

A common stereotype pegs primal religions as polytheistic, and this is not altogether wrong if the word means that the divine can congeal in hallowed places and alight on certain objects. But this does not militate against a single Ultimate of which the many gods are instantiations or expressions. The Yoruba of West Africa never rank their Supreme Being, Olodimave, with lesser divinities *(orisa),* nor do the Edo confuse Osanobuwa with the *ebo.* The basic issue, however, is not whether tribal peoples explicitly identify a Supreme Being who coordinates the gods; but instead, do they *sense* such a being whether they name and personify it or not. The evidence suggests that they do sense it. Primal religions separate the divine Unity from its expressions less than the historical religions do, and in some cases seem even to veil it; but they contain nothing that is comparable to the anthropomorphic polytheism of the early Europeans. It is just that the holy, the sacred, the *wakan* (as the Sioux call it) need not be exclusively attached, or consciously attached at all, to a distinguishable Supreme Being.

Something may even be lost *by* so attaching it, that loss being the removal of holiness from the world that remains when God is factored out. This brings us to the most important single feature of primal spirituality; namely, its symbolist mentality. The symbolist vision sees the things of the world as transparent to their divine source; whether that source is specified or not, things are sensed as containing its light. Physical sight presents a lake in existential isolation, for as far as the eye reports, its water exists as a reality in its own right. From there, modern thought may go on to reason that the water is composed of oxygen and hydrogen; and if a spiritual gloss is desired, it may attribute to the water allegorical significance. Normally, however, modernity recognizes no ontological connection between material things and their metaphysical, spiritual roots. In this respect primal peoples are better metaphysicians, though their metaphysics, where articulated – it need not be – is naturally of mythic cast.

When ethnologists declare that for the Algonquins "there is no *manitu* [spirit] outside the world of appearances," this simply shows that they do not understand that for primal peoples, appearances are never self-contained.

This section should not end without mentioning a distinctive personality type, the shaman, who can bypass symbolism and perceive spiritual realities directly. We can think of shamans as spiritual *savants,* savant being defined as a person whose talents, be they in music (Mozart), drama (Shakespeare), mathematics or whatever, are exceptional to the point of belonging to a different order of magnitude. Subject to severe physical and emotional traumas in their early years, shamans are able to heal themselves and reintegrate their lives in ways that place psychic if not cosmic powers at their disposal. These powers enable them to engage with spirits, both good and evil, drawing power from the former and battling the latter where need be. They are heavily engaged in healing, and seem to have preternatural powers to foretell the future and discern lost objects.

CONCLUSION

Primal peoples have tended their passion for the earth and its web of life as a central, sacred fire.

A S BETWEEN THE PRIMAL and the historical religions, time seems to be on the side of the latter, for though millions would now like to see the primal way of life continue, it seems unlikely that it will do so. *"Civilization"* is seductive where not imperious, and we cannot quarantine the tribes that remain, preserving them for anthropologists to study and the rest of us to romanticize as symbols of our lost paradise. How industrial peoples will comport themselves toward the primal in what seems to be the short time they have left to share this planet together will be the final topic of this chapter. The historical religions have largely abandoned their earlier missionary designs on "the heathen," and if anything, the pendulum has now swung in the opposite direction, toward romanticizing the primal. Dismayed by the relentless utilitarianism of technological society and its seeming inability to contain its power to destroy both people and nature, citified peoples have come to hope that a fundamentally different way of life is possible, and latch onto primal peoples for support. Guilt enters the picture too, as the descendants of those who had power face up to the ways their forebears looked down on, despoiled, and destroyed those who lacked it.

On the positive side, we now recognize that we were mistaken about these people. Primal peoples are not primitive and uncivilized, much less savage. They are not backward. They are different. With this realization in place and disparagement of the primal behind us, we should think for a moment longer about our current propensity to romanticize the primal, for there is an aspect of that impulse which is not widely perceived.

Disenchantment with the complexities and mistakes of industrial life has (as we were saying) produced by way of reaction the image of tribal peoples as wholly nat-

ural. We regard them as sons and daughters of the earth and sky, brothers and sisters of animals and plants who live by nature's ways and do not upset the delicate balances of its ecological zones; gentle hunting folk who are still in touch with the magic and myth that we ourselves so badly need. Seeing them thus, we assume that our ancestors resembled them in these respects, and we celebrate them as our heroes. There is a deep, unconscious reason for this bent of thought. Every people needs to think well of its origins; it is part of having a healthy self-image. So modern peoples, who are no longer confident that God created them, transfer some of God's nobility to the source from which they assume that they did derive, namely early man. This is the deepest impulse behind "the myth of the noble savage" that the eighteenth century invented.

What may be hoped is that we are now ready to put both prejudice and idealization behind us. If so, perhaps we can live out our numbered years of planetary partnership with primal peoples in mutual respect, guided by the dream of one of their spokesmen that "*we may be brothers after all.*" If we succeed in doing this, there is still time for us to learn things from them. For, tabling shortcomings that are not the issue here, it is not just romanticism to affirm what John Collier, one-time United States Commissioner of Indian Affairs, said of his charges. "*They had what the world has lost: the ancient, lost reverence and passion for human personality joined with the ancient, lost reverence and passion for the earth and its web of life. Since before the Stone Age they have tended that passion as a central, sacred fire. It should be our long hope to renew it in us all.*"

Above and opposite: *Ritual masks created by the Sepik River tribes of Papua New Guinea.*

A FINAL EXAMINATION

THE RELATION BETWEEN RELIGIONS

LOOKING BACK ON THE ROAD we have traveled, three questions suggest themselves. We have met the world's religions individually; how should we configure them — see them as related to one another? Second, have they anything to say to the world collectively, in concert? And third, how should we comport ourselves in the world they help make pluralistic?

To the question of configuration, three answers come to mind.

The first holds that one religion is superior to the others. There is nothing in this book to suggest that this is the case; but equally, nothing that argues against it, for comparisons have not been its province.

A second and opposite position holds that religions are basically alike. Their differences are incidental compared with the towering truths on which they unite. This appeals to our yen for togetherness, but on inspection it proves to be the trickiest position of the three. For as soon as it moves beyond vague generalities — "every religion has some version of the Golden Rule" — it founders on the fact that the religions differ in what they consider essential and nonnegotiable.

A third conception likens religions to stained glass windows that refract sunlight in different shapes and colors. This analogy allows for significant differences between the religions without pronouncing on their relative worth. If peoples of different cultures have different temperaments, God may have taken those into account in addressing them.

Leaving it to the reader to configure the religions

as seems appropriate, we proceed to the second question. Have they anything to say to the world concertedly — in a single voice?

THE WISDOM TRADITIONS

ONE OF E. F. SCHUMACHER'S LEGACIES to the world was his conviction that "we need the courage to consult and profit from the 'wisdom traditions of mankind.'" Those traditions have been the subject of this book. What wisdom do they offer the world?

Modern science has retired their cosmologies, and the social mores of their day which they reflect – class structures, gender relations, and the like – must be reassessed in the light of changing times and the continuing struggle for justice. But if we single out their conclusions about reality and how life should be lived, they begin to look like the winnowed wisdom of the human race.

In the realm of *ethics,* the decalogue pretty much tells the story for them all. We should avoid murder, thieving, lying, and adultery. These are minimum guidelines, but they are not nothing, as we realize if we reflect on how much better the world would be if they were universally honored.

Proceeding from this ethical base to the kind of person we should strive to become, we encounter the human *virtues* which are basically three: humility, charity, and veracity. Humility is not self-abasement. It is the capacity to regard oneself as fully one, but not more than one. Charity shifts the weight to the other foot; it is to consider one's neighbor to be as fully one as you are. As for veracity, it extends beyond basic truth-telling to a sublime objectivity – the capacity to see things exactly as they are, freed from subjective distortions. The Asian religions extol these virtues by noting the obstacles that debar them. The Buddha called these obstacles poisons, and identified them as greed, hatred, and delusion. To the degree that they are expunged, selflessness (humility), compassion (charity), and seeing things in their

Wall tapestry depicting Adam and Eve in the Garden of Eden.

Suchness (veracity) replace them. Finally *vision* – the wisdom traditions' perception of the ultimate nature of things.

It begins by seeing things as more integrated than we normally suppose. Mortal life gives no view of the whole; we see things in dribs and drabs, and self-interest skews perspective grotesquely. It is as if life were a great tapestry which we face from its wrong side. This gives it the appearance of a maze of knots and threads that look chaotic. From a purely human standpoint, the wisdom traditions are the species' most prolonged and serious attempts to infer from the hind side of life's tapestry its frontal design. As the beauty and harmony of the design derives from the way its parts interweave, the design confers on those parts a significance they are denied in isolation. We could almost say that seeing ourselves as belonging to the whole is what religion – *religio,* rebinding – *is.* It is mankind's fundamental thrust at unification.

This first motif – unity – leads to a second. If things are more integrated than they seem, they are also better than they seem. Paralleling the astrophysicists' report that the world is bigger than it *looks* to our unaided eyes, the wisdom traditions report that it is better than it *feels* to our unregenerated hearts. And in comparable degree we should add, which means that we are talking about light years. Yahweh, God and Allah; T'ien and the Tao; Brahman and Nirvana, carry the signature of the *ens perfectissium* – perfect being. This perfection floods the wisdom traditions with an exuberance nowhere else to be found. It includes their estimates of the human self which, as we have seen, is astounding. Wherever human beings go (a Rabbinic tradition relates), they are preceded by a host of angels, crying, *"Make way! Make way for the Image of God!"* In Saint Paul's formulation, *"Beholding the glory of the Lord, we are ourselves changed from one degree of glory to another."*

To the unity of things and their inestimable worth, the wisdom traditions add (as their third surmise) mystery. Murder mysteries have debased that word, for detective mysteries are not mysteries at all for having solutions. A mystery is that special kind of problem which has no solutions because the more we understand it, the more we see that we don't understand. In mysteries, knowledge and ignorance advance lockstep. As known unknowns become known, unknown unknowns proliferate; the larger the island of knowledge, the longer the shoreline of wonder. It's like the quantum world. The more we understand its formalism, the stranger that world becomes.

Things are more integrated than they seem, they are better than they seem, and they are more mysterious than they seem; this is the vision that the wisdom traditions bequeath us. When we add to this the baseline they establish for ethical conduct and their account of the human virtues, one wonders if a wiser platform for human life has been envisioned. At the center of the religious life is a particular kind of joy, the prospect of a happy ending that blossoms from necessarily painful beginnings, the promise of human difficulties embraced and overcome. In daily life we have only hints of this joy. When they arrive, we do not know whether our happiness is the rarest or the commonest thing on earth, for in all earthly things we find it, give it, and receive it, but cannot hold onto it. When we possess those intimations, it seems in no way strange to be happy, but in retrospect we wonder how such gold of Eden could have been ours. Religiously conceived, the human opportunity is to transform epiphanies into abiding light.

The world, however, particularly the modern world, is not persuaded by the religious view, so what do we do? This is our final question. Whether religion is, for us, a good word or bad; whether (if on balance it is a good word) we side with a single religious tradition or to some degree open our arms to them all, how do we comport ourselves in a pluralistic world that is riven by ideologies, sacred and profane?

We listen.

LISTENING

*I*F ONE OF THE WISDOM TRADITIONS claims us, we begin by listening to it. Not uncritically, for new occasions teach new duties; but nevertheless expectantly, realizing that it houses more truth than a single lifetime could fathom, let alone enact.

But in addition to our own traditions, we listen to the faith of others, including the secularists. We listen first because our times require it. Daily the world grows smaller, leaving understanding the only place where peace can find a home. Those who listen work for peace, a peace built not on religious or political hegemonies, but on mutual awareness and concern. For understanding brings respect, and respect prepares the way for a higher capacity which is love.

Understanding, then, breeds love; but the reverse also holds. Love brings understanding — the two are reciprocal. So we must listen to understand, while realizing that to the extent that compassion increases we will listen more attentively, for it is impossible to love another without hearing that other. If we are to be true to the wisdom traditions, we must attend to others as deeply and as alertly as we hope that they will attend to us. For as Thomas Merton once noted, God speaks to us in three places: in scripture, in our deepest selves, and in the voice of the stranger.

Said Jesus, *"Do unto others as you would that they should do unto you."*

Said the Buddha, *"He who would may reach the utmost height, but he must be eager to learn."*

If we do not quote the other religions on these points it is because their words would be redundant.

A Phoenician goddess figure.

ACKNOWLEDGMENTS

Every effort has been made to trace all present copyright holders of the material used in this book, whether companies or individuals. Any omission is unintentional and we will be pleased to correct any errors in future editions of this book.

Chuguji Temple: 2. Premgit: 6/7, 24, 25, 31 top, 33, 35, 41, 42, 79, 82, 83. Don Farber: 9, 255. Rijksmuseum, Amsterdam: 10/11. Scala, Florence; 12, 48, 96, 164, 176, 178, 180, 187, 188, 190, 202, 204, 210/211, 214/215, 218/219, 221, 222, 223, 246/247, 251. Yatri: 15. Bibliothèque Nationale, Paris: 16. Prince of Wales Museum, Bombay: 19, 20, 22, 26, 52, 53, 97. Hans Wichers Collection, Hamburg: 23. Archeological Survey of India, Bombay: 27, 34, 47. Hodalic Arne: 28, 30/31, 54, 55 top & bottom, 56, 70, 72/73, 80, 146/147, 159, 172/173, 244/245. Tantra Museum, New Delhi: 36, 38, 39, 93. Image Bank for Teaching World Religions, Cambridge USA: Diana Eck 44/45, 46, 69; Spencer Palmer 98; Robert Weller 132; Chris Joachim 133; Aramco World 153, 165; Sabra Weber 162; Anne Batteridge 163; Thomas Hartwell 166; Eric Oey 169; Judah L. Magnus Museum; 182/183, 184, 192, 193, 194, 198, 200; Edith Turner 201 top & bottom, 227; Edwin Bernbaum 236/7; Judith Gleason 242. Arts Council of Great Britain: 51. Gianluca De Santis: 57, 114, 115, 137, 177, 243. Derik Gardiner: 58, 84, 87. British Library: 61, 99, 149, 155, 156, 157, 160, 161. Museum vor Volkerkunde, Vienna: 62. Carol Neimann: 66, 67, 118, 119, 128, 129, 130/131. Gulbenkian Museum of Oriental Art, Durham: 76, 121. Graham Harrison: 86, 88, 94/5. Yakamoto Photo Research Lab., Tokyo: 89. Japanese Tourist Organisation: 90. Stein Collection: 100, 108. Everson Museum of Art: 101, 102. Michael Holford: 103. William Gardner and Annie Hough Funds: 104/5. National Palace Museum Collection, Taiwan: 107, 112, 113, 124, 125, 134/135, 140. Peking Museum: 117. Pat Fok: 122, 126/127. Keith McLeod Fund: 142/3. Rohit Chalwa: 144. Topkapi Saray Museum, Istanbul: 148, 150, 151. British Museum: 152. Comstock Photolibrary: 167. Ann & Bury Peerless: 168. Labyrinth picture library; 170. Mick Sharp: 174/175, 224, 225. Juliette Soester: 197. Louvre, Giraudon: 207. National Gallery, London: 208. Staatsbibliotheek Munich: 209. Novosti Press Agency: 212. John Hillelson: 230. Prism Press, Bridport: 233 top & bottom. Museum of American Indian, Heye Foundation: 235. Axel Poignant: 240. Israel Department of Antiquities and Art: 249.

Special thanks to the Image Bank for teaching World Religions contributors; supplied by Harvard University Center for the Study of World Religions, 42 Francis Avenue, Cambridge, Massachusetts, U.S.A.

"Autour d' Elle" by Marc Chagall.

INDEX

I N D E X